THE
BODY SNATCHER'S
WIFE

MY LIFE WITH A MONSTER

BARBRA REIFEL

WITH JOHNNY RUSSO

Post Hill
PRESS

NOV 2 7 2019

Post Hill Press
New York • Nashville
posthillpress.com

Published in the United States of America

To my angels here and above...
and most in my heart, my two innocents.
From my heart, this is for you.

Contents

1

The Move

The garage door opened. So did my eyes. Three in the morning. The alarm started blaring at a piercing decibel. Michael took too long to turn it off, finally ceasing before the police call. Expecting screams of terror from Gerry on the monitor, not a rustle in the crib. Beside me, Mike still asleep by some miracle, nestled close to me. Thumps quaked the stairs.

He must be hammered. Late business dinner.

Still as a corpse in bed, my slit-open eyes appeared closed. The door flung open as he stumbled into the room, swaying like a pendulum toward my side of the bed. He loomed over me, slouched, peering down at me, then sluggishly raised his hand. I held my breath, praying he wouldn't strike. Suddenly, he dropped his heavy hand, dragging it through my hair as I braved the pain. A drunken caress? A sign of affection? I took anything. He crawled into bed on his side. Closing my eyes, I let it go.

With his new business ventures, he had more and more late evening meetings with associates. He always had, but this was different. He was different. Something was off, not right. Loving and trusting him for so long, offering the benefit of the doubt was second nature. When I needed reassurance, he gave it to me. The one exception was telling me I was crazy, all in my imagination, and I should talk to someone. Since we first met in 1989 eleven years before, I remembered the love, how he gazed at me as if only we existed. Where did it go? When did it go? Or was that in my imagination as well?

* * *

Fresh outta college back down to my hometown, Brooklyn was in my heart, no place else like it! Hair half foot high, slammin' accent with snappin' gum, big earrings, acid wash everything, glitter, frosted makeup, and what else but a Caribbean tan.

Speaking of, Caribbean Tanning Salon was the pulse of Brooklyn, my second job. Always funny crazy shit happened there. That's why I moved back down to Brooklyn! To experience life! Grab it! Live it! Be close to the city, land of opportunity! And I'd never seen so many beautiful people in one place, but when they opened their mouths, Madonna mi, that accent! With a language all their own! My accent was only eight years deep, but it was there. You name it, they walked in, tough guys, wannabes, pro athletes, models, porn stars, celebrities, celebrities in their own minds, "wise guys" in their own minds, muscle heads, "family" heads.

One night, a reputed "family" boss walked in, always sharply-dressed, a reserved gentleman. Newer generation was a bit louder, their daily wardrobe, velour sweat suits, donning thick gold chains around their necks, and the strut with the shoulder shrug and foot stomp. Just couldn't take them seriously.

As I greeted Mr. G, my eyes drew right to the guy holding the door for him, reserved like him. My heart raced. They knew each other. Did they come together? Oh no, what did I tell myself? Never get involved with a mobster, let alone melt over one. A romanticized, yet very difficult life. They were cheaters, beaters, and criminals from what I'd heard. Stereotype or not, I wasn't taking any chances.

He had his eyes drawn right back on me, his silent smile searing right through me. The heat rushed through my body, filling my head, burning up inside, instant electricity between us, all a shock to my system. Tall, dark, and gorgeous, dimples with that grin, and a cleft to die for. And big! So big, but not a meathead. His neck lined up with his chiseled jaw, shoulders just fit through the door. This guy had to be Mr. G's bodyguard. Hoped not. He had this strong, quiet presence.

Just the way he looked at me. Damnit, I melted instantly inside, but played it real cool, at least I tried, especially as he walked by and caught me bent over cleaning a tanning bed with my little acid-washed jean skirt, ridiculously tanned legs, and white sneakers and socks. Yeah, that was '80s Brooklyn. He made no idiot sexual comment that most of them would have, just sweet fun conversation. He won my heart.

He came over to the side of my desk after his tan. His name was Michael Mastromarino, Mr. G's neighbor, not his bodyguard. Thank you, Lord!

An ex-U of Pitt football player, NYU dental student, president of his freshman class, studying to be an oral surgeon, he knew what he wanted and went after it. He was perfect and exuded this cool confidence. Envious, I wanted some. And he wanted me.

It was undeniable. The attraction, magnetic from the first moment. I fell for him so hard and so deep. He knew I was the one. He told everyone, said I belonged with him. He wanted to take care of me, have a life with me. I wanted to take care of him. He wanted me to have his babies. I believed him.

* * *

His craniofacial surgery practice and businesses had expanded, but the money was not coming in, or at least I wasn't seeing it. Things were not adding up. The money started spreading as thin as he did.

We shouldn't have bought the house. His silence was an admission, to what I wasn't sure. We were there less than two years and needed to move quickly. So, I'd make a new beautiful home for us elsewhere. Home was where I was, as comfortable and happy as could be. My upcoming tri-fitness obstacle course competitions I had worked so hard for, looking and feeling the best of my life, canceled. What more could I have done? Smart, independent, confident, not over-demanding but no pushover, as sexy as I could've been for him seemed never enough, treating me as nothing more than a trophy wife. Spit-shine me up, show me off, and stick me back on the shelf.

The house sold in less than two weeks with the help of Rue, my savvy real estate agent, who was like an aunt to me. We found a townhouse in Fort Lee, New Jersey, a nice gated community, and half the price. The entire move and closing was on me. Michael wasn't big on being a team player, unless it was a sport or a profitable business deal.

Staying at the local Hilton with his parents as we awaited our move into our new home, Michael noisily stumbled into the hotel suite from a business meeting, unreachable throughout the night. Voicemail. Voicemail. Always voicemail. Four in the morning. He left at eight. Gazing at my boys in sound slumber beside me in the king bed, the questions would wait. Fixated on our doorway, enough time had passed. What the hell was he doing? As I approached the door, his mother pushed me back in grabbing my arm, frantic, her face inches from mine.

"I'm worried about Michael! I walked into the bathroom and he was putting a needle in his arm! He told me it was vitamins. Something's wrong!"

My heart skipped, coolly taking a breath. First, she needed to be defused and removed. "It's most likely for his back pain from his football injury. He gets epidural shots in his lower back from Dan, his anesthesiologist friend from the hospital. I'll check on him. It's okay. Go back to bed."

She did. Approaching the closed bathroom door, the light underneath shining in the dark hallway, glass clanked. Reaching for the knob, the door swung open. Almost falling on me, Michael staggered past me as if I wasn't there. My heart jumped into my throat. His eyes rolled behind as his lids fluttered half-closed like slot machines, his undershirt stained with dried blood, pants half undone. My eyes shot to his arm, blood dripping to the floor, a trail of drops behind him. Wait, he was in his undershirt. Where was his tailored shirt? It'd better have blood on it, otherwise he was unclothed while he shot up—which alluded to an affair. There was no way he unbuttoned his shirt or unbuckled his pants in this condition. Then again, he got here alive, just filled a syringe and shot it in his arm.

His briefcase was by the front door and the shirt peeked out. Clean, not a drop of blood. My stomach sank. A dinner meeting in his undershirt? Shooting up? I imagined him in bed naked wearing only an undershirt, shooting up with some dirty whore. Sharing needles? God, no! Twisted inside, the vision hurt. All my years with him, he wore an undershirt to bed, sex or no sex. He said his back was sensitive from stubble. My mind ran wild with painful possibilities, but he wouldn't, would he? Then again, I never thought he would drug himself up. My husband was not as strong as once I thought. The wall holding him up, his eyes closed, body trembling. I shook him, snapping his name. No response. Holding his head with both hands and his eyes open with my thumbs, slapping his face, his lids shuddered closed. He mumbled incomprehensibly. I shook him. Nothing. But I continued.

My teeth gritted, voice low, the questions could not wait. "Michael! What did you take? What fucking slut bitch were you shooting up with?"

My hopes of truth serum were impossible. Too far gone. Damnit! None of his jumbled words made any sense, except one, "Frank," our lawyer friend. Could it have been my imagination, jumping to too many conclusions? I hoisted him with all my might under his shoulder and dragged his six-foot-three, 220-pound sorry ass into bed. Letting him fall over, I swung his legs onto the bed and covered him, nudged him, again. He was out. Time to find some answers. His cell phone was locked. No time to break codes. The search was on. His toiletry bag was tucked under a towel on the basin. *Way to hide it.*

The side pocket had two small bottles of Demerol, empty. He used this shit to put his surgery patients to sleep. I kept on. One small bottle of fentanyl, horse tranquilizer, half-full, an uncapped bloody needle, and a tourniquet. I'd seen enough. My stomach knotted. The trek to the bedroom seemed forever. Whether the kids were in bed between us or not, Michael and I couldn't have been any farther apart.

My heart tugged, kneeling over them, my hands clasped so tightly my fingers numbed. *Dear God, give me the strength for whatever may come. Keep my babies safe. Help me protect them.*

Curled away from his children on the very edge, my eyes could've seared a hole through this man. *Where is my husband? Who are you? The devil?* As if he was possessed, a shiver ran through me. This was clearly not the last of this nightmare. What would tomorrow bring?

Slipping in on my side of the Great Divide, my arms cradled them, caressing their heads with a gentle fierceness I'd never known. *My sweet innocent babies. What will this life hold for you? No worries, Mommy's here.* Lying awake, not knowing if my eyes would ever close, feeling in my bones this was only the beginning.

My eyes sprung open to clanking noises from the hallway. Not a stir from my good sleepers. Six o'clock. Bracing myself, I followed the noise to the front door. The mirror reflected his steady, smug mug. Not turning around, he fixed his tie as if it were any other morning, this time completely lucid. My husband was back.

He glanced through the reflection coolly. "What's wrong?"

"You're kidding, right?"

"Honey, if you're talking about last night—"

"Last night? You mean two hours ago! Michael, you were out of your mind! We need to talk."

"Later. I've got to get to the hospital." Out the door, he couldn't escape me fast enough. A sure no-show for dinner.

Later came, no Michael. His parents, the boys and I sat at the hotel restaurant table, ordering. As the door opened, the breeze could have blown me over. Michael strutted in. Tension was tight as steel, table talk short and strained, silence uncomfortable. The kids brought levity just being kids. When dinner was done, we hid away in my truck.

"After the meeting, Frank, Keith, Kevin and I hung at Lou's place watching the game," he said. "Everybody dozed. My back was acting up, so I went into the bathroom and took some, maybe a drop too much. Strong shit, worked like a wonder drug! My back felt no pain!"

His excitement about the drugs and indifference about his condition scared the hell out of me. "So, you just happened to have a bottle and needle handy? What about your undershirt with blood on it and your shirt had none? You shot up in your undershirt, and your pants undone? Who were you with, Michael?"

He took my hand tenderly, in earnest. "Honey, do you really think I could do something like that with anyone? I'd be so ashamed. Call Frank, he'll tell you."

A wise woman once told me, beware when one answers an accusation with a question. I tucked my fears away, hoping they'd never again rear their nasty head.

"The next time you think about taking that poison for pain again, you imagine the faces of your two beautiful boys before you do! And don't! Please!" All I could do was hope and pray.

Days after settling into our new Fort Lee townhouse, as I unpacked boxes in my new kitchen, the caller ID flashed Michael's MRI office. My stomach jumped with a bad feeling.

"It's Keith, how are you? The kids? How's the move in going?" Pleasantries transparent.

"Good, thank you. Is everything okay?"

"Have you noticed anything 'off' in Mike's behavior, any changes at all?" And there it was. The time of truth.

"Well, for his back, he took a little too much—"

"Demerol?"

"Oh, God."

"He was found passed out on the floor in the bathroom with a syringe in his arm and a bottle of Demerol while his patient was asleep in the chair prepped for surgery."

The floor fell out. How badly I wanted to be wrong.

"Please, tell me the patient is okay! Is he okay? Did anyone call an ambulance? Is he still there? Was he alone?"

"The patient is fine. We woke her and canceled the surgery, explaining the doctor had an emergency. When Mike came to, he was completely incoherent and belligerent. He flew into a rage and plowed through everyone that tried to stop him. Barbra, this is serious. We can't have him here like that."

"How long ago?"

"About four hours ago."

"Right now, I'm a bit more concerned for his well-being and anyone else in his path! It took you four hours to call me? You let him leave and get behind a wheel?"

My mind flew into a frenzy. *Is he dead? Did he kill someone else? Is he alone?*

"I'm sorry, Barbra. Of course, I'm concerned for him. I didn't mean to sound that way. We didn't know what to do. We continuously tried to reach him. And the last thing we wanted to do was worry you. Bad call on our part."

"I understand. Bad call on Michael's part!"

"Listen, I love Mike. We love you guys. We're not abandoning him. Anything we can do to help, tell me, and we'll be there. But please understand we can't let him come back here until he agrees to get some help. I'll help you find a place for him."

"Thank you. Right now, I need to regroup and find him. He's not home yet. Will keep in touch. Thank you!"

Michael's cell. Voicemail. "Hi, honey. Wondering if you're making it home for dinner. Let me know."

I couldn't do it alone. Michael listened to his dad who was already on his way from Brooklyn. The boys needed to be removed from this. Ingrid would take the boys for a sleepover with her kids, who were friends with mine. I trusted her. Excited, they packed their Pokémon roll-a-way suitcases then watched TV until she came. Minutes passed like tree sap in the winter petrified to the bark. I reached out to every hospital and police station—nothing. Just as I carried the boys' overnight luggage to the kitchen, the front door opened. Michael. As I approached, he appeared torn apart and sloppily pasted back together. So disheveled, his hair was messy, twelve o'clock shadow, face gaunt, shirttail out, dried blood on his hands, shirt, and pants. The bulge in his pocket unmistakable...a Demerol bottle and needle.

Hand on my hip, I mimicked Mae West. "Hey, big boy, is that a bottle in your pocket, or are you happy to see me?"

Unresponsive, head down, he dropped his keys, phone and a couple of index cards on the hallway table.

"Honey, I tried to call you."

He plodded by, not a glance my way, as if it made him invisible. He staggered up the stairs, then disappeared around the corner. "I was probably in surgery."

Quietly behind him, I stopped at the top. He was on the phone. I couldn't make it all out. His office was conveniently an open space off the living room. I made out enough.

"I forgot my index cards there."

Where the hell was *there*? Couldn't be the office. Rounding the corner, the sight of him slumped at his desk, blindly shuffling papers, sickened me. My eyes pierced him, keeping my cool. "Keith told me what happened at the office."

His face in his papers. "He did? What did he tell you?"

"You were found passed out in the bathroom with an empty Demerol bottle and a syringe in your arm. You left the office in a rage almost five hours ago."

His eyes shot up at me. "That's it?"

"Isn't that enough? What else is there? Michael, you promised you'd never take it again!"

"You look at me with such disgust! Look at you!" He snatched some papers from his desk and stormed past me.

9

Following him. "Where are you going?"

"The office!"

Fearless, my razor tongue had a mind of its own. His volatile temper, on drugs, who the hell knew what he was capable of? At that point, who the hell cared? "How can that be if you're not allowed back in the office until you get help?"

Michael stopped, spun around in my face, his bellow shook the house. Eye to eye, finally. "Keep your fucking nose out of my business! Who the fuck do you think you're questioning, you nosy bitch! I'll take care of it!" He charged to the stairs.

He was not leaving if I could help it, my safety not a thought. "I called your father! He's on his way."

He swung around and lunged. Grabbing my shoulders, shaking me, he shoved me into the wall. Still standing my ground, I stared into his dead eyes as he roared in my face.

"You called my father? You fucking cunt! You called my father? Who the fuck do you think you are? What gives you the right? How could you do this to him? If he gets a heart attack, I'll fuckin' kill you!"

He shoved me harder. This time I fell into the folding closet doors, which broke my fall as they collapsed. I immediately jumped back on my feet. He wasn't going to keep me down! He paced back and forth savagely, clenching his fists, ranting, motioning to strike, but didn't.

Unshaken, I didn't care. I felt eerily calm. "You have that a little confused. Take a good look in the mirror. Your actions will be what kills him, you asshole!"

A whimper from the kitchen doorway. Mike guarded Gerry, both frozen, petrified. My heart wrenching, I ran to them as Michael obliviously continued his pacing rant. Dropping to my knees, I hugged them tight.

"I'm okay. Everything is okay."

But was it? Or would it ever be again? I would make damn sure of it. The doorbell rang. Michael halted like a deer in headlights. Saved by the bell!

Smiling at my precious innocents, I said, "Grandpa from Brooklyn came to see you!"

The boys beamed at each other. Mike squealed. "Grandpa from Brooklyn is here? Yes!"

Gerry joined in, prolonging the "S" sound with his brother. "Yes!"

The kids darted down the stairs to the door with giggles, ready for their white-haired Grandpa in the doorway. Referred to as GM by most, he had the thickest Brooklyn accent ya ever did hear, "th" replaced with "d," "ir" with "oi," "ar" with "aw" and on and on. I had only the faintest Brooklyn twang but it always felt like home to hear. You can take the girl outta Brooklyn, but you can't never take Brooklyn outta the girl!

"My boys! How are you?" He scooped them up with hugs and kisses.

Mike pulled him close. "Is Daddy going to kill you?"

Grandpa raised his brows to me, belly-laughing. "Never happen! Don't you worry! Hello, daughter-in-law. How are you?"

"Thank you, Dad." I hugged him, not wanting to let go.

"You go take care of my little boys. I'll take care of my big boy right now!"

The boys ran up to the living room ahead of me. I stayed back, remaining out of sight, peeking. They faced each other, nose to nose, Michael's head bowed, shoulders slouched. His father hollered up in his face, reaching up, slapping his head. "Mikey! What da hell is goin' on here? What da hell are you doin'"?

Michael cowered, his head still bowed, unmoved as this little man slapped him around. Amazing. Thank God for Grandpa. "Nothin', Dad. They're blowing it all out of proportion."

"Dey blowin' shit! You better get your head straight or I'll take dose kids and your wife da hell outta here and you won't see us no more! You hear me, you cocksucker!" His father smacked his head again. "I love you, you son of a bitch! You wanna kill yourself? Go right ahead! I can't stop you. Ya ain't takin' your family wit' ya! And another ding! I hear you talkin' to your wife like dat again, I'll knock your fuckin' teeth in for ya! You dink I didn't hear trough da door? Remember who you're talkin' to! Dat's your wife! She's da best thing dat ever happened to you! You treat her wit' respect, ya hear me?"

The doorbell rang again. Mike and Gerry flew past me down the stairs. My second angel of the night, Ingrid. I came down with their bags, seeing both kids already wrapped in Grandpa's arms. Michael reached to give the boys kisses and hugs as if they were his last. Gerry hugged and kissed him back. Mike shrunk into me, his fearful eyes searching.

Caressing his head. "It's okay, love."

As Mike walked toward his father he wouldn't let go of my hand, as if the bad man was going to take him away. Stiff, he let his father hug him. I followed my two big boys, rolling their Pokémon luggage out the front door behind Ingrid. Before letting them go, they needed to be filled with my love and security. I squatted down, each taking a lap, my arms secure and holding them close.

"Don't worry. Everything is okay. Mommy will never let anything happen to you, or me. Promise."

Gerry reached his soft, tiny hands out holding my face, heaven on my cheeks. "Everything is okay. I love you, Mama."

At three, he still called me Mama. My heart smiled a mile wide, bursting and breaking for my children all at once. Gerry wrapped his cherubic little arms around my neck and squeezed so tight, then slid off my lap and climbed into the car. He stopped himself, turned back around, and kissed my cheek with his sweet little lips. Priceless. Mike was still on my lap, his eyes questioning.

I held him tight. "Mike, has Mommy always protected you?"

His troubled hands on my shoulders, protectively. "Yes, but what about you, Mommy? Daddy hurt you. I saw him push you and yell curses at you."

"I don't remember him pushing me." Still feeling the sting where his fingers gripped me, the ache on my back from his force. "Are you sure you heard curses?" Reaching.

Mike shot me an *are you kidding?* look. "Mom. I know curses, and I know what I saw."

Trying to brush it off lightly killed me almost as much as lying so ridiculously. "Mommy called Grandpa from Brooklyn to help Daddy feel better, and Daddy didn't want me to call him, that's all."

"That's not a good reason to push you or call you curses."

My pride bounded—such a good heart, precocious as hell, and sharp as a tack for five. "Mike, you're absolutely right and so smart. He said he was sorry and will never do it again."

"Mommy, can I talk to him to make him feel better?"

"You are the sweetest boy. It's okay, love. Grandpa will be with him." I stroked his hair. "Baby, nothing will ever happen to me. I'm magic. I'll always be here for you two, no matter what! Always remember that. Now, let me see a smile."

What a beautiful sight. As long as he felt better, I was good, sealing my promises with hugs and kisses. Mike climbed in. I squeezed Ingrid's hand, no words needed. We waved as the car drove away and pulled into the driveway five houses down. Close, but far enough away. Many more questions to be answered, many more white lies, many more promises I hoped I could keep. My tears creeped back up as I turned to the house.

"Breathe. Just breathe."

Faltering up the stairs and turning the corner, I held my breath. Michael and his dad were hugging. His father had calmed him down. He had calmed his father.

Michael trudged toward me. "Honey, I'm sorry. I was upset but understand why you did it. It won't happen again."

I took two steps back. He was upset? He understood? He was out of his fucking mind! And lying through his sorry face! Seeing through his act, I intended to play my part until this all played out. The momentary hug was disingenuous on both parts and a moment too long. I pulled away. Michael immediately retreated to his office. A pit of panic ripped through my core, knowing I would be left alone with him. I needed to keep my promise.

"Dad, can you stay over? Please?"

"Believe me, I wish I could! Dat dope of a son I got! I gotta go home and take care of your mother-in-law. I can't leave her alone too long. She's worried sick!"

I don't care how worried sick I was, nothing would ever keep me from my kids in any time of need. "I understand. Give her our love. Thank you for coming, Dad. I'm sorry."

"For what? You didn't do nuttin'. I'm glad you called. You call me whenever you need me, y'hear? Let me know what's goin' on, anytime. Take care now!"

My stomach rattled, steeling myself as I closed the door, his car pulling away. As I approached Michael's office, he barged past almost running me over, phone and keys in hand and a folder under his arm, determined, as was I.

Holding my bladed tongue. "See you later."

The door closed. His car turned the corner. I waited a minute, then double-locked the door, alarm on, just in case. It was Michael, after all. First, his office phone. Redial. The bypass number to MRI, no one picked up. *69. Last call in, unknown number. I combed through his desk, cabinet, closet, drawers, papers, in every unassuming crevice. Jackpot! Under his hanging files in the very back of his drawer: an empty Demerol bottle, another half-filled and two unopened, two bloody syringes, and bloody tissues. Poof! A sleuth was born! I embarked on a game of cat and rat, me the prowling cat pursuing my lying sneaky rat of a husband and his dirty secrets. How much he was hiding I was going to find out. Would he even notice these things were missing? How out of his mind was he? Where would I hide it all? My fine china cabinet in the dining room, buried and covered. He'd never find it. The bar one cabinet over, one level up, no need to move. A large snifter glass and a tall bottle of Frangelico, the monk. No children, no husband, so alone, so many unanswered questions. Truth or lies?

My brain blurred, I glazed at the monk. "You and I are gonna become good friends."

Cuddled with a blanket and my companion for the night, cradling my glass, I lolled, swaying on my living room balcony loveseat. The cool spring night, so quiet. What a beautiful starry sky, so clear. Though nothing was clear to me.

To God, to my angels. "I can't do this alone. Please, guide me. I'm scared. So scared. Protect my innocent babies. Protect me. They need me. I beg of you. Help Michael find his way. He's lost."

The sky a seesaw, the bottle was empty. So was I. Under the stars with my new-found buddy, the monk, I fell asleep.

2

The Shock

"Thursday, twelve, in the Edgewater McDonald's parking lot next to the drive-through, got it."

"Stay in your vehicle. I will come to you wearing a blue baseball cap, jacket and sunglasses. Bring the information we discussed."

"Will do. See you then." Sneaking, playing his game. I hated every minute of it. What was I to do?

My cell still in hand, Petra's name flashed, Michael's New York City office manager. She never called from her cell midday. "Barb, you gotta come now! Michael collapsed in the hallway!"

Loins girded, I veered to the city in a blink, unusually cool. "Is he unconscious?"

"He was out for a few minutes, then came to, but he's really out of it. He didn't want me to call you. I had to. The ambulance is on its way. I don't know what hospital yet."

"On my way. Thank you."

I needed to get there, fast. He promised he wouldn't use the Demerol anymore for his back and would make time to see Dan. His words had become selfish lies, out of control. I was losing him to his secret love affair with this Demerol, this poison. I felt it, but I loved him.

Katia, my house cleaner, my sitter, my trusted friend, answered, thank God. "I can't explain now, but please pick up Mike and Gerry from school today. Can you stay until I return? It's an emergency."

"Yes. Don't worry." Unspoken, Katia knew, probably more than I. We were good to each other.

"You're an angel, I love you!"

The ride up felt as though the elevator had gorilla glue for cables laboring up each floor. As the door opened, I flew into his office. Petra greeted me with a hug and led me to Michael on the floor in the hallway, hunched against the wall with four paramedics surrounding him. Two police officers, onlookers everywhere, it resembled a crime scene. I waited for these guys to break out their yellow tape. Was he in trouble?

Arms crossed, Petra's eyes shifted from him to me. "Hellina fled the scene."

His surgical assistant? How much of a dirty rat was he? Couldn't be. She wasn't even close to his type. I was beginning to believe I didn't know my husband at all. My "cat hair" stood up along the back of my neck. Stopping myself from jumping to conclusions, I played it cool. "Why did she take off?"

She shrugged her shoulders, lowering her chin. "Maybe she was afraid of getting caught."

"Caught for what, Petra?"

"I don't know." Her eyes told me differently.

Putting it aside, wondering how anyone else could not know, I turned to the matters at hand and the towering officers. "I'm his wife." They let me through.

"Honey, how are you doing?" Scanning his arms, nothing. No matter, I knew.

"Why are you here? I told Petra you shouldn't come."

"I'm your wife. Why wouldn't I be here? Let them finish taking care of you. I'll meet you at the hospital."

"The fucking hospital? Get the fuck outta here! I'm fine! There's nothing wrong with me! You're all fucking crazy!"

Hoping the hospital was Pandora's box to break open his dangerous hidden drug problem, I pulled aside one of the paramedics. "He should go to the hospital and be tested for what's going on and why this happened, shouldn't he? Please?"

"Yes, he should. We'll do our best, ma'am."

"Please make sure they run a thorough blood panel on him. And keep this conversation between us."

"What conversation?"

"Thank you." I watched, conflicted, wanting him exposed to get him help yet not get him in trouble.

The paramedic reasoned with Michael. "Sir, given your stats, under these circumstances, we're obligated to take you to the emergency room."

"I'm fucking fine!" He tried to get up with a vengeance but fell to the floor like a rag doll.

"Please stay seated, sir. You may be having an attack, heart or anxiety. You need to be monitored."

Michael relented and they lifted him onto the gurney. "Which hospital, sir?"

"Lenox Hill. I'm an attending doctor there." Michael's sunken eyes shifted to me. "Barbra, go home. I'm fine."

"I'll meet you at the hospital."

I kissed his forehead, whether he liked or not. Chasing the ambulance on the streets of New York? Impossible.

I made it. "Oh yes, Mrs. Mastromarino, he's been expecting you. Come right this way."

Still on the gurney. "What took you so long?" He immediately sensed me. "What's wrong?" His lofty eyes told me he could fool the whole damn world!

"What did the doctor say?"

He gave himself the cavalier once over. "See? I'm fine."

Unbelievable. "They didn't find anything on the blood tests? Nothing? What about urine?"

He grinned, clasped hands resting on his chest, tapping his thumbs in victory, so smug. "Nope, I told you." He felt me searing right through him. "Don't believe me? Ask the doctor."

On the hunt, I found him. "Excuse me. I'm Michael's wife. What were the results of his blood tests and urinalysis?"

"When he came in, his blood pressure was high, his heart beat somewhat erratic for a short time. Otherwise, he's fine. We're ruling it as an anxiety attack."

"But, the blood tests. They were normal? All of them?"

"Yes, he's strong as an ox according to our tests. He does need to take it easy for a few days. Knowing Michael, that's asking the impossible."

How the hell did he do that? He's becoming a master of deception. I need proof exposed!

"He's free to go. I've already signed off on his chart."

"Thank you, Doctor." Stupefied, I careened back to Michael.

He lounged back like the rat that ate the cat. "So?"

"They couldn't have tested for everything."

"Honey, they take a battery of tests. Really, I'm fine."

I studied this man I thought I knew so well, completely thrown, but knowing.

Thursday, 9:30 a.m., at the Englewood Cliffs MRI location, Lou, Michael's associate, reached out and swallowed me with a bear hug. "Barbie baby! How you doin'? Meetin' with the boys?"

I had known him since their NYU Dental School days together before Michael went on to his oral surgical residency. Word was he found Michael passed out on the bathroom floor. I was surprised he didn't call me. I surely didn't know the whole story, yet, instantly a crusader against the old adage, "The wife is the last to know."

"They're waiting in Keith's office. Good to see you."

Keith's door was open. At his desk, he greeted me with a hug. It all felt surreal. Who could I trust?

"Kevin is finishing the morning meeting with the staff. He'll be in shortly, but let's get started."

"You mean he wants you to pave the path, the diplomatic one, right? I'm sure he's quite heated about all this."

"You know us better than I thought."

We laughed. The ice was broken.

"It's not the first time I've been underestimated. Back to business. What is the next step as far as you're concerned?"

"We heard what happened at the Manhattan office. Doctor Miles concurs with the agreement we have drawn up for Mike to concede. He needs to seek help to show good faith for business's sake. We'll leave it at that."

He needed to show more than good faith. Exactly what were they thinking? Business. They believed Michael was brilliant and far more of an asset than ever a liability, given his little problem. I wasn't so sure.

"I understand. I will handle the personal matters."

"And Barbra, trust me, we understand. We're here to help."

That's what they all say. I couldn't believe anyone, with their own damn agendas.

Keith sat forward with conviction, his expression sad. "Our mom, now passed, was an alcoholic. We'd been through it most of our lives until she finally gave out, more difficult than I could ever describe."

What they must have gone through. I thought of my boys.

"Whichever the loved one, or the substance, it's all the same. It's hard all around."

Now, I was the one who underestimated them, so grateful for the unexpected understanding, support and guidance, though my terror remained. "I am so sorry, Keith. There are no words that could be enough."

"Barbra, I'll only tell you two things you need to remember at all times. Beyond anything, make sure you take care of you and your children first. You need to protect yourself. Get yourself a lawyer. And don't take anything personally. This is his problem, his choice, not yours."

"A lawyer? That's an extreme measure for me right now. I'm out to be there for him and help him through this. And don't take anything personally? That's a little tough since he's my husband. Is there something you know that you're not telling me?"

"Please, take your precautions. You'll understand when the time comes."

I took it all in, not quite sure how to process and proceed. "Thank you, really. I'm assuming I should set this rehab up, like yesterday?"

Keith chuckled. "Pretty much. He won't be allowed to practice here or his other sites until he gets treatment. Look into a rehab, Hazelden, in Minnesota, specializing in treatment of doctors—highest success rate. Let me know how you make out. We'll help as much as we can."

"You've helped more than I could have ever asked for. I can't thank you enough. I just want him to be okay."

"Our sentiments exactly. But remember, you first."

"Without question. I should go. With no office hours in Manhattan, he'll be heading up here from there sooner than later to meet with you."

"Keep this between us. Let Mike tell you."

I hoped he would. "Tell the staff I was never here."

I hugged him, my voice trembling. "Thank you."

Gliding through the office, I withstood the stares, whispers, and phony smiles. I had put all the bits and pieces of rumors together like a puzzle I didn't want to believe as true of Michael meeting Hellina, a dancer, one night at a restaurant years ago, of them together for a long time, or maybe not for long. So many conflicting stories floated around, too many to ignore. All I had gotten for my trouble were cagey answers from our friends, colleagues and even his family, I held my tongue until it was real. No matter how he denied it all, showering me with love, I could never look at him the same, feeling as if a serrated knife twisted in my heart. Still I smiled and said good-bye to everyone as if it were any other day. But Michael had changed everything. I left with my dignity. No one could ever take that from me. Hazelden would be my pitch. Minnesota or West Palm Beach? No contest. West Palm Beach in the spring? Perfect lure.

On to my meeting. Parked in my truck by the Golden Arches, aroma of fries and grilled burgers. Couldn't remember the last time I had either but didn't miss them. A nice piece of carrot cake from Whole Foods in the next plaza was worth it, something sweet to take away the sour taste of it all. Lies to my family. Lies to my dearest friends. Lies from my husband. Lies from who knew else. No fitness competitions. No anniversary trip to Italy. No stability. No direction. No certainty. Just chaos. In the dark.

A man with a baseball cap and sunglasses came to my window. "Barbra?"

"Yes. Jim?"

"Yes." He slid into the passenger seat, folder in hand.

"I can't believe I'm doing this. I never thought—"

"Don't worry. Most people who come to me feel the same. Modestly, ninety percent of the people who call me for a reason they don't think they have, come to find out they did. If you're feeling something is there, it probably is."

"I don't want to believe he would do that to me."

"Nobody does, and, believe it or not, a good percentage end up going back to their spouses after discovering they've cheated. It takes seven times for a woman to leave her abuser and cheater."

"Really? I came to you to validate or negate the suspicion. If it's true, I'm done."

"From what you told me on the phone, drugs are involved."

"Yes. Rumors are he does the drugs with his surgical assistant, Hellina."

"Drugs and cheating usually go hand in hand. I'll prove or disprove the hearsay for you. Do you have the information?"

My folder had all the intel he had asked for, and all I found. He asked me questions and warned me some I may find offensive or invasive. They were. But I was all good with it. Who had any shame after childbirth anyway? Like an unspoken "Bold Bitch" club. But these questions needed to be answered to get the full picture. He took notes. What was he scribbling? How funny, feeling deceitful to Michael. He left me no choice. I trusted no one. Alone, I had to get the truth. Odds were, it was not going to be what I wanted to hear. My new trusted confidant, sadly my private investigator, told me to get a pre-paid phone for contact. Radio Shack set me up, my PI phone under my sister, Raven. Everything was ready to roll.

In my car hiding away, along the Hudson shore enjoying every bite of my cake, I traced the strong waves flowing south. The water tumbled over the pretty stones beyond the walk path. Gazing across at the most exciting city in the world, my city, where Michael and I started our lives together and his career, it was simply beautiful.

Lost in the blue sky, calling to my angels, I said, "Help me."

Later, back at the house, without a second thought I sleuthed through phone bills and credit card statements, hoping to God nothing would jive. The door chimed. He was home. I hid the evidence. Straight or high? Did he smell like another woman? Hellina, his haughty assistant perhaps? Seeming coherent, he came toward me, but stopped...as if he knew I needed space between us.

"I spoke to Keith and Kevin. I need to appease them by going away for a little while to get help. I don't need it, but I need to show good faith."

I kept catching myself. Trusting his word had always been second nature.

"We need to find a good place, specific to doctors. I'm not going to a dump! It's gonna be as close to a vacation as possible." Vacation? *Delusional, a rude awakening was coming.*

"Already on it. Hazelden, West Palm Beach caters to doctors and professionals. They'll have a bed for you Friday."

"I could get into that. Come with me."

"To rehab?"

"No, stay at a neighboring hotel so you're near me. I'd feel better if you're with me. Don't leave me. Could you stay with me until we leave? I want you with me every minute. I trust you. I don't trust myself."

Pinch me. Didn't trust him either. Didn't care. He let me in. I was his wife. No one could take care of him like me.

"There's a Days Inn around the corner from the center," I said.

"Fuck the Days Inn! It's bad enough we need to cancel the Italy trip. Besides not speaking at the conference, that was our anniversary trip. Book yourself in the best hotel around in a suite. Stay there as long as I need to stay. Then I might just join you."

"The Ritz-Carlton is five minutes from there, but—"

"Book it." He grabbed and held me, fighting for me. I never wanted this feeling to end, it felt so damn good. My suspicions still tugged, hoping I would never need Jim. My gut told me that was not likely.

Pulling back. "Michael, look me in the eye and tell me nothing is going on between you and Hellina."

"Honey, nothing is going on. Why would I want you with me, and only you? You're my bashert." He held me closer.

It felt too good to be true. Second to my boys, nothing mattered more than him getting better. I stayed as close as he'd let me. There was no easy fix. How could I tell Tiana, Maria, and Rayne the truth? Lies to my trusted besties killed me inside. Worried, there for me in a heartbeat, they would know my business trip with Michael was a ruse. I was reduced to hiding because of him. I hated it.

Palm Beach was gorgeous, the weather beautiful, Hazelden Rehabilitation Center fundamental. I escorted him in to make sure they received and kept him. He signed a release for his dad, Keith, Kevin, and me to call for updates. Really, he could have trotted out of there as soon as he walked in. Only the law could've coerced him or anyone into rehab, with the threat of losing an important license/certification, or jail time.

Simply magnificent. Breathtaking views, the beach, the ocean—my therapy. The hot sun kissing my skin, sand cascading between my toes, running my hands through the water as the waves washed up on shore. Beautiful rhythmic waves resounded through me. The horizon beyond the ocean seemed endless, leading to where? I could only see heartbreak. My husband was falling apart. My marriage too? The doctors assessed that he should stay for three weeks, at least. No visitors before seven days. A knock on my hotel door broke my trance, but I hadn't ordered anything. A dozen roses and dark chocolate. My heart leaped, hoping Michael did this from rehab for our anniversary? Could he be that thoughtful? The card read, "Happy Anniversary," compliments of the Ritz-Carlton. Nope. Such a nice gesture couldn't take away the pain, though the roses were beautiful, and the chocolate the sweetest thing on my lips since kissing my boys' cheeks goodbye. As decadent as the Ritz was, my broken heart wasn't in it.

The next day there was another unexpected knock. Peephole, nothing. Another knock. I opened the door to Michael with two champagne glasses in one hand, a bucket of ice with a nice chilled bottle of Diet Pepsi (in lieu of alcohol), and one red rose in his teeth. "Happy Anniversary, honey!"

A happy anniversary it was. He came to me. I forgot the world, the doubt, the drugs, enraptured in our getaway. He enraptured in me. Newlyweds again! Everywhere we went, the beach, the gym, dinner, people actually asked if we were recently married. Together, we rediscovered each other.

Fear struck me. I was afraid to leave the hotel, this dream, to go home, to face reality. "Michael, look me in the eye. Promise me nothing was going on with Hellina." The thought was like fingernails on a chalkboard, clawing at my mind.

"Maybe you should get some help and talk to a shrink," he suggested playfully, with a borderline mocking tone.

"You're telling me to get help? You just ducked out of a rehab facility after three days for Demerol abuse. You haven't stopped lying to me. The only help I need is the truth!"

Kissing my neck, he slipped his hand under my robe. "I'll show you the truth."

Affection? I'll take it. Nice diversion. Into the night we cozied together on the balcony, mesmerized by the ocean shimmering in the moonlight.

"So, tell me, Houdini. Release or escape?"

"I checked out." As if it were a hotel. "I'm fine! They should take care of people who really need it. I don't belong with *those people*. I'm smarter than everyone there! Including the doctors! They came to me for advice!" Ego unbounded.

"Three days? You really think that's enough? And what about Keith and Kevin?"

"Don't worry your pretty little head, they'll be fine."

No fight? Again, I caught myself. I didn't recognize my husband, but I liked him. Nothing made sense. *Use instinct, reason. Don't trust his word. Doubt what is dubious.*

3

The Slip and Fall

A week later, the boys jumped into our arms, squealing with joy. "Mommy! Daddy!"

Hugs and kisses. "My babies! We missed you so much!"

I hugged my mom and dad close. "Thank you."

With loving eyes, their silence told me they had faith in me and supported me despite my husband. Michael pensively hugged them, telling them all was okay. They were not convinced. Mike strutted into his grandparents' living room and climbed on the coffee table, his stage, glancing at Grandma for approval. She gave him a nod with a smile, waiting for her grandson's show.

With his toy mic. "Guess what! It's almost our birthdays!"

Leave it to Grandpa, the big kid, to remind the kids of their birthdays way too early for Mom to handle!

Gerry climbed up next to his brother with his toy mic and held up three sweet little fingers. "I'm gonna be three! I want chocolate cake, please! Oh, yeah! And lots of toys!"

"So what! I'm gonna be six! I want strawberry ice cream cake. And I want more toys!" We all laughed and applauded. Mike took a bow, then Gerry.

The next two weeks were like a dream. Michael and I brought our newlywed mood home from the Ritz. More importantly, he surprisingly brought his recovery persona home from his self-prescribed three-day rehab stint. Day after day, he looked clean as a whistle, spending time with me and the boys as much as he could. Still, the feeling nagged. This was too easy. Nothing is ever that easy. I planned to take every good day I could get, enjoy every moment for as long as it lasted. To keep my perfect picture I kept a distance from everyone. But I had Jim in my side pocket, paid and ready. Hellina's profile was etched in my mind. I could independently track Michael, her, or them together in a pinch.

Gerry's birthday dinner arrived. His favorite, macaroni and skirt steak with salad set, Mike and Gerry kneeled over their plates, forks in hand ready to pounce. No Daddy.

Mike stared at the food. "Mommy! I'm hungry!"

"Me, too! If the food is ready, why can't we eat?" Even at three Gerry had inarguable logic.

I had enough. "Dig in, boys! We have chocolate cake tonight! You need to help each other blow out your candles and open presents, okay?"

"No problem, Mom. Where's Daddy?" Mike never missed a trick. Nothing got past him. His senses so keen, we all called him hawk ears and eyes, with an elephant's memory.

"He should be here any minute. I'll try him now." His office—answering service. His cell—voicemail. My stomach fermented. Trying again, my heart burned. Not again. "Boys, Daddy missed a lot of work. He's probably still catching up."

They pouted instantly.

"Hey! Let's take some pictures of what he's missing, so he can feel like he was here! We'll show him later."

Mopes turned to smiles in a flash. Snapping the Polaroid, pictures popped out of my two posers, eating dinner, blowing out Gerry's candles, eating cake, tearing open presents. Voicemails left over and over. Nothing. I knew. Did the last few weeks mean anything? These last eight years? Us? Our family? After cake and presents, they had the biggest birthday bubble bath the tub could fit. At that point, I didn't care if they flooded the bathroom! If they were happy, Mommy was happy. The fine art of distraction, for them and me.

"It's powder time! Michael Anthony, you are not to touch the powder. I will place it in your hands. And no clapping, got it?"

He put up three scheming little fingers close together and giggled. "Scout's honor, Mom."

I cracked up. "You're not a Boy Scout, wise guy!"

I opened my drawer to reach for the powder. Michael's drug paraphernalia tucked in the back stung my eyes. It all came rushing back. Calmly, I took the powder, closing the drawer and visions behind me. Eyeing Mike, I sprinkled powder in each of their hands to powder themselves in the right places.

Mike clapped his hands with a big grin and sang. "Happy birthday to you! Happy Birthday to you! We just took a bath! Now we don't smell like poo!"

The boys giggled. I couldn't hold back my smile if I tried. To the bedroom, through the lingering powder cloud.

"Come on, get your jams on."

After we read a story, they clasped their sweet little hands under their chins, closing their eyes. "Thank you for the yummy dinner and our presents, and for Mommy. Please, make sure Daddy is okay." Tugging at my heart with every word.

"Mommy, when Daddy comes home, don't forget to show him the pictures, okay?"

"I won't forget, babydoll, promise. Sweet dreams, my loves."

Three a.m. Michael staggered in, all lights off, the house still. He clomped to his office, feeling for the switch. Lights on. Bam! He almost fell over, shocked. Reclined in his office chair, my eyes stabbed him. A drugged mess, he glanced down at his desk. In plain sight, Demerol bottles, needles, bloody tissues on one side, and Polaroids of his boys spread across the other. I kept my promise.

I leaned forward, hissing. "Which is it going to be? You can't have both."

He reached out to touch my arm. I left the room as if he was not there. Motioning to speak, no words could come. Over his desk unsteadily, squinting to focus on the pictures, his eyes gravitated toward the bottles. His heart skipped, seeing one half-full. Sobbing, his tears fell to the beautiful image of his babies. He was a broken man, torn. Having left the pitiful sight of my sorry husband, I continued upstairs and retired beside my children, cuddling close to them, feeling their warmth. His sobs resonated through the house. I closed my eyes.

He had a different excuse for consistently not coming home after work: late nights, cases at the hospital, the schedule at the office, meetings. Gone. I had lost him again. How could I fight for him? Amazing, a drug that aids in surgeries can take over souls like the devil. No more breaking news from any offices, but my forced expertise gave me no choice, I knew. Everything more distinct, the signs were enough. His eyes sunken in, brows and facial muscles drooped, aging him thirty years. Complexion cadaverous, trembling, sluggish, unbalanced, gibberish, blood drops on his shirts and pants, marks on his arms and hands, his pitiful cast of fright and confusion. One or all, a dead giveaway. He resembled the walking dead. My virile, handsome husband diminished to a sad sight. My heart bled for him. I didn't know how to help him. It was where he wanted to be. I didn't understand it. He fell deeper into his problem, becoming more careless, yet more skillful at trickery, more cunning, all a paradox. Every day was the frightening unknown.

I needed a new approach. Beat him at his own game. He isolated himself on our bedroom loveseat at the foot of the bed, staring at the TV as if he was invisible. He appeared to be somewhat straight, but edgy, having come down from using earlier. Seizing the opportunity, I joined him. His body stiffened, eyes not veering from the TV. I needed to get on the inside again and bring him back over, snuggling closer, rubbing his shoulder and neck without a word.

He leaned forward, loosening up. "Ooh, that feels good."

Melting to my touch every time since our beginning, this was my leverage. Though his back injury remained the bane of his existence from his football days at Pitt, he would do it all over again, not erasing a moment. Scars are funny that way. They don't hurt anymore, but they have a great story behind them, and many a lesson learned.

Facing him, I took his hand. "Honey, look at me."

He turned to me, caressing my fingers, listening intently.

Keep five steps ahead, two not nearly enough. Speak kindly of his coveted painkiller. For his back? Bullshit. That's what his epidurals are for.

"I love you. Just listen. Please, be truthful. I know you've been using the Demerol and understand your back has been killing you. But using it the way you are is hurting you more than it's helping you. Sometimes, I think you may be taking too much. I want to help you. What can I do?"

He dropped my hand and looked away, defenses rising. "No, I haven't." He started to get up from the couch.

Trying to tame a wild hangry beast was a cakewalk compared to him. I gently tugged him back down. "It's okay. You left a drawer open. It was out in the open and I couldn't miss it. I'm not mad, just worried. I love you."

He took my hand again and perked up. "Don't be worried. Honey, you have no idea how good it makes me feel! I feel great! I have some in my closet. Try it! You'll know what I'm talking about. I'll get it." He jumped up from the couch, with spring in his stride to his closet, as if sharing a new toy!

Oh, my God! He's not kidding! Steady. Steady.

"I'll take your word for it. I don't need to try it."

He emerged from the closet filling a syringe from his bottle of poison, coming toward me, smiling. "Just a little, you'll see. Here, I'll do some first."

He so naturally put the needle in his arm. Injecting the Demerol into his vein, his entire body loosened within seconds. He came toward me with the rest.

Panicking, I backed away as if we were playing tag. Oh shit, I was It! "Please! I don't want to! Stop! No!"

"Really, honey! It's great stuff!" He cornered me between the bed and window against the wall.

"Michael! No!" Nowhere to escape, I struggled against him, trying to pull my arm away as he took it bracing tight.

He brought the needle close. "Here. Just a drop."

My entire body tensed. "Stop it! You're going to rip me with the needle!"

"Hold still." He held me still, so calm, with a smile, happy to be bringing me to join him on his side—the other side.

The cold steel on my skin, fear paralyzed me. God forbid it broke off! The needle penetrated beneath the surface. The hot sting rushed through my veins instantly.

"See? That wasn't so hard, was it? You'll feel it any second now. You'll love it!"

He is out of his mind! He wants me to be his drug partner! This is insane!

"Damn you! I told you I didn't want to! How could you force that on me! And the same needle!" The thought he shared needles with Hellina scared me to death.

"Come on. What's marriage all about? We're sharing interests." Such a cheeky asshole.

His nonchalance infuriated me! I attempted to scream, but nothing could come. The Demerol overtook my body, feeling dizzy and nauseous, so sick. My entire body started to shut down. Everything went dim. "I don't feel so good, like I'm going to faint, vomit and go to the bathroom, all at once."

He helped me onto the bed, fixed the pillows, put the covers on me, placed a cold wet cloth on my forehead and gave me a bottle of water, without a shred of regret.

Mike appeared in the doorway, his arm around Gerry. Those innocent, angelic faces were so worried. "Mommy, are you okay?"

As I motioned to speak, Michael answered. "Mommy's fine."

Mike, still holding Gerry, glared at his father shooting back to me. "Mom. Are you okay?"

"I'm okay, baby. Just a little headache, don't worry. Go back to your game." I had to be okay.

"But I heard you yelling something about 'Michael no, stop ripping you.' What did he do to you?" Mike shot his father another dagger and took Gerry's hand to approach my bedside.

"Oh, baby! Daddy didn't do anything! You must have heard a TV show. I do that sometimes, too, when I think something is happening in the house, but it's really on TV."

Mike was insistent. "It sounded just like you, Mom."

"But it wasn't. So, you go finish up your game with Gerry. It's almost time for bed. Now, I need a hug sandwich."

My boys gave me a double hug.

Michael chimed in. "Go ahead, guys, go play. Mommy's fine. Daddy will take care of her."

Mike's eyes shot one final dagger at his father as they left the room. Boy, if looks could kill! They scurried down to resume their game. The inventor of this miraculously distracting video game called Nintendo 64 deserved a medal of honor! Michael sat down beside me, stroking my hair. How I wanted to push his hand away but didn't. What was I doing? Love can mess a girl up, beyond reason.

His beeper sounded. "Lenox Hill. I'm on call tonight." He wobbled into the bathroom as he dialed, then emerged from the bathroom as he closed his cell phone. "Honey, I have an emergency, bad motorcycle accident. Sounds like it will possibly go all night. I'll most likely grab some sleep in the residents' room at the hospital."

Wow. He forcibly shot me up. I got sick. He got a beep and made the call from another room. He had to go. What a damn coincidence, remarkable timing. I failed as a drug partner, so back to the same old? Still, I had to play this right. If I asked for another shot of his favorite "toy," would there be an emergency? Should I have asked to see his phone? Not yet. A time and place for everything.

He entered his closet, reappearing in his scrubs. "I'll call you later to see how you are, okay?"

Examining him in his stupor, hastily and excitedly packing his bag, more questions flooded my mind. My heavy drugged head didn't stop my visions of him meeting Hellina, spending the night with her, shooting up with her, the hospital, his car, Hellina's bed. Cut through me like a serrated knife. "Who's your assistant for the surgery? Hellina?"

"Honey, nothing is going on. Come on now. I don't know who can make it in. Most likely just the hospital surgical nurses will scrub in."

"I have too many doubts. Hellina living right here, just one town over, just blocks from us is too close for comfort."

"Tomorrow, I make all your doubts disappear, promise." He kissed me on the forehead and left in a hurry.

On to the things that mattered: putting the boys in bed. We read a story and I tucked them in with kisses, my two little reasons for everything. Back into my bed, being alone wasn't so bad, peaceful, though hell still ensued. Cell in hand, Bellevue Oral Surgery Department, no one gave me a straight answer about Michael being on call. Were they playing stupid? Or just stupid?

Put nothing past him, five steps ahead. Okay, smoking gun. I'm gonna find you.

Pulled out my PI phone. It was time for Jim. "Wednesday, Michael has office hours from about 12:00 to 5:00 up in Rockland County, New York, at Ken's dental office, a very dear friend of ours. Sometimes, Michael leaves early if a case cancels. They always park in the back and use the employee entrance. I'd say get there for 3:30 and wait. Hellina will be assisting him that day. I'm sure they will travel together."

"I'm on it. Is there any way you and your kids can take a trip that day? Usually when the cat's away, the rat will play."

"Should I plan a trip or let him believe we're gone and hide out in Edgewater while my kids are tucked elsewhere?"

"Risky. Besides, you all could probably use time away."

"You don't have to ask twice. My boys' school year is over. I'll take them to the beach for a couple of days."

"Two or three days in succession is even better. He'll think his window is wide open. I'm available on Thursday, but not Friday. I'm locked in to another job."

"Hopefully Wednesday is all we need, but keep Thursday open, please. Thank you."

Alone again. Jim, a paid professional, a complete stranger, the only one I can confide in. How pathetic. What happened to my husband? How much should I be willing to bear? This cat-and-rat game has become lies begotten of lies. This is not me, I hate it. How low will I have to go because of him?

Beyond lost, finding the truth was the only answer, no matter the pain. If I left him, what would he do? How could I save him from himself? My husband was sick. He needed me. No truth, no trust, no certainty, no direction, so many doubts, so tired, so very tired, I slipped away to sleep escaping to my dreams from my nightmare awake, no pain, just peace.

4

The Plan

Wednesday, my plan ensued. Michael's schedule at Ken's was on. I'd hear from Jim soon. On the beach in Montauk, a quiet, scenic, faraway beach town, PI cell in one hand, my cell in the other, soaking in my boys digging a crater in the sand and having the time of their lives—carefree and happy. These unknowing innocents had no idea what loomed around them, capsizing their lives. Agonizing, I couldn't stop it. Whatever it took, I'd kill or die trying before I let anything happen to them, their preservation at any cost. Sadly, I needed to protect them from their own father. The absurdity of it all...my children at the beach enjoying a beautiful day, while Mommy was having Daddy followed for cheating and drugs. The façade of bliss and normalcy laughable.

Just then, two guys on WaveRunners whizzed by offshore. Why didn't I think of it before? I was so busy shutting myself off from the world. I needed to call Maddie. Sandals, Antigua, we had met them on our honeymoons eight years ago. I remember how Michael and Reid had pulled up to the shore on their WaveRunners, strutting over to their smokin' hot bikini-clad, colada-sipping brides, posing on our lounges for our approaching studs. Those were the days. Life was so simple then, our biggest concerns dinner and lots and lots of drinking. The best of friends ever since, we didn't live close, but no matter. We had seen each other through many good times, and some hard. Our friendship was so deep, knowing no time or distance. Reid and Maddie lived close by in Stony Brook, two of the best, most genuine people I knew.

"Mad! How are you, my love? I'm so glad I caught you."

"Barbie! I was just thinking about you. I had this crazy feeling. Are you okay?"

"What a coincidence! I am crazy right now. Our telepathy is uncanny. Michael and Reid always did say we were witches. I just say we're mystical. Do you think you could blink over to Montauk? I need you."

"I knew it! Wait, wait, I have a vision. I could hear the ocean. My mystical powers tell me you're on the beach right now sippin' a cosmo, aren't you? And if you don't have one, you want one. Order two! I'll be there as soon as I can. I have the kids with me."

"I have mine here. We're at Gurney's. They'll keep each other busy while we have a sip and talk. I'll free up a hand for a drink when you get here. I'm holding two phones right now. Don't ask. Prepare to have your ears burned off. Get your ass over here!"

"Oh, God! I'm on my way."

I felt better already. As I hung up, the PI cell rang.

"I'm in place, but I don't see the white Eldorado."

"I know he drove it up. I'll conference in Ken's office. Stay quiet. Hi, Sheila, it's Barbra. Is Michael still there?"

"Let me put Dr. Ken on."

Ken's voice sounded shocked. "Barb, what the hell is going on with Mike? I was just calling you. The girls told me he was in the bathroom for a very long time and wouldn't come out. He had a patient under anesthesia ready for surgery. He finally stumbled out, completely out of it, slurring, and just took off. Blood was all over the sink, on the floor and the doorknob. If you know something, please tell me."

"Ken, wait. You don't know what's happened with Michael?"

"We were blown away today, Barb! This is insane!"

"I thought you knew, I am so sorry!"

Filling him in on Michael's incidents, all I could do was apologize for Michael, and make sure Ken had all his associates' numbers to stay connected.

"The girls are sending his patients in the waiting room home and canceling the rest as we speak."

"Good. When did he leave?"

"About fifteen minutes ago."

"Was he alone?"

"He left with Hellina. I think he drove her up."

Damnit! "I hear a call waiting. That might be Michael. I'll call you back!" I stayed on with Jim.

"Got it. We'll do our best to locate him. He usually takes the Palisades back to Fort Lee, correct?"

"Yes."

"I'll call you back with status ASAP."

Checking back with Ken, we'd talk later. Michael answered his cell, incoherent. My gut wrenched thinking of him behind the wheel. I tried to keep him on the phone to solve the riddle of where he was, but it was impossible. He answered yes to everything, unintelligible. Click. Out of my hands, I was learning very quickly I couldn't save him from himself. Above all else, I prayed for him and anyone in his path. My children blissfully frolicking in their superhero crater kept my head above the quicksand that was my life. I needed to disconnect. What else could I do three hours away with no clue of where he was, or more importantly, of how he was? Detach and decompress.

"Jim, just abort for now. It's useless." To be continued.

Maddie and kids arrived, finally. The four superkids played together in their superhero crater, while we mystical moms watched them from our enchanted beach chairs, sipping our magic potions, catching up on our crusade against evil.

"Maddie, what am I going to do?"

"I felt something wasn't right, but this? Our Michael? I'm blown away! Honey, I'm so sorry. I truly hope you don't find anything. He adores you. You were that last couple I ever expected. You're my Doctor and Mrs. Perfect Couple friends. I couldn't take it if you two broke up. I brag about you guys to everybody, y'know." Maddie grew misty, then pissed. "We're supposed to go to each other's kids' graduations and weddings. Barbie! The drugs! What's wrong with him? He's got a beautiful family and life, a soaring career. And if he is, what business does he have cheating on you? He couldn't ask for more! He's got a knockout wife who is ridiculously devoted to him, and is too damn good for him, by the way! You're a dream wife! I even wanna marry you!"

We busted out laughing. I lifted my glass. "I'll drink to that!" We toasted. "He rarely ever touches me, y'know. And on the rare occasion he does, he can just never hit it! Never! He's just not good at it. I don't think he cares. I do play a good Sally. He thinks he's King Kong, gets off, grunts, rolls over and goes to sleep. WTF?"

Maddie choked on her drink, roaring. "Oh, honey, you deserve some serious pampering."

I lifted my glass. "Me, myself and I, girl. We take care." I winked. "With the most delicious faceless man." I tapped my temple. "Anything else would be cheating, right?"

She lifted her glass. "To toys!"

I lifted mine. "No need."

She lifted her dropped jaw. "I'm jealous! We'll talk. Seriously, he's an idiot."

"I'm scared to know. I would need to leave him." Gazing into the bright horizon over the water, feeling the waves roll in, I dug my feet deeper into the sand. "But I love this man who hurts me, who hurts himself. How do I leave him in his abyss? He's lost. Michael's world is his little glass bottle."

Maddie took my hand. "If we can help in any way, we're here. First things first, you need to take care of yourself. You can't do this alone. Doesn't matter that you're the strongest bitch I've ever known. I remember when Mike was born like it was yesterday. You were my hero."

Smiling, we both welled up.

* * *

Lying on the examining table, just a routine exam due in three weeks, Dr. Schwabner had let me listen to little Mike's heartbeat, his stethoscope on my belly and his little box in hand. The most beautiful sound, his heartbeat echoed through the room, through my heart. My baby inside of me, a part of me, it was all so wondrous. He kept listening and listening. He listened from all angles around my belly. Oh, God. I felt the heat rising through my head.

"Barbra, I'm going to put some electrode pads on your belly for an EKG of the baby's heart. I hear a skip."

My heart had felt a skip of its own. "What could it be from?"

"It may be nothing at all, or the baby may be holding or resting on the umbilical cord. Let's see."

He hooked me up. "Are you comfortable?"

Tense and knotted up inside. "Once I know my baby is okay. The stirrups I can do without."

Dr. Schwabner laughed. "I will be back in a few minutes. Rest, and please try to lie still."

"That's funny."

He left the room. My mind reeled, trying to keep breathing. Everything would be all right. Blessed with "cool under pain or peril" from Mom, still, my heartbeat could've won the Indy 500.

Back, he examined the reading, expressionless. "Get dressed and meet me in my office."

What? Just leave me hanging? Dressed in record time, nerves frayed, his office door was open.

He motioned me in. "Barbra, I'm going to be frank with you. I don't like the way the heartbeat is dipping."

He showed me on the long roll of paper. The dips burned through my eyes and into my heart.

"I'm not comfortable letting you leave this office unless you go directly to the eighth floor to have this baby today. At thirty-seven weeks, you're far enough along to deliver. I'll give you Pitocin to induce you."

The room spun, stunned, yet collected. I trusted him with my life and my baby's. Was that enough? I prayed, terrified.

We're having our baby today. Please, God, take care.

Before I made my way to the delivery floor, outside NYU, the sun shining, air fresh, the fruit stand the best around. Enjoying my plum in all my fullness, something wasn't right, and I was going to have my baby early because of it. *What are you doin' in there, little guy?*

Michael met me on eight. After all was set and done, my Pitocin drip started working. As I was coming along, Dr. Schwabner placed electrodes on my belly and reached all the way inside to place electrodes on my baby's head. I could only see up to his elbow. More fun—the doctor held what looked like a mega-giant crochet hook.

"I need to break your water." He slid that in, no pain, just the warm rush. Holy shit. That was crazy.

Staying calm was easier said than done, knowing why I was in that room, three weeks early, monitors surrounding the room, all attached to me and my baby. My epidural, a wonder drip. We heard rhythmic screams of a woman coming from another room. Our eyes bulged and locked, grinning.

"Honey, I just want to apologize now for any scratching, biting, or name-calling I may attack you with during the delivery. Remember that I love you, okay?"

Michael laughed, lovingly gazing at me on the gurney as I watched TV, ready to have his child, ready for anything. He was in awe. I felt it. My labor and delivery, like a workout, quick and easy, no emergency C-section, my perfect baby came out. I barely touched his heel before they rushed him away to a table. My eyes were glued. Something was very wrong. Michael was still cradling my shoulders, caressing my head. As we intently watched more and more scrubs surround our son on that table, Dr. Schwabner directed them all, yelling. Knowing my mild-mannered doctor and friend for years, never until then. My head turned to the table as the assistant surgeon still tended to me, in plain English, to stitch me up. So much commotion, so scared, I was deaf to all noise, waiting to hear my baby cry.

His tiny body blue, struggling, gasping for air as they put an Ambu bag over his face for oxygen. Michael tried to distract me from looking. He knew. Our boy couldn't breathe on his own. Our son met eyes with Michael as they still held him up. He saw the fight in our boy's eyes to breathe. He tried to hide his tears from me.

Terrified, I watched our baby taken away with a team of at least a dozen doctors, suddenly so drowsy, fighting to stay awake. "What's happening? What's happening to my baby!"

When my eyes opened, I didn't know where I was. It all started coming back to me, the nightmare. They must have given me a sedative in my IV. Lying in a recovery room alone, it was just me and the IV. No baby. *Is my baby alive?*

Ready to push the call button, Dr. Schwabner came in.

"How are you feeling?"

"I don't know yet. Is he alive?"

"He's breathing on a respirator. He has what's called a diaphragmatic hernia. When his diaphragm formed, it did not fully close, leaving a hole big enough for his intestines to grow up into his chest cavity. The intestines moved his heart to the right and depressed the left lung. He has a good chance of surviving if his stats remain stable for seventy-two hours. At that point, corrective surgery could then be performed. I'm sorry."

No breath, frozen, stinging, tears. "This wasn't detected on the sonogram? Could it have happened from anything we did?"

"Your sonogram was at the normal sixteen weeks, as you were not in high risk and couldn't have been healthier. The diaphragm does not fully form until twenty weeks. Nothing you could have done. We just need to wait. He's a lucky little boy. Most babies don't survive birth. Dr. Henry Gilburg has already examined him. He said your baby is in a fairly good success group for survival. Gilburg is the top pediatric surgeon in his field. Your baby is in good hands. Speak to you later. Hang in there." Dr. Schwabner squeezed my hand.

"Thank you for saving his life, for everything!"

As he was leaving, Michael walked in, hugging him before letting him leave. "Thank you, Doc."

"Michael, how many pieces can my heart break into?"

He just cradled me, as if he was guarding us against the impossible pain. Insisting I needed to see my baby, the nurse finally let me walk. Michael took me to see him. He wasn't where all the other babies were. Little Mike was in the Neonatal Intensive Care Unit in a clear, enclosed case, hooked to tubes everywhere. The vision took every breath from me. I just crumbled. I had to turn away.

"He's never even had a chance to cry. My poor baby! Oh, God, take me! Spare this child, please!"

Holding me, his face buried in my hair. "I would take my life for both of you, but you're not going anywhere. I have to be the one to go first. I could never live without you."

We both knew we would always have each other, despite the unthinkable. Life stood still, not moving a moment forward in time until we were able to take him home. Those next three days, we intently watched those monitors. Soft Disney baby music on the kid recorder, singing and talking to him was all I could do. My little fighter knew his Mommy's voice. They allowed me to bring the softest, floppiest stuffed animal, Sammy, to sit outside of his bubble. Day three, he made it! Day four, it was time.

As they wheeled him in for surgery, we stayed with him. "Fight, baby, fight. Mommy and Daddy love you!"

"No Admittance" doors were where we needed to leave him, in his little bubble with all his tubes. It killed Michael that he wasn't walking through those doors to help save his son's life. Invited to observe, but he couldn't. It was time for me to comfort him as he sobbed, clutching me, unable to do anything. Hour after hour, our family and friends filled the waiting room, all of us waiting for the doctor to reveal himself with an answer. Finally, after over eight hours, Dr. Gilburg came in. He called us over to talk to us privately. His face blank, I couldn't read him. My stomach clenched.

"The surgery went well without complication."

As the words released from the doctor's lips, so did my breath and the circulation back into Michael's hand.

"We just need to see if the left lung will expand, and what limitations there may be, if any. The heart should take care of itself and shift back into place with healing and time. We will know within forty-eight to seventy-two hours and keep a watch on his progress from there."

I didn't care. My baby was alive.

Dr. Gilburg shook his head. "You have one tough little guy. He's a fighter."

"Thank you! Thank you so much!" My hug could've never been big enough.

Michael and I held each other. We all rejoiced. Tears of a joy I never knew I could feel, it was a good day. Within a few days, little Mike's left lung expanded fully without limitation. My baby was filled with miracles. Thank God. Every day, I cared for him as much as they would let me, to be the mom I was dying to be, but only through the rubber gloves attached to his incubator. Little Mike felt his mommy's love. The day finally came. They let me hold him, two weeks old, skin so soft, his sweet cheek resting on my neck, his tiny fingers wrapped around my own. Heaven. I never wanted to let him go. Giving him back was the hardest thing I'd ever had to do, and I prayed for the day when I could take him home.

Another week later, my prayers were answered. His vitals reached healthy levels and he had gained enough weight after losing so much over the course of IV and surgery. Little Mike came home! At that moment, my empathy for my parents was like I had never known before. They never took my sister, Toni, back home, only nine. Her liver had killed her. I was fourteen. It still hurt. My heart and prayers went to fellow NICU parents we had met, knowing they may never be able to take their baby home. My child cradled in my arms, there was no richer blessing. Thank God for the miracle of my little Mike, and for sharing life and love with my soul mate.

* * *

"Maddie, you have more faith in me right now than I have in myself, or than Michael has shown me."

"If only you could step outside yourself and see. You're 'Beauty with Balls'! Trust me, listen to your friend. Make an appointment, talk someone as soon as you get home. Get a schedule of Al-Anon meetings in your area. I know you can walk on water, you just haven't tried it! Bring that strength to the surface, you're gonna need it. He's gonna need it." Maddie pretended to write something on a pad. "Okay, that'll be five hundred dollars for the hour."

I welcomed the levity. "You really are my therapist. The only pro I have right now is Jim. I'm in the dark. Hopefully he could help me shed some light."

Hugging tight, we wept together, hiding our faces.

"Mad, you have no idea that you are literally saving my sanity and my life right now. You're the first and only person I've been this open with."

"Don't worry, you always have us. We love you. You have too much for one to bear right now, but you're doin' it!"

"I've shut myself off from everyone who truly loves me. My parents don't know all the nasty details. My friends suspect. I'm alone on this sinking ship, in the dark."

"They're your lifeboat. If you're drowning, how are they supposed to pull you up if you don't reach out to them? And, by the way, you can never be in the dark. You shine too bright, baby! You'll always find your way!" Maddie winked.

After ice cream, Maddie and her kids left. While the boys were distracted with Nintendo, Michael answered, still sounding muddled, gurgling his words. I hung up.

5

The Accident

Friday night came quickly. Michael and I had a date, not the good kind. We needed to talk. He promised to come home directly from the office by eight. He sounded so sincere, willing to try again. But he was using, hiding it. *All* that he was hiding I wasn't sure. Mike's strawberry ice cream birthday cake for Saturday was already ordered, presents wrapped, candles ready, skirt steak and fries for dinner.

Petra told me he left at seven. Eight o'clock came and went. The boys were in bed, sleeping soundly. Nine, voicemail. I left a sweet message. My bad feeling worsened. Hour after hour passed, no Michael. This time, a concerned message. Thoughts of him with Hellina high on drugs stabbed at my mind. My PI was off tonight, the night I really need him.

On my balcony, sipping my old friend, the monk, keeping me company through my unclear circumstances, my eyes were fixed down the block. I waited to see headlights. Gazing at the stars so bright in the dark sky, I closed my eyes, calling on my angels, chanting over and over. "Please, let me know the truth…"

Suddenly, a very bad feeling shook me. Alarmed, I needed to find him right then. No time, it was midnight, no calling anyone. I carried my sleeping babies out into their car seats with pillows and blankets. Catching him with her would make it real. But there was no sign of his car at Hellina's. Disoriented and desperate, scouring the unfamiliar streets of our new neighborhood in the dark trying to spot them, my truck had a mind of its own.

A fleet of flashing lights just ahead, I slowed to a roll. An ambulance with a slew of police cars blocked off the area in front of Mike's school, a white SUV almost split in half by a telephone pole, knocked slanted. Thank God, his Eldorado was nowhere in sight. I scanned the scene for anything familiar driving by. Nothing. I slammed on the brakes, my breath a vacuum. Michael was slumped and unsteady against the last patrol car, handcuffed, with an officer on each side of him.

I stuck half my body out the window. "Michael!"

He half-glanced up, then disappeared as they ducked his head into the car.

"Is that Daddy?" A shadow of movement in my rearview mirror. Damnit!

"No, no, it's only a dream, baby. Put your head down. Go back to sleep." Mike laid back down and stayed.

The officer warding off traffic motioned me. "Lady, remove your vehicle from the area now!"

"Officer, I'm his wife. I have my children in the back."

"I don't care if you're the First Lady! You're in the middle of a crime scene! Back up or I'll bring you up on charges, and you can join your husband!"

"Thank you for being so kind, officer. I appreciate it. You have a good night now!" In other words, Fuck you! Asshole!

Backing up with one hand, my other rummaged for a mint in my bag. Eureka! The monk couldn't be on my breath. The officer standing in front of the ambulance appeared approachable.

"Excuse me, officer. That's my husband in that patrol car. I have my sleeping children in the back. That policeman over there just threatened me. Could you help me?"

Leaning into my window, inching myself back, my breath held, he peeked back at the children and stood back up. "That guy? Don't mind him, he's an asshole. Nobody likes him, not even on his squad. But I'll deny it if anyone asks." He grinned.

I laughed. "My lips are sealed. I'm glad it wasn't just me. Could you tell me what happened here?"

"What is your name, ma'am?"

"Barbra Mastromarino." I showed him my license.

He dished. "Your husband is arrested for possession and distribution of narcotics."

"Demerol?"

"Yes, and cocaine." More than I was fishing for. "They're taking him to the town jail. He refused to go to the hospital. He's pretty messed up. They had to remove him through the sunroof. He's lucky. The woman that was driving was already taken to the hospital."

The woman. My heart and stomach twisted, switching places in an instant. From the pit of my stomach, I started to shiver uncontrollably, freezing in July.

"Once released, she'll be taken to the jail on a slew of different charges, including possession of Demerol and cocaine and reckless endangerment. She's got some serious problems."

Needed to hear it. "Hellina, right?"

He nodded. My heart shattered into a thousand pieces. A two-ton weight pressed into the middle of my chest, burning, the pain only growing. My marriage was over, had to be, needed to be. Our wedding was a sham.

* * *

What a beautiful day. Our family and friends gathered. Writing invitations for his family was a trip. Five Johns, five Gerrys, four Louises, three Michaels, on and on and on. That's Italian! A perfect day. Except one thing. Michael lit his candle from the unity candle nice, no problem. But my wick directly over the flame would not light. I scraped wax off the wick and tried again. And again. And again. Nothing. So glad everyone at the ceremony found it so funny. I kept cool and cute about it, inside panicking. Was this a sign that I should not marry this man? Over a candle? What could this possibly mean? But I wanted to marry him with my whole heart. No candle was gonna stop me. I was gonna try until the damned thing lit.

Every time I tried, everyone bellowed with laughter. Turning to them, I shrugged my shoulders. They laughed harder. Monsignor Nonie marrying us took my hand with the candle and waved my wick over the unity candle. What'd ya know. It lit. The church applauded. It took a little divine intervention with a heavenly hand to get me through it. That day, I proudly became Mrs. Michael Mastromarino. From that moment on, I planned to live, love, and be happy with my dream man in my dream life...for the rest of my days. Truth was, my hand alone could not light that candle.

* * *

The candle showed me truth. That heavenly hand never left me. And, boy, did the truth come to me. Like a bullet to my heart. Even so, there was no stopping there. The search for more was not over. Many pieces to this poisonous puzzle were still missing.

Trying to stay cool. "What happened to her?"

"We don't give out information unless it's a relative."

With bright eyes and smile through my pain. "I am related to her in a way, not by blood. Just my husband by injection."

He chuckled. "A broken nose and leg."

"That's it?"

The policeman grinned.

"Thank you so much, officer."

"Don't go rushing down there first thing in the morning, now. He will need to stand before the judge before any bail is decided. It all takes a while, depending on how fast they feel like moving. Probably by noon."

Were their clothes undone? No need to ask. Sex, drugs, and crime. Was I terrible, feeling the justice of Hellina and Michael getting blown out of the water? Hell, no! Dad and my brother, Ben, came to rescue the boys to their safe haven at Grandma and Grandpa's upstate far away from this nightmare—their father. Calls needed to be made ASAP to everyone, our families and close family friends. I didn't care what time it was, or what his mother thought about it. This was serious. Max, Michael's childhood best friend and business associate in Brooklyn, and Mike's godfather came and helped me, and were such a great comfort. Sleepless and shattered, I was numb. Nat, Max's girlfriend, didn't come. No doubt, she woulda gotten the key from the guard, killed Michael, and locked him back up if she was close enough. She loved us, so pissed for me. Little bit of a thing, with six-inch heels, crazy and powerful, the only "made" woman. Her bad side was lethal. Literally.

Max and I strategized as we waited at the Fort Lee police station to bail Michael out late the next morning. The officer brought him out. He looked strung out and disheveled. He reached to touch me.

Pulling back, my eyes daggers, teeth clenched, I spat my words. "Don't touch me."

With regret and desperation, he dropped his head, dejected. Caught. Turning away, I couldn't look at him. Max and I told him the judge mandated he must enter a rehab program immediately after his release or he'd be thrown back in and his dental license would be revoked. He believed us. I knew nothing of drug addiction, cheating, or violence growing up. With every step, this forced wisdom was changing me, Michael the root of it all. Directly admitted into Bergen Medical Alliance for three days, he would detox before admitting into High Watch, a rehab community in Connecticut. My three weeks of peace from hell, filled with freedom, investigation, determination. So damn tired, but I was not nearly done.

Waiting for his room at BMA, on the landline phone, not allowed to have his cell phone, he scribbled on a pad. He took the paper and put it in his pocket. When they took him in another room for observation and pretesting, I took the pad, lightly brushing the side of a pencil point over where he had written. Hellina's contact info materialized! She was still in the hospital.

Proof in the pad, I backed him into a corner. "How many years have you been fucking her? Do you love her?"

"No! It was only a kiss!"

"Enough already with the ridiculous lies! She was a dancer! You met her out one night! I know so much more than you think I know!" As his face froze, I shoved the pad in it.

"Okay, yes, I had an affair with her, but it didn't mean anything. It's over. I just wanted to make sure she was okay."

A shred of truth finally, among sheets of lies. He admitted the affair. The rest, bullshit.

"Do not ever think for a second that I will ever believe a word out of your cheating, lying mouth."

I turned and left, realizing Michael's great love had turned to Demerol, with her. He was hooked on both. The man I loved was lost. His addiction and affair had been so dangerously intertwined, sharing needles, a bed, beyond insult to injury. Bad choices, and bad taste, he was still the father of my children. As he struggled with addiction, I struggled with some hard decisions. Hellina was released from the hospital and jail.

Her cousin answered. "Please, give her a message from her employer's wife. She is officially fired. And if she ever brings her dirty twat near my husband again, I'll rip it in half like a wishbone. Thank you."

That filthy rag went around talking about me. That haughty streetwalker wanted my life. You know what? She could fucking have it! They both deserve each other!

Speaking of dirty rags, since Max had filled me in that Michael never liked condoms from the beginning of time, Dr. Schwabner pretty much drained my blood and tested me for every disease under the sun. Clean, thank God.

Max also gave me the lowdown on my husband's M.O. with girls back in the day. "Before you, Michael had a knack for making every girl feel like she was the most important girl in the world, made promises he was never gonna keep, just to get what he wanted for the moment. I was straight up with girls, probably too honest. If I was just out for a lay, I told 'em, still got 'em. I used to tell him he was crazy. I'm tellin' you, Barb. He changed with you. He may have fucked up royally, and you have every right to leave him, but he really loves you."

"You mean he was worse?" I asked. "I am not feeling special. That kind of love, I don't want."

Michael away, my serenity, strength, and self-worth helped me past it, my building blocks. The fear was gone. He did it. Done. But I wasn't. Wanting to whack him in the head with a bat and say, thank you, made me laugh. Time to let Jim go and do the rest on my own. Jim told me to let him know when I was looking for a job, he'd hire me in a second. Speaking of jobs, Nat insisted I be an extra on a *Sopranos* episode.

"You just gotta do it! You're so damn hot! It could be the beginning of something for you!"

The hottest show, great opportunity, I graciously declined. They were using her cousin's boat on the show, and I would've been the hot bikini chick on the boat. I watched that show. We all know what hot bikini chicks were required to do on *The Sopranos*. Would I even have a bikini on at all? Or would the guy take it off and bend me over or put me on my knees? Ah, no. Besides, my own private detective job needed attention.

Everything had a trail—mapped out, trips, gifts, her apartment, her truck, destroyed by the accident. The manager at the MRI place was so kind to give me copies of all the bills of charges he ran up on the company card. Rumors of him being a drug dealer and having extra life insurance policies on himself were still unsolved. The extra cell phone on our account he took for business was their hotline to each other. Michael was obsessed with her, calling a ridiculous amount of times a day, and the calling cards. Nat clued me in to check on the insurance checks. Retrieving info from the bank, I investigated. Sure enough, countless insurance checks signed over to Hellina. On many of them I didn't recognize his signature, forged. Thief! Damn! My girl, Nat's got eyes everywhere! So thankful for her help.

Next target, Carmela, Nat's cousin who did his office's accounts receivable and lived with Hellina in Cliffside Park. She caved with my threats, the checks, and so much more.

"Hellina had sex with dealers to score cocaine to sell. I walked in on her blowing a dealer for blow. She tried to get me into it. I couldn't. And her trips to the Dominican Republic were shady, but I never got involved so I never asked. I want to move out, but I have no place to go."

Another nugget I didn't want to hear. She knew more and wouldn't dare lie, too simple, scared. I highly suspected she was lured into an attempted ménage, but no matter. Maybe Hellina made Michael one of her pimp drug dealers. Maybe he was willing, sex and money. Damn, the pain never had a chance to dull. Michael never seemed to disappoint me, with more lies and deceit. The pieces were coming together. But "maybe" didn't cut it. I needed hard facts. He was not himself. She and the drugs together had taken him over, it seemed. His choice.

My new life lease. Let go and start living, breathing and smiling again, even when it hurt. Take care of myself, my kids. Open up and share with my lifeboats, my family and friends.

My besties were relieved I was okay. Maria hugged me. "It's about time! We're here for you, girlfriend. I got a great guy I want to set you up with. He's good-lookin' and loaded!"

I couldn't help but laugh. "Didn't I just throw one of them back?"

"Damn, you're right!"

Tina had no patience for Michael. "Baby! Forget about that stiff! Give me five minutes with him. I'll loosen him right up! We're on for next Thursday night, right?"

"I have no doubt, Ti! Loose is your specialty, girlfriend! We are so on for Thursday!"

"You know it! And lose the name Tina. My name is now Tiana. I needed an exotic name to fit my exotic persona."

"I think exotic may be too tame for you babe!"

"Erotic is more like it, honey!" Maria was so right.

"All I know is there'd better be some young studs lined up to service me all night long. I'm in my prime, darlin'! I want some prime cuts! Ooh! I'm gettin' wet."

She was just what I needed. "Get a bath sheet, you crazy bitch! So, what's the plan, Ti?"

"Love it when you talk dirty, B! Maria, you're escaping from the salon to my place to do up my hair. Rayne is gracing us with her presence—"

I put my hand up. "Don't start! Be nice!"

Maria cackled. "I love it. You're fuckin' crazy, Ti!"

Tiana and Rayne competed like two virile cats. A sight to watch them show each other up!

Tiana acquiesced. "Fine. Rayne better dim her shine Thursday night! I'm the star! She can go steal all the attention she wants on-location in LA Monday. She ain't stealin my oxygen! Elle is closing the boutique early. If not, she'll meet up with us. I need to be surrounded by hotties. Makes me look good! Everybody who's anybody in the city will be following. A couple of my people from LA will be in town. I got a party train lined up wherever we go."

How I loved the distraction. "I don't know if Manhattan can handle you!"

"Never happen! You're a nut!" Maria grinned slick at Tiana.

"Damn straight, gorgeous! We'll start out at the Four Seasons for cocktails and hors d'oeuvres. A light dinner and drinks at Tao. Marty will take care of us. Lord knows I take care of him enough! Then, we'll hit the VIP lounge at Lotus. Let's see. After that, whoever's still standing will float to the fourth floor at Float for after hours. Manny's got a stretch lined up for me all day Thursday until Friday morning. My sitter is sleeping over. Rick can't take the kids."

I was listening, but my thoughts drifted. The distraction was great while it lasted.

Tiana couldn't help but notice my silence. She knew me too well. "Hellloo! Are you listening to me? You'd better make sure your sweet ass is there! Who's gonna keep me in line? Oh, speaking of lines I got some great shit for that night unless I treat myself to an early birthday rush."

"Here we go!" Maria threw her hands up.

"Hey, I'm turning thirty-nine and I still got it goin' on! Live like there's no tomorrow, baby!"

"Count me right by your side! Don't mind if I skip over the lines." Tiana knew I didn't.

"I know my girlfriend. You could use a good stiff one right now, and I don't mean Michael. I'm here if you need to talk."

My girlfriends made sure my social life revived in a way I'd never known. Lunch by day, private parties, VIP in every lounge and club by night. Feeling free, sexy, validated, an escape from real life, putting my babies to bed first, Raven or Katia with them, never letting them miss me. Yet I was still so sad inside, the family I wanted for my boys would never be—broken, because of him. Michael stole my heart and my dream.

"Mommy? I had a bad dream." Mike nudged me awake.

I scooped him up into the bed and gave him a snuggle. "You okay, honey? Tell Mommy what happened."

"A giant snake, like bigger than this house, big as the tallest tree, came and took Daddy away. Then he was gone! Mom, it was so real! I was so scared!"

This child and his sense. A snake bigger than all of us did take his daddy away. *Drugs.* "Baby doll, you know he's away working helping people, right? That was just a dream, not real. He'll be back in a few weeks." Killed me telling him another necessary lie, knowing my dreams were never just dreams, neither were his—foreboding. The thought tore at me allowing my boys to visit their father at rehab, aka work, the whitest lie ever. Just too young, they should not need to know. But their father kept striking like a snake. We traveled with Michael's parents, his brother, John, and sister, Louise, for the High Watch family weekend. Its community farm setting, a picnic-like day made it tolerable. They left for the visit. A picnic with Michael? Not on my worst day. I chose peace. Michael would be completely deflated. Good little Barbra wouldn't be there as expected. He would not get the best of me anymore.

Powerwalking alone on that warm beautiful summer day, my sweet, innocent, beautiful children were visiting their father at rehab. The words alone hurt my head. The fear gone, fierce empowerment growing inside me was palpable, never feeling stronger. I planned to stand up for my life. Feeling refreshed and serene, my pen splashed passion and inspiration for life and fitness, every thought to every word, page after page, to save my life with hope for helping others. Savoring the moments alone, I missed my babies, praying they were having a safe and good time. They all returned with smiles, telling me Michael seemed well and how crushed he was I didn't come. He had no idea what crushed was.

Louise had me alone. "Between you and me, I understand you not visiting him. No one on this Earth could not. Barbra, you have been so gracious in all this, given what Michael has done. I love my brother and wouldn't want it to happen, but I couldn't blame you if you left him."

A deep and knowing empathy, I appreciated her quiet support. It spoke volumes. "Thank you, Louise. That means a lot."

The boys carried on about their day, the games, the barbecue, seeing their dad, Mike relieved. Their blissful oblivion relieved me yet twisted my insides. "Mom! You gotta come tomorrow! They're gonna have a tug-of-war and you have to help! Please? It's gonna be so much fun!"

How could I deny my boys? "I'll think about it, okay?"

Showering me with hugs. "Please, please, please?"

"I'll come!"

"Yay!"

"We're gonna kick their asses tomorrow!"

"Mike!"

"Sorry, Mom! Butts."

"Remember, 'sorry' is only as good as you trying to not do it again, okay? That goes for grownups too."

"Okay, Mom." My boys hugged me tight.

The visit came. I walked toward Michael. The tears streaming down his face could never be enough to wash everything away. Stiff and stern, my strained greeting told him to keep his distance.

"Guys, can you take the boys to play the games, so I can talk to my wife? We'll be over in a few."

"My wife? That's rich."

His words through his sobs, broken, clinging to me. "Barb, I am so sorry. I can't believe I did this to you, my boys, my family. I took from you and my boys. I'm so sorry."

Silent, blank, I listened, but didn't walk away. He couldn't expect more from me. Genuine? For the moment? Or complete garbage? Wasn't sure of anything.

"Can I show you around?"

He took me to the eating hall, the kitchen, the recreation area, introduced me to his new friends—adding how they all had jobs doing work in the community. Michael proudly proclaimed he scrubbed toilets. I laughed on the inside. Humility, momentary? Me staying, temporary? He worked jobs beneath him? For no pay? He contributed his valuable time, getting nothing in return? Incredible. Wait a minute. That's right, he had no choice. His license was the carrot. We played tug-of-war and won. My boys enjoyed the day, which was all I needed. The day ended, not a moment too soon. Back home to peace, without him.

6

The Counsel

Dr. Rich Griffith, Michael's court-assigned sponsor, warned me. "No matter how noble the intentions, active addicts can't keep promises. They're liars and count on you believing their lies. You must take care of yourself first, then the boys. Michael is a big boy and needs to take care of himself. AA for him when he gets out, and Al-Anon for you to start. Therapy should come soon after."

After researching, Al-Anon kept identities anonymous, and meetings seemed to be located nearby from town to town at churches, houses of worship, prayer and peace. St. Matthew's was close. The church was locked. Alone, left lost in so many ways, I hoped to change that. A man noticed my confusion and helped me find the open door. Both early, we chatted outside the church.

"My wife is an alcoholic. We have four daughters. They're my life. She's still drinking but is trying to stop. I had enabled her for longer than I care to admit...a co-dependent, meaning either do something, or not do anything, to help them stay in their addiction, most times based on one's own fears or insecurities."

Am I a co-dependent?

"For way too long, I let my wife leave the house to drive our girls to school with her coveted cup of coffee, allowing my daughters in harm's way every day. I thank God they escaped harm before I finally put a stop to it. I was in DENIAL, as all active addicts and co-dependents are, stands for Don't Even kNow I Am Lying."

Everything was making sense. Different story, same fit. A crash course before my first meeting.

"I'd ask for a sip of her coffee. Never happened. The problem is we have no control over anyone but ourselves. But I make sure I protect myself and my girls. I love my wife, and my family, and am doing the best I can. One day at a time. You'll hear that a lot."

"You have helped me so much already." My story about Michael flowed out of me with ease.

"Barbra, you'll need to find a sponsor. Someone who has been through it, your support whenever you need, and you will need it. My sponsor helps me beyond words, just to know he's there. It took a while to find someone compatible."

"You have been so helpful in just these few minutes. Can you be my sponsor?"

He blushed and chuckled. "If my wife ever met you, I'd be in the doghouse. Usually sponsors are the same sex as the co-dependent or addict."

"I understand. Thank you for everything. I hope one day to help someone in need. Right now, I'm trying to help myself."

He led me into the meeting room. All welcomed me with hugs. It was amazing the different people and stories Al-Anon brought together. A woman's violent active-alcoholic/drug addict husband threatened her life daily if she were to leave him, tracking and watching her every move on surveillance 24/7. A young man's alcoholic wife was in recovery for five years. A man's sixteen-year-old son was in recovery from heroin for six months. A young woman's alcoholic mother was in recovery for ten years, and her drug addict father relapsed two months ago after three years clean. The woman herself had never taken a drink or a drug. The woman running the meeting inspired me. Her husband had been in recovery for nearly twenty-five years, but she was still giving. They all inspired me.

My turn. "Hi, Barbra here. My husband is a drug addict."

I opened up, poured out. They listened. I cried. Some joined me, comforted me. I asked for guidance. They fed me. We all held hands and ended the meeting with the Serenity Prayer:

God grant me the serenity to accept things I cannot change,
the courage to change things I can,
and the wisdom to know the difference.

My mantra, still. After the meeting, they gave me this small hardcover book, *One Day at a Time*. I planned to read every day of it. They also recommended the book *Boundaries*. Trying to give them ten dollars, I couldn't give them enough.

"Thank you. Usually attendees donate a dollar if they can. We never turn anyone away. If it's more than five dollars, put it back in your pocket."

Floored by their humility and integrity, five it was. This education opened my eyes and my world.

"Assume every word out of an addict's mouth is a lie. Only trust myself. Be careful who else to trust. Accept help from people who love me, and love Michael. I couldn't do it alone. Set boundaries to protect myself and my children. Don't let him manipulate me into helping him feed his addiction, and he may find a fighting chance. I cannot take responsibility for his rise or demise, that's on him. I can control no one, but myself."

Michael arrived home, welcomed by his family and friends. I welcomed him back into my heart and my bed, apparently, as if I needed to prove something to myself and to him! Wasn't quite working. After returning from an MTV Music Awards After-Party at Sache in the city with the girls, my escape, Katia reassured me all was okay. No trouble. Michael would not be alone with the children. He couldn't argue me going. He wouldn't dare. Crawling into bed next to him, I was distant. Flat on my back staring into the darkness, visions of Michael and Hellina danced across the ceiling, burning into my wild imagination. I closed my eyes. Couldn't escape the nightmare in my head. My tears fell, but not a sound. Michael reached out to me, wiping my cheek. I turned away, my back to him.

He whispered to me, his breath on my ear. "I love you."

Why couldn't I leave him? "Don't! I don't want you to love me! It hurts! It hurts so much! I can't get it out of my head! You, on top of her! Inside of her! Kissing her! Why don't you leave me! If you care about me at all! Please! Just leave me! You need to leave me! Please! I can't take it anymore! Please!"

"I can't." He kissed my head, whispering into my hair. "I love you so much."

My body inched away. "I wish you didn't." I closed my eyes.

Since I was a young girl, I dreamed of love. True, devoted, breathtaking, passionate, can't live without, love. Find the man of my dreams, a good man, just like Dad. He would marry me and love me like no one else ever could. And to be a mom, like mine, my heart could not wait. A once in a lifetime love, beautiful children, the perfect family, a happy home, dream come true. Our family didn't have much, but we had a lotta love and laughter. My parents struggled at times but never against each other, always together. Dad would not leave the house to work until he kissed her goodbye, a sweet peck on the lips, with a little grab-ass when he thought no one was looking. With parents like that, was there any other choice but to be a hopeless dreamer? I was determined to have it all, just like Mom and Dad. This was not it.

He forged ahead, healthy and eager to get back to everyday life, apparently. On the top of his list, work. What else? His associates gave him a wary reception. A welcome, nevertheless. Truth was he was a brilliant surgeon and businessman, when lucid. He had a sobering schedule, with his probation officer in Hackensack every week, Dr. Griffith in Westchester, assigned AA meetings, all mandatory. He let it be known he would do whatever it took to prove himself, most importantly to me. Hard to believe. *Doubt what is dubious*, Dr. Griffith's words and Al-Anon were in my brain.

Michael shared a proverb from rehab. "The opposite of love is indifference, not hate." Noted.

In a matter of weeks he started using again, couldn't stop. His skills honed, lies evident. I saw right through him. Did anyone else? Passing urine tests for Dr. Griffith, his offices, his probation officer. Escaping consequences of the car accident. Thank God, no one was ever hurt. His pharmacies, his hiding places, his deception, how could I make everyone see? How did he get past it all? He was so cunning, possessed, as if by the devil. I felt trapped.

Dick, our accountant and friend, reviewed our policies for me. If Michael died under the influence, no life insurance. If he died under the influence in a car crash and killed someone else, no life or auto insurance, nor liability coverage. Everything would be in default, only lawsuits. As his wife, his consequences may have very well become mine. Why wasn't I thinking legal separation? Would it have even helped me? I wasn't thinking. I thought of him, our vows, my sick husband, father of my children. How could I abandon him, leave him to die, possibly to kill others?

Keep my boundaries steadfast.

Damnit! I knew this. Should I have told him to get out of our house and our lives until he could stay clean? Yes. Who did I think I was, thinking I could save the world? Trying so hard not to be a co-dependent, but I was, trial and error. I could only pray, for each and all of us. One day at a time. My vow to make damn sure my children and I would be okay, no matter Michael's decisions or actions, would carry us through. How far would I need to go?

My trusted friend, Nat, gave me a suggestion she thought might ease my pain, in a permanent way. "Life's a bitch and then you become one. Or get rid of one."

At first, I laughed. Oh, no, she was dead serious. "Honey, this bitch is going to be the death of your husband. I knew it the minute I met her. I told Max! He'll tell you. If you want to save the father of your children's life, she's got to go."

Well, when she put it that way. "Sounds like a plan."

Nat was right. His chance of survival was better if Hellina was out of the picture. The drugs and Hellina were as one to him. Why chance it? Give him a better one. The stats: Dr. Griffith informed me only 6 percent of addicts reached sobriety and maintained recovery, most didn't make it. The odds were against him.

His AA sponsor, Dr. Boylan, who worked very closely with Dr. Griffith, had warned me. "Michael's type of addiction is very aggressive. The longer he uses, even days longer, his chances of survival are slim to none. You must mentally prepare yourself that he will die."

The only way to handle it was to disconnect. Better and better at it, I still needed to do something.

Nat headed up the plan. "Tell no one, especially not Michael. Not even Max."

Nat's reasoning and encouragement with my desperation and confusion was the perfect cocktail for me to really consider it, believe it was the answer, to save him, us, and our family.

"My people will take care of it. She's a junkie. We make it look like an overdose. Perfect plan."

"I want to be there for her to look in my eyes before her last high."

"That's my girl!"

Who was this girl? Murder? I was Michael's perfect prey to hide his horns under my halo. He knew me, chose me, used me. My halo got darker and darker, shade after shade, battling his demons with my own. But Hellina was terrorizing me. The threatening phone call from some guy with a message from her, someone skulking around my townhouse late one night, followed and taunted in my car by two people behind me, all while Michael was in rehab. The madness needed to stop. Nat's crew had tried before to take care of Hellina and "talked" to her, and so did the town detectives. But after everything, only one remaining option stared me in the face.

It was happening. Nat by my side. They held her down. An overdose. Terrified. "What did I do?" Desperation was a bad place.

My eyes shot open, alone in bed, relieved. A dream! My clarity like crystal through my cloud of hell.

How could I even think? He's not going to drive me crazy and convince me I am! Who am I to play God? I'm not going to the Dark Side he so enjoys with her! Michael is not the victim here at all! He never was. Neither am I.

Michael was the master of illusion. Why did everyone believe it was only her fault? If not her, it would've been someone else. What will be, will be. Everyone gets theirs. God will take care. No clear answer, that was surely not it. Nat's idea had been anything but a dream, but thankfully she called it off, respecting my wishes. She understood. Tough spot being the wife of a cunning drug addict and mother of his kids. What would every next moment bring? "One day at a time" turned into "one moment at a time."

Michael said he had to check on a couple of cases at the hospital and would be back by noon. It was two o'clock. We waited, packed, ready for our annual trip to Gurney's in Montauk with Max, Nat, and all their kids. Mike and Gerry were so excited. This time we invited our family, given all the close calls with Michael. We geared up for a great time. My family couldn't make it down, but his would be there.

The phone rang, like a siren in my head. "Hello, is this Mrs. Mastromarino?"

"Yes, may I help you?"

"This is Officer Kern from the New York City Police Department. Your husband has been in a car accident—"

"Is he okay? Was anyone else hurt?"

"He's a little shaken up, but he's fine. No one else was hurt. His car is pretty banged up. He crashed into a rail on the north side of the FDR by the 132nd Street exit. We'd appreciate if you can come down to the scene of the accident. Then, you can follow us to the precinct and you can pick him up there."

"I'll leave now. Thank you, Officer."

"Thank you, ma'am."

I had no choice but to take them. "C'mon, boys! We gotta go pick up Daddy."

They came running down the stairs.

Mike stared up with his sweet eyes. "Are we going to save Daddy again?"

Like taking a bullet to the heart. "Yes, honey. Daddy needs us to pick him up. As soon as we pick him up, we're driving straight to Montauk! Everybody's going to be there! We'll get to stay the whole week, okay?"

"Awesome!"

Gerry echoed. "Awesome!"

They hopped into the truck with delight. Driving on FDR south, not a car on the north side of the highway. The scene of his accident blockaded the highway completely by a fleet of patrol cars, two fire trucks, and an ambulance. As I slowed, the front of Michael's car was completely smashed in and smoking. Absolutely sure he was fine as always. His M.O. was to wreak havoc everywhere and flee the scene. How could he flee this one? Driving south past the accident to loop around, miles and miles of traffic trailed the accident, waiting for my arrival to open the highway again. I wished I could blink us there, wishing I could blink this all away, blink him away. Just ridiculous, if these drivers only knew what was really holding them up. A drug-doping man-child who dozed off at the wheel.

We finally arrived at the scene. The children had fallen asleep. The police had Michael in the patrol car. By regulation, he needed to travel with them. After following them, how nice to walk my six- and three-year-old children into a Bronx police precinct. My fury was off the chart. Oblivious to it all, they were still zoned in on getting to Montauk as fast as they could. The art of distraction. An officer directed me to Michael. He looked a mess, expecting nothing better.

We all sat, waiting, as I pumped the boys up about the trip. His sleeve, blood stains, Dick's warnings rang through my head. What were they going to slap him with that would fall on me?

My quiet whisper couldn't have been louder. "Roll your sleeve up! There's blood on it!"

Again, enabling to preserve me and my children! Furious with myself, because of him! His pant leg, blood. Did they see? Do they know? What next? We squirmed there for what seemed like hours. The volcano that was my stomach seethed with every move of every officer.

Finally, the officer called him over. "Dr. Mastromarino."

The volcano was bubbling over. Michael, somewhat collected, but still a wreck, swaggered his way to the desk. He signed some papers they put in front of him.

They shook his hand. "Take care, Doc. Have a good one."

Wait, what? "That's it? He can go?"

Amazing! He passed the Breathalyzer! Therefore, he escaped? Didn't they see the blood? Check his urine for drugs? Check his record? Cross-check state records? See his arrest on drug charges and all his auto accidents in New Jersey? He had "Dr." in front of his name and flashed his New York City police surgeon's get-out-of-jail badge, no doubt. Or did they make a deal with the smooth-talking devil? What's wrong with this system? Wait, maybe he did pass a drug test. He'd passed every test he had taken. Why not with the police, too? He needed to be caught, to go away, be saved! Fear silenced me from asking the police. Down to Montauk we went. I drove. Michael continued to fool the world with his handsome mask, absent, still using, as if no one could see. Or maybe no one wanted to see.

7

The Insight

My eyes darted to his shirt sleeve rolled up to his elbow. He had used recently. He was coming down from his high. Watching a movie with the boys, I didn't get up from their low beds to greet him.

"Hey, guys."

"Hi, Dad." Their eyes never left the TV.

"Barb, I'm leaving for Ken's in about twenty minutes, my hours are from three to eight."

"Okay. Change your shirt."

My eyes directed him, the bright red blood stains, fresh, unmistakable.

His ol' faithful. "That's old."

I turned back to the movie. "Okay."

His brow raised, upper lip curled, teeth clenched. "You don't believe me? You fucking cunt! Fuck you! Nobody believes me! I'm never gonna live this down!"

He stormed out of the room, slamming the door behind him. The trim pulled away from the wall, falling to the floor. The children's doe eyes gaped at me for reassurance.

More lies. "Everything's okay, Daddy's sorry for cursing. Watch your movie, I'll be right back. Stay here or the movie goes off, deal?"

"Deal." They turned back to the movie, comforted by my protection and Mommy's magic.

I raised the volume, gently shutting the broken door, knowing soon I would need to have him leave. I locked our bedroom door behind me, planning to diffuse. "What is wrong? And don't curse in front of the kids!"

"Fuck the kids! And fuck you! You'll always be scrutinizing me! Everyone will! I didn't use today!"

"'Fuck the kids'? You selfish son of a bitch! Don't you ever say those words again! I took all your blood-stained shirts out of your closet! Those bright red stains are new, and you know it! You're a damn liar! Tell the truth for once!"

He lunged at me, grabbing my shoulders, shaking me. My arms twisting to get free, he slammed me into the closet folding door. I fell back as the door collapsed. Another closet. He started pacing, ranting. This was getting old.

"You think I'm using? Yeah? I'll throw you out the fuckin' window! You fuckin' cunt!"

Pushing myself up from the shelves, I came right up to his face. "Go ahead! I dare you! Throw me out the fuckin' window! Go ahead! Leave your kids without a mother! All they'll have left is a piece of shit junkie for a father! A lot of good you'll be to them!" Shoving his chest. "Do it! I dare you!"

He put his face closer to mine, nose to nose. "Don't you fuckin' touch me! Who the fuck do you think you're pushin'?"

"C'mon! Throw me, big shot!" I stomped to the window and opened it. "I'm waiting! You fucking cunt!" I hate that word.

He retreated, grunted and thundered out of the house. I checked on the boys, still fixed to the TV. Thank God for Disney all day. Mike went downstairs to play Nintendo, while Gerry stayed to finish watching the show. Therapeutically folding laundry, what was my next move? Like a dark twisted game of chess. A momentary sober apology later was meaningless. He, his drugs, and his violent temper needed to leave, for real.

As I carried the boys' clothes down the hall, Gerry walked out of his room, his eyes fixed on something in his hand. Trying to make out what it was, I picked up the pace toward him. Gerry's eyes sparkled up at me and held up his newfound plaything, waddling faster toward me. As he came closer, his toy came into focus. My baby was holding a syringe with no cap, needle exposed! Dropping the clothes to the floor, steadily moving toward him, I smiled excitedly, softly coaxing him to show me. He handed it to me with a proud smile.

"Look, Mama!"

"Thank you!" I safely tucked the needle right up on a high ledge where we stood.

He started crying and reached his arm up toward the ledge, his hand motioning to grab. "Mama! I want it! It's mine!"

Calming him, as I checked his entire body for any accidental pokes, perfect and pure, thank God, pointing up. "Gerry, that's bad! Bad boo-boo! Ouch-ouch!" I waved my hand as if it hurt.

Gerry stopped crying instantly without a blink. He understood. He was happy with his juice cup, joining his brother who was completely unmoved by all the commotion, playing his video game. Back to their room. Where did my child find this needle? Surely there were more. Gerry's sock drawer lowest to the floor for him to reach was open, in plain sight an empty Demerol with a syringe cap and some bloody tissues. My mind reeled, rummaging through the drawer, under and in every pair of socks and underwear, another syringe and bottle, not yet used.

"Is he serious? In the children's drawer? That's it! He's not stepping foot back in!"

Every inch needed to be checked. Mike's drawer above his, every drawer, piece of clothing, pocket, shoe, their closet, clean. The search was not done. He needed to leave with every drop of his poison. Michael's closet, the inside pockets of hanging jackets and pants, every shoe, sock, the shelves, in, under or behind his drawers, the pile of my findings grew. Tearing the bathroom apart, smelling every cologne and bottled liquid for that distinctive Demerol smell, more. On to the guest room, more.

Stop. Take a minute. Breathe.

Startled by my cell ring, Ken. "Barb, you gotta come up here right away and get Mike out of here! I found him in my office shooting up into his leg! He had a patient in the chair going under! Thank God I caught him! No one is hurt. My dad is furious! You know we love him, but this has to stop!"

Keep breathing.

"My dad called the Board of Dentistry and the DEA. I'm not sure if he'll press charges against him. I reached out to all the guys to let them know what happened."

Finally! Real help at last.

"I'll be up as soon as I can. I'll inform Michael's sponsor. He'll get things done."

Once again, Mike and Gerry to my parents' house for shelter, conveniently in Rockland as well, just a couple of miles from Ken's office. I wasn't his wife. I was his damn keeper. On my way to Ken's office, Dr. Griffith confirmed this was grounds for him to coerce Michael to enter a more intensive program dictated by him. Jail or his license? Behold the carrot. At their office, I apologized to Ken and his dad, sharing details of Dr. Griffith's plan.

Ken's father hugged me, then held my hand sternly.

"Sweetheart, don't you apologize. This is not your fault. He's a grown man. He knows what he's doing. You just take care of yourself and those boys."

Our ride home was silent. No mention of Dr. Griffith. He would soon find out. Michael entered a four-week program the following week in Tully Hill rehab center near Syracuse, New York. This one he couldn't leave. While he was away, more evidence uncovered that he had never lost touch with Hellina. The more I dug, the more I unearthed, wanting to find nothing. No more living in his lies. Everything about Michael was not true. I was leaving him. How many times can one man break a woman's heart? A woman he claimed to love and couldn't live without?

First, my children. They'd seen and heard too much. The schools were made aware of our home situation. The boys, unknowing of the severe reality of it all, believed their father was away for work again. Their teachers and counselors, on guard for their welfare, commended me keeping balance and stability for my children. I appreciated their support. Given the circumstances, I was trying. Through all of this, since I abandoned my fitness competitions to be there for my family because of him, I achieved my certifications in Master Fitness Trainer/ Sports Nutrition Consultant to help others, especially moms. It was mine. He couldn't touch that. And it would allow me to make my own schedule around the boys' school and activities.

Michael knew I would be visiting him. Much thought went into my very long "Dear Michael" letter, every suspicion I ever had about him cheating I deemed as true. The list was endless, rendering it almost too incredible to believe. Nevertheless, blasting him with every bit of it was long overdue. The letter was my final contribution to this marriage for him to read and choke on.

Details of phone calls from girls to his house in Brooklyn when I first dated him, his ex-girlfriends, Griselle and a few others from NYU Dental School, Val and Kim from residency on call with him, nurses at NYU and Bellevue Hospital while he was on call, girls from our Manhattan apartment building when Michael and I were married starting a family, Kathy his assistant, Molly the rep, that other rep who left him a message on our home phone that she "owed" him dinner and drinks—forgot her name—and Danielle the marketer. And who knows how many others!

I even suspected Brandi, Ken's wife. She had a bad habit of hitting on all her friends' husbands and boyfriends after a bit of Baileys.

I hoped she wouldn't do that to me. I had hoped that of my husband. And look what happened.

I ended the letter with "I don't feel like your wife anymore. I can never forgive you. When you get out, you'll have to find somewhere else to stay. Your whore's place, perhaps? You paid for it anyway, right? Or maybe one of your whores here?"

Michael denied it all. Of course he did. The words "I didn't do it" flowed so easily from his lips, too many times to count, too many lies to keep track of. No fairy tale here, all my dreams were gone. The man I thought I married, gone...Or was he never there? Aside from my hunt for more lies and betrayals, I was now on the hunt for a good time. I became a regular of the New York City night circuit. Classy restaurants and VIP lounges with Rayne. Tiana was a direct line into the VIP section of the hottest clubs. Maria was up for anything. I found myself very much like her. I admired her and looked to her for sound advice. A lifetime friend, no doubt. Maria's nephews ran some A-list city clubs. Elle's sister was a model living in the city and promoted A-list clubs as well. Rarely ever cost us a dime. We ran with some heavy hitters in the fashion scene, the entertainment world, TV, movies, pro sports. As big as their names were, they were regular people. Some were iconic and amazing, some cafone and phony. This coat designer with a worldwide company hung with Tiana. We had all been out a couple of times. He gave her a gorgeous coat. I didn't ask.

One night he flipped. "You called my fucking house? And spoke to my wife?" Turned out he had an apartment in the city with a secret life that his wife didn't know about. It was obvious Tiana was just fucking with him. He did tell her to never call his house.

She chortled, "Fuck him! It's his problem he's cheatin' on his wife! At least I got a couple o' nice coats out of it."

In my warped unknowing sense of love, still, for Michael, I felt thankful that my estranged husband wasn't that bad. Yes, I really thought that.

My wild ride with my worldly friends was a trip. Alcohol and being out with Tiana seemed a dangerous combination. Landed me with a guy every time. At Float, VIP, third floor, this guy, Bruce, turned out to be a dentist in the city, through Ti's friend. He knew Michael. I remembered meeting him a handful of years before and thinking he was a dick. But he was striking me right that night. Not far from the club, nice bachelor place and a dog. He disappeared under the sheet. I moaned and groaned, playing a little Sally. One would think doctors in the oral field might know what they're doing. I didn't know who was worse, him or Michael. Zero for two. He came up for air. And fell the fuck asleep. I slipped out of bed, got dressed and left, just like a guy.

He called me a few hours later after the sun was up. "Come back, baby. Cuddle with me."

"It was fun. Trust me, you don't wanna get involved with me." I kept in touch with him for a New York minute.

Continuing on, all around the clubs this adorable young JFK Jr. look-alike club promoter, funnily his name was John, always had his eye on me. We met through friends and they assured me he was a good guy. Back to his place. Without a condom, the line was drawn, teasing to the point of blue balls. He wanted to see me again, take me out, make dinner, spend time with me. Either he was full of shit or trying to move too fast in a direction I was not going. He was twenty-five, ten years my junior, and promoted clubs. Come on! Besides, I was a hot mess and I knew it. We'd smile, hello, if we saw each other out, as far as it went. Lee, visiting from Miami for the weekend, was cute, quiet, a good guy, perfectly temporary, and safe, family friend of Geo, my soap-star friend. Again, empty. Geo's soap best bud, Tino, coincidentally my all-time hall-pass soap desire, made a pass at me. Still married to a beautiful model with a child together, damn gorgeous player extraordinaire. A hard no. My own mess was enough.

A dangerous thing, a woman in my headspace could get lost in the Big City out with the girls. Especially Ti. It was time to back the hell up and chill. Done with the crazy fling circuit, all Band-Aids to my broken heart. What was I doing? Reckless, with no passion. Just a "Sally" girl, hoping to find the real thing? Michael stole something from my core I was afraid I would never get back. He used to be my dream man. Now, he was my worst nightmare.

Released from Tully Hill, he stayed at his parents' in Brooklyn. The boys accepted it, used to him not around, sad but easier, more peaceful. My ground rule. "Do what you want, but you will not bring your cheap whore around my children. Over your and Hellina's dead bodies!" Michael came over to pick up more clothes and spend time with Mike and Gerry at the house while I was there. He needed to be supervised, no objection.

"Barb, did you find those papers for me?"

Wasn't interested. "I didn't have a chance to look yet."

"I asked you a couple of weeks ago."

"You asked me three days ago. This was a last-minute visit." Disconnected. "I don't jump when you say 'jump.' I do not live to run your errands. I have children to raise and a lot of other things to do besides find your papers."

"I'll find 'em myself!"

He flew into the home office, rummaging through papers, flinging them across the room, howling. "You don't fuckin' do a thing for me! Everything and everybody comes before me! I'm fuckin' last on your list!"

Emotionless. "How does it feel? Not so good, does it?"

"You fucking whore bitch!" Michael yanked out my wallet from my bag on the desk, and took a scissor to my credit cards, as he raged.

Tightened, I kept cool, just a call to get new cards. He would apologize. "I'm the 'whore bitch'? You're kidding, right? Does that make you feel like a big man? Go ahead! This will really help you get on my good side! You make me sick!"

He tore out the computer, grunting as he threw it against the wall, then stopped, dropping to his knees, in front of me, hugging my waist, sobbing. "I'm sorry! I'm so sorry!"

"Mom?" Mike shook in the doorway.

Pushing Michael off me, I swept my son up in my arms. "Baby, are you okay? Nothing hit you, did it? How long were you standing there?"

"I'm okay. Why did Daddy throw the computer? And why is he calling you those names?"

Michael walked over to give Mike a hug. Stiff as a board, Mike crawled deeper into my arms. Damnit! As much as I tried to protect my boys, the moment he came back in there was destruction and wreckage everywhere.

Carefully calculating my words to help Mike understand just enough, but not too much. "First of all, none of this is your or your brother's fault. This is between Mommy and Daddy. Honey, when two people get married, they take vows and live by them together. Vows are marriage laws, like the laws we all have to live by. If someone breaks a law, that person gets punished, like going to jail. Well, Daddy broke a vow in our marriage, and he hurt my heart. Now, Mommy needs to decide if I can forgive him. I'm gonna try my best, but I don't know if I can."

"Then why is he the one mad all the time? Not you." Good point. That's my boy.

"Daddy gets mad at himself and tries but doesn't know how to make it better."

"He keeps making it worse, Mom. What was the law?"

Michael was silent, knowing his son, six, was right.

"This is why we need time apart, so we can try to make it better. Baby, the law between Daddy and me, you don't need to know."

"What happens if you can't?"

"Then, we can't get back together."

Mike started to weep, my arms hugging him tighter.

"Baby, we have a better chance of staying together if we're apart while we try to make it work. Remember that Mommy and Daddy love each other, and we want to stay together, okay?"

Another lie. Michael gave a nod. This was about Mike and Gerry. "Whether we're together or not, we love you and Gerry, no matter what!"

Mike nodded, his eyes filled. He watched his father put the room he destroyed back together. In one motion, I opened the file drawer, pulled out papers and handed them to Michael. Time for him to go home, back to Brooklyn.

January 2, 2001, two months later, day of reckoning or day of doom? I took him back. Damnit, love was still messing me up like a yo-yo. My mind and heart struggled. My heart won. His parents vouched for his sobriety. I had to hope they were truthful. He agreed to go on a weekend retreat for couples, Retrouvaille. The children were excited to see him. Hellina had gone back to the Dominican Republic. The feeling of her looming presence and his betrayal, my doubt still nagged.

Michael told me he could still perform surgeries at the hospital. His truth or pride didn't matter. I knew he was banned from every office. Where he was going "to work" I had no idea. Truth was I had started to harden, numb. Truth was he had never stopped using. He seemed to cheat with Demerol alone this time, somehow easier to cope with, at least emotionally. My searches turned up only his drug paraphernalia. Symptoms instantly pronounced, his condition grew dire. I grew strangely disconnected, robotic. Dr. Griffith told me to monitor him and use my judgment.

Judgment—I questioned mine. The words "co-dependent" and "boundaries" rang through my head. So I asked Dr. Griffith, "Is it wrong of me to not kick him out?"

His tone was grave. "At this point, his family won't make a difference if it hasn't before. He is over the edge, but won't say yes to going away again right now. Keeping him close keeps him and everyone safer." Dr. Griffith's words: Gospel, trusted. What he suggested was what would be done. "However, it is your choice. How much are you willing to tolerate?"

A month later, in our bedroom, Michael slumped back on our loveseat, jaw dropped, deep asleep. He was barely breathing. My head to his chest, his heartbeat sluggish. Shaking him, yelling his name, smacking his face did nothing. Waking for a second, his eyes rolled back, lids fluttered, then closed. He dropped back into the same breathing rhythm.

Dr. Griffith, voice message. "At what point should I call the ambulance?"

Fuck! What do I do? Is this the moment?

"What's wrong with Daddy?" My boys at the door gawked at their father. "Is he okay, Mommy?"

"Don't worry, guys. He's gonna be okay. He's just taking a really deep nap. He's so tired."

"But, why did you say ambulance?"

"How about if you guys go in your room and watch a show. I'll call you to help me wake Daddy in a few minutes."

They skipped to their room, excited.

The phone rang, Dr. Griffith. "Get him awake. Keep talking to him and throw water on his face. Let me speak to him."

Yelling his name, I held the phone on his ear. He seemed more responsive for a few moments, then his eyes rolled closed.

I took the phone back. "He fell asleep."

"I will call William Farley rehab in Williamsburg, Virginia, right now. They will get him in ASAP. Their program has a great success rate with a different approach, a long-term group buddy set up, three-month minimum, structured in everyday life settings. I will get right back to you with the itinerary. Keep him awake!"

Three months? Hallelujah! The boys stood on the loveseat ready for their cue.

"I have an idea! Let's splash daddy with some water and wake him! Just this time, though. Jump and yell, 'Daddy, wake up!' Okay? And be careful, don't fall off!"

Thrilled for the game, they splashed water on his face as they jumped up and down, all giggles, singing. "Daddy, wake up! Daddy, wake up!"

Jumping on their father clueless, my heart was breaking. He slowly came to, still groggy, too out of it to get pissed. The boys hugged him, then me and scurried back to their room.

"Michael, do you remember talking to Dr. Griffith? You almost stopped breathing."

He didn't move. I slapped his face.

"What'd you do that for?"

Got his attention. He called Dr. Griffith. Again, the carrot, his license. He bit. Always did. He was going away but hated me for it. Again, unaffected, composed, my best strategy.

Go ahead, you son of a bitch! Hate me. Maybe it'll save your life.

No way Dr. G could break it to me gently. "They can't get him in until the day after tomorrow."

My heart sank. "No sooner? I would leave with him now!"

"Best I could do. It's only two days. You can do it. I have complete faith in you."

A lifetime away, how would I keep him alive for another day? I got hold of his car keys and hid them, his extra set already tucked away. He was so wasted, he'd just think he couldn't find them. Or another way? It was Michael, after all. He exited the bathroom, fresh blood on his arm, spiraling down at full speed. I put him in bed, shook him. He was out still breathing. I called our housekeeper, Katia, filled her in and told her not to come tomorrow. I needed to deal with him alone. She told me she once saw him from the balcony over the driveway go into his car. Our secret. Damn, he was a master, so devious. Machiavelli got nothin' on him. His car keys in hand, my next mission. The entire front console came up, a bottle of Demerol and needle. What was a dashboard without a console? Lifting it exposed another bottle with two syringes, and bloody tissues. I swept the car, inside and under. Was I just spinning my wheels? Really, nothing could stop him.

The morning came. My boys once again in Rockland at Grandma and Grandpa's safe haven, Daddy off to work again. Sadly, they were used to goodbye with him, adapted, so resilient. When he was away, all was peaceful and right with the world. Time to drive him down. The door chimed.

"Michael!"

"I'm going for a bike ride. I'll be back in a half-hour."

I forgot about that set of wheels! That sneaky fucker!

"Wait! Michael!"

Frantic, I dashed out the door. He was nowhere in sight. The guard at the gate said he saw him riding a bike out. As I called his cell, it rang, perched on the kitchen table, beside his wallet. In my truck I scoured the streets once again. Every local pharmacy had not seen him, promising they would never dispense to him ever again. I even drove by Hellina's old apartment. Nothing. He was nowhere in sight. Maybe he was back home. Was he looking for his last high? Or was he escaping? Unstoppable. Two hours passed. I called his two frequent pharmacies in Teaneck to see if he had shown, ripping into them for dispensing to him so regularly in the first place. I mentioned the DEA if they ever dispensed to him again. They apologized. The door. He practically crawled in, flying high. I let it go. The car was already packed.

"Do you want anything to eat before we leave?"

"I don't want anything, you fucking bitch! You ruined my life! I fucking hate you!"

"Okay. Let's get on the road."

He spit hate every time he spoke to me for the entire eight-hour trip. No violent outbursts thankfully. He was probably too high. Or he deep down loved me for it. Let him hate me for the rest of his life. I didn't care either way. Maybe he'll live. They held his car and keys for the first two weeks until driving privileges around town, only with a buddy or group. I hoped this one would take. Fourth time's a charm? On the plane home I came up for air, Michael a choke chain around my neck, with a two-ton weight at the bottom of a river. My deeds were done. Life was crashing down, his business was done. I needed to sell our townhouse. Rue, our real estate agent, helped me put it up for sale and find a rental. She made me cry, offering us to stay at her house in Alpine for a while if I needed. Who does that? A saint, she had seen me through it all. I loved her. This rehab was different. For the first time, "Superman" realized he was powerless against his Kryptonite. The revelation of recovery.

"Barb, you make me a better person."

Though I appreciated his sentiment, I knew that. "The new Michael can stay. The old Michael will need to go."

Ready for anything, what Michael was I gonna get?

8

The Second (Tenth?) Chance

This was truly our second chance...well, more like tenth. Michael came home in complete recovery, apparently "staying under the radar," as he put it. What would he do now? Thank God for his disability policy, surprisingly covering him for his condition—addiction and the supporting circumstances. In one year, would we make it? Or would I leave him for good? Renting was the smartest move in the face of such uncertainty. The moving date set for the following week, staying in Fort Lee, we were moving to a duplex rental just blocks from our sold townhouse in the same school district.

My fitness training, speaking, and writing for *NY Power*—for Dr. Nick Barnaman, my mentor and friend—was staying. It was all a big part of my life, and a lifesaver. It didn't hurt he was also a crisis counselor for drugs, alcohol, and suicide for many years. He knew my story, had a place on my angel list. With so many good people around me, why couldn't I think for a second of my husband as one of them?

He was the reason for everything bad. Was I doubting my decision? Yes. I'd try to give him a chance. Again.

Leaving my boys with their father, fresh out of rehab with anger management issues, was not an option. Mike had only become more precocious, and they weren't used to having him around. Opportunity after opportunity passed me by: fit modeling, fit news show guest as a fit mom coach and trainer, writing a fitness hand bible for moms. Some passed and gone, some on hold. No regrets—though this life is a delicate dance with every step, my boys came first. My day would come whether he was in it or not.

His voice unmistakable, he was using again, like a thousand bee stings to my brain. He'd either go away to rehab for at least six months, to prison, or six feet under. My first instinct was call Dr. Griffith, because Michael was still under his jurisdiction. Really, he seemed my sponsor more than he was Michael's! His support saved our lives. He really did genuinely care about us. His advice was to stick to my boundaries and call him back after I confronted him with it.

Michael denied it, laughing at me. "I just returned from three months of rehab! I've never been better!"

Letting it go ostensibly, I didn't. Cat and rat game back in play. "Sorry, honey, just my paranoia, I'll get past it."

Wouldn't be long, inevitable. Michael's signature was all I needed and all he contributed for the closing. Standing over his desk in his office, papers in front of him, my finger pointed to every line. A life-sized bobble-head face down to sign, his head almost hit the desk a few times. His hand trembled, pen to paper, his lids fluttered, his signature that of a three-year-old. Pathetic.

The move tomorrow needs to happen, with or without him. I wish he would disappear.

No such luck. The movers started packing up the truck. The children were in school, Mom and Dad set to pick them up and keep them overnight. I transported breakables in my truck to the duplex, Michael presumably the same. Katia, my angel, my right arm through everything, helped with her truck as well.

She pulled me aside at the duplex. "I drove behind Michael. He swerved bad, almost crashed a few times!"

I stayed hard and steady. "Where is he getting it from?"

"I saw him go into the front bush by the townhouse."

She was my eyes and ears, too! How could I ever thank this girl enough? Nothing could never be enough to show my gratitude. When Michael arrived at the duplex and into the house, I snatched the keys from his ignition, and drove away in my truck back to the townhouse.

Not a minute later, he called me, his slur undeniable. "You have my keys? Can't find them."

"I don't know, I'll check. Be back in a few."

Sticking my head in the bush, the bottle and syringe stared back at me. "This is way past old."

The hiding places could be countless. No time. Packing more in my car, I headed back to direct the movers.

I pulled up. He staggered to my car. "You find them?" He followed me into the basement.

I closed the door. "Michael, I have your keys. You're high and almost had a few car accidents driving here. You were all over the road."

"Give me my keys! Now!"

"I can't. I hid them. Just, please, wait it out."

He leaned into me to yell again. One of the movers knocked, needing me outside. Following the mover to the driveway, Michael was right behind me, the heat of his breath on my neck.

He grabbed my arm and swung me around, his face too close to mine, my nose gone if there was one snap of his jaw. "Give me my keys, you fucking cunt!" His roar heard down the block.

Every one of our new porch-sitting elderly neighbors stood, if they were able, and stared. Welcome to the neighborhood, motherfucker!

Ridiculously unruffled. "What did I tell you about calling me that disgusting word! For your own safety, I can't. Please, try to remember everything you got out of the three months in Farley. Please."

Staying cool, taking back my arm and pulling away, I continued to unpack the car. Unsteady, he stood in my way, with his chest puffed out, like a cock ready for a fight.

"Fuck you, you fucking cunt! Give me my keys or I'll crack your fucking head open!"

All eyes on us, the movers and neighbors froze.

My tone temperate. "We're gonna do this again? Is that what you want? Crack my fucking head open? Why? Because you can't get to the drugs you hid in the bushes, you idiot?"

Caught off-guard. "What the fuck are you talking about?"

My temperature rose. "Do you need to shit all over everywhere we live? We haven't even moved in yet! You're making a fool of yourself! And I'm a fool for being here! You need to get a hold of yourself! Get it together, Michael! Or get out!"

Why am I here?

He charged away, then cooled off, and apologized. Hollow. I apologized to half the free world for his behavior. He promised he wouldn't use again. Empty. How could I let him mistreat me like that? Again and again? How did I ever get used to his abuse? Was it my strength? No reason was good enough! Not the man I thought I married, cracks showed through his strong handsome mask, weak beyond my wildest nightmares.

Two days after settling in, on a sunny June day, I took one step into the house with Mike and Gerry from fun at the park and pizza with their friends, their first day of summer vacation. From the door, up the steps in plain sight a trail of blood spots, as if acid splashed in my eyes! I smoothly commandeered the children to the kitchen table with a healthy snack and TV and told them to stay there for a couple of minutes. Hastily, I cleaned the trail of blood in the hall and up the stairs leading to Michael sleeping in bed. That was it. No more.

From the next room, his local sponsor, Tim. "Barbra, leave. You have no other choice. Remove yourself and your children from the situation. His career carrot is gone. You and your boys are all he has left. Take yourselves away from him, give him an incentive to get back on track. He has a solid three-month foundation under him." In the very next call, Dr. Griffith agreed. He would call Michael once I had left him. His father was on his way, so he shouldn't be alone. All our clothes already in suitcases from the move, the car was packed.

As I sat on the edge of the bed, he jumped. "What the fuck are you doin'? Don't sneak up on me like that!"

Not even worth it, I let it go. "I found a trail of blood in the hallway and up the stairs."

"Barb, I cut myself! I swear! Look!" He showed me a scratch mark of blood across his forearm.

"From the needle, Michael." The rat caught in the trap.

I gave him an eleventh chance. "You are going to end up dead or in jail. You should immediately put yourself back in the program, and you need to stay there for at least six months. You've only been out for a couple of weeks and you've been using for a week already."

Eerily stoic. "I'm not going back in."

"I'm taking the kids to my parents' indefinitely. I love my husband, Michael. This man that sits in front of me is not him. He's a liar and loves his drugs first, not his family, nor himself. You are not my husband. When he comes back, maybe I will. Do you want to say goodbye to the boys? Or should we just leave?"

He acquiesced. "Let them come in, I'll stay here. I don't want to see you leave."

As I gave him a hug, he clung. I pushed away. "Goodbye."

A week later, Michael's dad told me he had been clean the entire week. Michael never left his sight. I trusted my father-in-law, though he wanted me with his son. How far he would go to keep me I wasn't sure. The three of us met and sat in the kitchen for a talk. We hashed it out, Michael falling back into the drugs, his depression about all that he had lost, his career, his friends, all the people he had hurt, everyone turning their back on him, what would he do, going forward. As we laid it all out on the table, Michael got up in tears, swung around and punched a hole in the wall.

Ooooh! I couldn't stand that temper! "Does that make you feel better now? Destroying things?"

He sat back down, as if he threw a weight off his shoulder. "I'm sorry."

"You're going to fix that. Everything you're pissed about is all your own doing! Do you really think 'sorry' fixes all the shit you create? 'Sorry' is only as good as trying to change what you're sorry for! And not letting it happen again! The drugs! The cheating! The lies! Your temper! Cursing at me! Hurting me! You can't come clean to save your life! Right now, all your 'sorrys' mean nothing until you show me a difference. I don't and won't believe a word you say until you prove it." I sprung up. "Sorry." At the doorway with my bag. "Whatever step number it is, take inventory of the people you've hurt, and own it! The people who cut you out of their lives were the smart ones!"

Leaving it all behind me, I closed the door and left. I felt so free without him. Why did I keep going back? A prisoner of love, literally. Good to get back to my boys so enjoying time upstate with my family, their safe place, Raven and Bill had a beautiful little boy. They got to see their new baby cousin, Aidan Hunter. So happy for them! Michael's father confirmed another two weeks of sobriety for Michael. He had kept up with his AA meetings, with Tim and Dr. Griffith, confirmed by both. Not enough. Another few weeks, we came home. Day after day, examining him, studying his behavior, no signs, Michael was sober. Recovery, please stay. Was this really my station in life? Monitoring this weak, senseless man? For drugs? Cheating?

"I just gotta keep doing the next right thing. I'll make it up to you guys. I will! I promise!"

Promises. There wasn't one he hadn't broken. We'd see. Michael feverishly worked in his home office, the third bedroom. His door was closed much of the time. As long as he wasn't doing Demerol or a whore, I was good.

"Honey! I know what I'm going to do! A tissue recovery company for transplants and research. I have a good relationship with RTC."

"You said RTC stole two patents from you, and you never saw credit or a dime from it. But business is business, I guess. I'm afraid to ask, what would you do?"

Money trumped trust, it seemed. "I'll use my surgical skills on cadavers for tissue and body parts from hospitals and funeral homes, with consents and proper criteria, of course. It'll help a lotta people. And good money."

I put my fingers in my ears and closed my eyes. "Ugh! Okay! That's good. No more. Heard enough! Sounds creepy, but if it helps people, keeps you safe and provides for us, go for it."

"I have a lot of work to do."

"I'm happy for you. But from now on I do my own thing and you do yours, got it? It's healthier for me."

Independence from him was essential to my protection, security. My life, children, family, friends, fitness career was all mine, he could never take any of them from me. He had a hard time with me having my own life and doubting him. Too bad! If he didn't like it, leave!

Didn't take long before his humility went to shit again, ridiculing my work in fitness and training moms and elderly ladies. "You make pennies compared to me! I make more in an hour than you could make in two months with the disability alone! You don't even take money to speak or write!" He taunted, laughing.

"You sound like a cocky asshole! It's not always about money, Michael! It's about something for myself! About helping people! Fine, you make your millions! I'll make my way! I've turned down a lot of opportunities for the sake of my family and because of your trouble-making! Your arrogance is nauseating! And insulting! Keep bringing old Michael back and I'm gone! Check yourself!"

We fought more and more often. My doubts wouldn't leave me. He was irritated. I couldn't get it through his thick skull that trust needed to be earned, especially starting deep in deficit. It was a privilege, not a right. Our marriage needed time to heal. The wounds were deep and he was wielding the knife. Every single time.

Mike, only nine, was distraught about our fighting. "You two are gonna get divorced! I know it! Watch! It's going to happen! I just feel it!" His extra sense?

When I tried to reassure him, he didn't hear me. Time for help. We saw Dr. Will, a family psychiatrist. Mike felt better. Gerry didn't feel any different, at least on the surface. As the younger child he saw, experienced, and knew less. Many times, Mike shielded his little brother. Michael didn't want his drug problem discussed. It needed to come out, an inescapable part of our story.

Dr. Will was perplexed. "There is a piece missing to this puzzle. Barbra, you should have been the one unfaithful in this picture. You were existing, not living."

Michael gave. Everything made sense then. Not to me. Drugs or not, I should've been the one. Michael had started his affair with Hellina before they became partners in addiction. It was a swift kick in the gut and not what I was originally led to believe. She was also found with him in every bathroom he bloodied from the drugs. Another omission by all.

Dr. Will posed a question. "Either way, you both will go on in your lives without each other. The question you need to ask yourselves is, will your life be happier with or without each other? I'm talking about quality of life."

Though life was peaceful without him in our lives, so much easier, I did love him. We made progress. He started his recovery business. I stayed with my children and in fitness.

"Jay and I present this donor plan to the different funeral directors to offer it to the grieving family members as a gift of donation. In return, the funeral home will offset the funeral costs with a discount or a free casket. RTC and processing companies like them are looking for good tissue for transplants and research. With my surgical skills, I got it made."

"What do the funeral directors get out of this?"

"I rent facility space from them as I perform the recoveries. The processing companies pay me a service fee as long as the tissue fits the criteria."

"Is it all legal?"

"Yes. We have attorneys working on the contracts."

"Good luck with it all, honey."

He had come a long way, having found something so humane for people in need, for himself. He went out on calls all hours of the day or night. The pattern seemed to be either his partner, Jay, a funeral director and home transporter in Staten Island, or a contracted funeral director, would call him. Michael would leave. Every time he left, acid swirled in the pit of my gut. Did he really have a case? Was Hellina around? Or someone else? Or several? Trying so hard to rebuild my trust in him, I couldn't shake the suspicion. Was he trying hard? Or trying hard to hide things, again? Michael still couldn't understand why I couldn't just skip over my hurt already and move on. Offenders never do. He was lucky I hadn't moved on from him.

One of my mantras. "Do unto others as you want done unto you." How could I make him get it?

"What if I was cheating on you? I can't stop thinking about him. Him making love to me? Inside me? Touching me? Me touching him? Me lying to you to be with him? With him every chance I get? Sneaking around behind your back? He brags to his friends how I want him, and my husband doesn't satisfy me? How would it make you feel? Good?"

"Enough! I get it!" He got it. At least for a minute.

Michael's bullshit aside, at least he found a worthwhile profession. His business seemed to be moving forward. At times, I heard him taking a call. "Did you speak to the family yet?" "It's the funeral director. The case should go in a couple of hours," or "We need to wait for confirmation from the family."

The truth was, I really didn't care to know a damn thing about his business, just that he was being true. Too much explaining waves a red flag for covering dirty tracks. Sometimes, he would be back in an hour or two, stating the donor didn't meet his criteria. Sometimes, he didn't come home until the next day, trust still in serious contention. Another bone I couldn't wrap my mind around, locked freezers for "this tissue" as he called it, in our garage where my kids' bikes and toys were! Creeped me the hell out! He said he needed to save money to start the business.

I had almost no choice but to agree. "This is temporary."

I was getting ready for a 9/11 benefit Geo invited me and Tiana to. "Michael, come with me."

"I'm not into it."

"Why not? It's for a good cause. Will be fun. At Chaos, this hot club in the city. VIP. C'mon, you need to get out."

"I'm not in the mood but call me later."

"Call me if you change your mind."

Katia was on call, in case he decided to come. The place was buzzin'. Geo led us right up to VIP where they greeted him and showed us to his area where some of his entourage got it started. What a great night! Mourning, giving, celebrating, partying, dancing. A photographer from *Soap Opera Digest* took a group photo of us girls with Geo in the middle. I would make sure Michael never saw that. Trying to call him, there was no cell signal anywhere in the place. We were leaving in a few anyway. As I drove Ti's friend, Shari, home, five minutes from me, we talked the entire trip until we got to her house.

"Hey, honey. I'm two minutes from the house. I just dropped off Shari, the one who works for the school."

"I thought you were gonna call me from there! Why the fuck did you wait until you dropped her off?"

"I tried. There was no service there. We were talking the whole ride. I was driving. What's wrong with you? It's only ten thirty. I left the benefit early."

"Why did you wait until you're two minutes from the house? You fuckin' cunt!"

"I'm warning you! Don't call me that again! You need to calm down. I'll be home in a minute. There's nothing to be upset about."

What would I have to deal with? What would I be walking into? He wasn't finished.

Minutes later at home, I took a seat on the loveseat away from him, ready for words. "Can you please tell me what's really bothering you?"

He sat up in bed. "Why didn't you fuckin' call me?"

"I told you already. You could've come with me."

"Who the fuck were you with?"

"That's what this is about! I understand now. Because you cheated, you think I'm gonna retaliate? I'm not you! I was with Ti, Geo, and bunch of their friends. It was a benefit! Relax!"

"Don't fuckin' tell me to relax, you fuckin' bitch! I'll snap your fuckin' neck!"

"Try it! I'll call the police!"

I held the phone up in my hand. He sprung out of bed! I dialed 911! He jumped on me! The phone dropped! He grabbed my throat! Not before I could wedge my fingertips between his hands and my neck! Knees up! He was squeezing! I kicked at him with my knees!

Screaming over and over! "Get off me! Get off me!"

I fought him with everything I had! I wrenched at his hands clutched around my neck, trying to relieve the pressure! I squeezed my knees up as far as I could, got my feet on his stomach and catapulted him off me! He fell to the ground, feet from me! "Are you crazy! You animal!"

He got up and stood there. "You fuckin' had it coming! You pushed me to it! With that cunt attitude!"

I was still trying to catch my breath. "You could've killed me! You're disgusting! I hate you! Get out! Get the hell out!"

"Believe me! If I wanted you dead, you wouldn't have gotten me off you! It wasn't so bad!"

Flashing lights outside the window behind me, the doorbell rang. My eyes shot to the doorway. The door open, Mike stood there, frozen with tears.

I ran to him and held him gently, resting his head into my neck, rocking him.

"It's okay, baby. Mommy's okay. See? I'm fine! Remember? Mommy's magic." My chin down so he couldn't see my neck, Michael's fingerprints undoubtedly a necklace. "Mommy has to get the door."

He wouldn't let me go. Getting too big to carry, I hoisted him up in my arms and headed downstairs. Peeking in, Gerry was still asleep, God bless him.

Michael had let the police in already, eight officers. One of them was Nate, an umpire from Mike's baseball league, his son a few years older than Mike.

"It's okay, baby. You will be safe with the policemen. You'll be right in the next room. Mommy's okay." I gave him a big hug and a reassuring smile.

The officer guided Mike to the living room. Four officers detained and talked to Michael upstairs. Nate and another talked to me in the kitchen. In the back of my mind, he was just past the drug charges, doing so well. He just went and fucked everything up. Again!

"Tell us what happened. Be as descriptive as you can."

They took notes, detail for detail, truth for truth.

"Has he ever done something like this to you before?"

"He's shoved me around a few times in the past, cursed at me more than that, but no choking or hitting." Was I just rationalizing?

"Have you seen him violently hit your children?"

"He's been rough with Mike couple of times, which upsets me terribly, and I've had talks and fought with him about it, but never a beating." Did I just fucking do it again?

"Mrs. Mastromarino, we've seen this kind of domestic situation happen many times before. Usually the wife presses charges, and then bails him out and lets him come back. Think about your children. This was a one-time incident. Please, think carefully about your decision to press charges or not. Do you think he would do this to you again?"

"You know he has trouble already, right? You can see when the address popped up, I'm sure."

"Please, think about your issue at hand."

"If I press charges, does he go to jail right now?"

"Yes. We take him away now."

Thoughts rush around my head like a speeding bullet in a steel box. "I don't know what to do."

"If you're that unsure, I think you know the answer."

"He doesn't deserve a 'no.' What he did! The things he said to me!"

"We'll do whatever you tell us."

One of the officers entered the kitchen. "Your son is doing well, ma'am."

"Thank you so much, officer."

He directed his conversation to Nate. "He's calm, respectful, and abiding. Very apologetic."

I chimed in. "Sincerely?"

"Seems so. He keeps saying he's sorry and he loves you."

All eyes on me. How much of his words were lip service?

"Don't they all say that to get out of trouble? Nate, it sounds like you're all talking me into not pressing charges." What would he do to me if I have him locked up and he gets out?

"We've seen this a thousand times. Many times, the perpetrator remains violent, or reasons with us that it was her fault. He's showing remorse, sincerely. We know the difference." They didn't know my husband.

"I won't press charges."

Would this shock him into breaking his bad behavior? Or was his remorse temporary, like every promise he'd ever made? Or a good actor fooling the police? Was I fooling myself? Oh, God, was I making a terrible mistake? As much as he taught Mike to stand up to bullies and take care of the little guys that couldn't take care of themselves, *he* was a bully! My bully! Life wasn't easy in the first place, but damnit he made it so hard, borderline unbearable.

9

The New Beginning

More than a year had passed. Not a hand lifted, nor a curse thrown, the children thriving...we made it to 2003! Michael's sobriety appeared solid, my trust in recovery restored. Not exactly my fairy tale life, but I'd take it. I didn't know what drove Michael to recovery. Was it me and the boys? Was it the need to succeed? The drive to make it back? Could it be something within him finally clicked and made sense to him? Or was it his ego? I didn't really give a damn. He appeared clean. I lived everyday as if. I'd never say he was. I learned the hard way, one day at a time. *Show me. Don't tell me.*

After my nightmare with Michael, I saw my trusted friend, Tiana, spiraling down. I talked her into taking her kids and going down to Florida to be close to her family and getting the help she knew she needed.

"I'll miss you. And Ti, you know I love you. No more partying for us. You need to get it together and I need to try to make my marriage work. Hanging with you is only going to cause problems with him."

"Honey, I love you. But he is your problem, not me. Watch, in five years, he's gonna put you through the same shit. I respect you, so I respect your wishes. But you'll be sorry."

"Thank you. You might be right, but I have to try. He's my husband. You better take care of yourself. Don't lose touch! Let me know what's happening with you. If not, I'm gonna find out from Maria and hunt you down!"

She moved to Florida. We did drift. But I always knew how she was through Maria. She and her kids were doing well. I was happy for her.

It was time to become of a part of the community again as parents. Michael attended the kids' games with me and our dads. He got to know the other fathers, the kids, coaches. He coached our boys in sports. They knew fitness from me. Getting closer with the parents, moms mostly, questions came. "So, what does your husband do?" About his thriving new business, he told me to simply say medical research. People wouldn't understand and it might scare them off. Despite its gruesome undertone, how could the truth hurt for such a good cause? I didn't like it. He was hiding from the truth and it scared me.

Time flew and Gerry's first communion came. He and his little friends were simply adorable. After the church cleared, our vow renewal commenced. Twelve years, we made it. Barely. Truth, my parents, Raven, Bill, Ben, Aunt Belle, and Uncle Herm attended for Gerry. They would've rather gone to a diner than my ceremony, having seen me through too much. Michael and I stood at the altar, our boys beside us. I never felt stronger, more confident, readier. For what, only time would tell. My heart told me I had made the right decision. My gut? I chose not to inquire within.

2004 came fast. No more freezers in the garage! Michael had expanded enough to get his own office and lab in the center of town in Fort Lee by the George Washington Bridge. His main guys Leo and Carl, he called them "cutters," just rolled off his tongue like nothing. Nice job title. They handled the recoveries and lab. I had only met them a time or two. Funny, Michael was drawn to that word, "recovery," in one way or another. I hoped they both would bring him success. He seemed to come full circle from everything, damn hell of a road. The new business flourished. So happy for him. Most importantly, he was staying clean. Only visiting his office a handful of times, I kept my promise to myself to do my own thing, not his. That didn't mean that I wasn't gonna check on his staff choices. Marla and her mom seemed like good people, from the neighborhood. He'd stolen enough from my life, heart and soul with his addiction and cheating. Never again. Forgiven but never forgotten. Impossible.

Michael took me on his trip to Gainesville, Florida, to meet with RTC. Phil, the CEO, gave me a quick tour. Cold, sterile, but impressive. The coffee lounge felt a bit warmer while they disappeared to their confidential meeting, Michael a VIP. Afterwards we had dinner and headed back to the hotel. We watched a movie, made love, and he turned over and fell asleep. Making love no more than a gesture, he was selfish.

One thing was certain. My imagination fed my starving soul. My faceless dream man. In the bathroom, door locked, lights out. He took me against the door, clasping my hands with his above my head, kissing me hungrily. His broad, tight body pressing into mine, feeling every ripple of his every muscle so perfect against me, his massive hardness unmistakable. My heart beat out of my chest. His big strong hand cupped my breast out of my nightie, his lips like heaven on me. He perched me on the sink, lifted my teddy, baring me, spreading me. My God. I curled into him, pulling him into me, so deep, reaching down, stroking each other as he drove into me, spanking me, caressing, kissing, holding so tight, jolting together as if lightning struck, sending shock waves through me. Good night.

Two in the morning, I woke to Michael's body twitching, his eyes half open, rolling behind his fluttering lids. Too much déjà vu from his drug days. Panic of our history hitting me, I backed away, holding my breath. Out of nowhere, he grunted and reached around swinging his fist, punching my pillow with a force that could've broken my face, just missing me! I jumped off the bed! He was still asleep!

"Michael! Michael!"

Whites of his eyes, body trembling, as if he was possessed, he rumbled in a deep tone I had never heard from him, like in a horror movie.

Suddenly, he thundered, "We'll get them all! We'll lead them to slaughter! Like lambs!" Echoing the devil.

Chills ran up my spine. Was someone leading him? Or was he leading? Someone must've been leading him. He was helping people, doing good.

"Michael! Michael! Wake up!" I poked him with the TV remote from a distance.

He jerked awake. "What the hell are you doin'? What did you do? Hit me?"

"I only tapped you. Michael, do you remember your dream at all? You were having a nightmare, shaking and talking in your sleep. You swung at my pillow and almost hit me! You scared the life out of me!"

"Really? I'm sorry, honey! I don't remember my dream at all. I never usually do. What did I say in the dream?"

"You bellowed, in this crazy deep voice, 'We'll get them all! We'll lead them to slaughter like lambs!' Does that mean anything to you? Do you think someone's out to get you?"

He was taken aback. "I said that?"

Returning home, he submerged himself into expanding his booming business. He traveled to Brooklyn, Rochester, Philadelphia, Connecticut, Florida. I couldn't keep up. Michael swiftly became the "king of tissue." Only having access to our personal account, I could only go by what he told me. House hunting? Hell, no. The memory was too vivid. My God, the hell he created. The devil with some kind of hold over me, as if his possession, he wouldn't let me go. Thinking back, why I stayed was still an enigma. We'd already moved five times in ten years, evading Michael's drug messes. That was enough. We weren't moving so fast if I could help it. I needed to feel some solid ground for a while.

Time passed quite happily, beyond a breath of fresh clean air. He seemed to have more free time for me and the boys, our Doberman puppy, Duchess, and our three Bombay cats from the same litter, Nero, Cicero, and Simba. Picture perfect? I could only hope. He took me to check out this new construction in the Bluff, just about completed by Reece, our friend and builder of our first Englewood Cliffs house that we had to sell. A nice tucked-away neighborhood of grand homes in Fort Lee, overlooking the Hudson and Manhattan, just a couple of minutes away from our duplex. The layout eerily resembled our first Englewood Cliffs house, so surreal, slightly smaller with a fraction of the property only a minute from the George Washington Bridge into the city, backyard enough for the kids and Duchess. Perusing around, loving it, taking it in, warmer, cozier, it felt right.

"Do you like it, honey?"

This place stirred emotion in me. "It's perfect."

"I knew it. That's why I already gave Reece the down payment from the disability money. It's ours, honey! We can finish the kitchen the way we want. You stuck by me through everything. I told you I would make it up to you. Anything for you, honey." Michael wrapped his arms around me. "Happy?"

My eyes welled, holding my breath. "Are you sure we can afford this?"

He nodded and pulled me closer as we stood in our new home. "I'm killin' it, honey."

After everything, we were starting over. No more unsettling, moving, shuffling the kids around. No more of him shitting where we lived. No more drugs, cheating, violence, upheaval, troubles with authorities, destruction. Should I go on? Life was good. Cloud nine. Not too good to be true, I prayed.

The end of July 2005, as I unpacked from our family Disney trip, every minute of it warmed my heart. My boys were elated—they even had fun with Dad. Pool only, of course. He loathed the parks, lines, crowds. I took them everywhere. Everybody was happy.

Mike had confided in me a while back. "Mom, I know it's not nice, but I like it better when Dad doesn't come. He's always mad. We have such a better time when he's not here."

Me, too! "I know, honey. He's never there for long when he does come. Keep it between us."

Days of sugar-coated lies done, older now, eleven and eight, they understood. No idea of their father's past, the dangers of drugs were better learned in school than from their father.

Michael called me from the office, voice tight. "Barb, detectives are at my office right now."

My gut tight. "Why?"

"I don't exactly know. They have a search warrant from the Brooklyn District Attorney's Office, taking records, equipment, all kinds of things from the lab and the office. I think it has something to do with Jay. He may be in trouble for something with his new partners in the funeral home. It seems they're investigating me to see what they can find out about him through me."

"Are you in trouble for something with Jay?"

"I don't think so. I have to find out what's going on. I'll see you at home."

Hardened by my experiences with him, panic wasn't in my vocabulary anymore, my heart rate steady, continuing to unpack as if he never told me. Gut still tense, in the back of my mind it sat. He came home with the same story, different words, no answers.

"Michael, is this anything I have to worry about?"

"Probably not. I'm not sure until I know what it's really about. For all I know, they may be questioning me to get to him, or trying to implicate me with him."

"Did you do anything for them to implicate you?"

"No."

"Okay, then, nothing to worry about, right?"

"No. I'll let you know as I find out. We're still going to Montauk next week and Point Pleasant Labor Day weekend."

Michael grew more edgy, easily agitated. I ignored it, his normal self, still on steroids from his college football days, never easy. The withdrawn part baffled me. Thankfully, he was straight. Mid-September, I flew down with Michael to a National Tissue Conference in Fort

Lauderdale. We ran into Leo, his chief cutter, at the airport, another edgy one, usually the easygoing one. What was this, a club? I was too happy to be joining them.

The ocean shimmered just beyond beach, the hotel paradise. Michael told me to wait by the couches as he checked in. Why couldn't I be next to him? What was I not supposed to hear? Maybe, go back later and ask the best way to reach Hellina and see what popped up. That lowdown bitch gnawed at me since their car accident and drugging together. At times, I would wonder where she was, if he'd ever been in contact with her, if they'd ever been together again, if he had a child with her, if she died in that plane crash in the Dominican Republic perhaps. I stopped the nonsense. Things had been great for a couple of years. Why question?

Very much in demand, he was constantly surrounded by his colleagues, vying for his time, the toast of the conference! He had come so far.

* * *

It was a beautiful summer day at Michael's family's house in Hunter, upstate New York. Good clean air. A serene getaway. We were together over a year. The sunset from the back deck was spectacular.

"When I was graduating high school, Admiral Farragut Academy, my counselor told my dad I was just a jock, no brainiac. A lawyer or doctor would never be in the cards for me. He put me at the city job level. My dad wanted to clock him for insulting his son, and insulting city jobs, as if they were low!" His eyes fierce. "I vowed I was gonna make it big! I'd show them I was smarter than them all! I had to study twice as hard. Damn straight, I'm doin' it!"

* * *

This time, Michael didn't boast about all the attention and status—he was uneasy. Lucky our flight home wasn't canceled. We just missed a hurricane, as if the storm chased us.

"Any more details about Jay?"

Without looking up. "No."

More and more unsettled, I kept going. "Let me know."

A couple of weeks later, Michael returned from a Princeton conference with his business associate, Mel, visiting from Georgia, white as a ghost. "My contact at Bio Cell told me they discovered discrepancies on a few of the donation consent forms! Phone numbers are not right! They called the families. All the numbers are bogus! I have to get to the bottom of this! I'm going to try some of the numbers myself! I'll see Todd and Syl in Connecticut first thing in the morning, and the Barone brothers later tomorrow in Philly to see what the hell is going on here! If they've done something wrong, I'm gonna be pissed!"

About time to start worrying. *Breathe, cool, calm.*

Michael stormed into the library slamming the doors as he made a call. Miraculously, the glass did not shatter. He threw them open, back to the kitchen table with Mel discussing this discovery, tension rough and coiled as steel wool. My cue to leave them coffee and bring snacks to my boys upstairs, my pure happy place.

Late the next evening, Michael came home, staring into space as he dazed into the kitchen. His dad and I both sat at the table raising our brows at each other, waiting.

He started reeling. "I called a slew of the numbers. All phony! The Barones didn't get consents from their donor families at their funeral home! They didn't fuckin' get consents!"

My stomach jumped. "You mean they just let you go in there and take tissue? And you didn't know?"

"Barb, they gave me all the information! It's not my place to check up on them! Or to call the family! The recovery team does not call the family! That's all their end! I'm not takin' the fall for them! Whatever they've done, they're going to have to face it! And I will give up whatever I need to!"

His dad shot up from his chair. "What da hell is goin' on, Mikey?"

"What about Todd and Syl?"

"They said they got consents. But had a flood and all their records destroyed. I told them God help them if they're lying!" He paced wildly.

A flood? Convenient. "Since you performed the recoveries, can you have charges against you?"

"I would hope not! I had nothing to do with it! Goddamnit! I'm halting all business operations from now, including my site in Rochester, until everything is straightened out!"

The following week, this vague plight progressed. "Cousin Mason is my attorney on this. He said they requested I come in to the Brooklyn DA's and make a statement in front of the grand jury. Tell them what I know. Oh, I'm gonna tell them, all right! I'm not taking the fall for no one!"

"The grand jury? That sounds serious, Michael."

What is a grand jury?

"Don't worry. I'll straighten this all out. I'll have this done, one two three."

The next morning, Michael, in his crisp suit and tie, beelined out the front door to his truck, a slew of photographers snapping his picture, reporters shoving microphones in his face. *Smooth.* He got in and drove away.

A lioness protecting my cubs, I decreed, "No one is to leave the house right now! And do not answer the door!"

All the media appeared to have left, most likely following him to the DA's office. Who knew if some were waiting around a corner for him to return home? This was all not going away so quickly. Where it was headed, I could never imagine. No doubt in my mind those pictures taken outside our home would surely make the newspaper and the news. Michael was news. I hoped he wasn't accused of anything because of someone else's actions. The doorbell chimed. Mike had answered the door while I was upstairs.

A man stood, with a recorder in his hand. "Hello, there. Are you Michael Mastromarino's son?"

Yelling down! "Michael Anthony! Shut the door! Now!"

He did before I finished my sentence.

Driving Mike to football practice, Michael called. "Hi, honey. Mike's here. You're on speaker. I'm dropping him off any minute."

"Hi, Dad."

"Hi, pal. Sorry I can't make your practice today."

"That's okay."

At the field, Mike kissed my cheek and jumped out. "Bye, Mom. Love you. Bye, Dad."

"See you at home, bud."

"Love you, honey. Have a great one! Big game Friday!" So proud of my sweet cub, tough as he was. He joined his team.

I braced myself. "What happened today?"

"They basically grilled me. I think I did okay. I answered their questions. Mason said I was candid. It should satisfy what they're looking for. Mason was against me talking to them in the first place. Fuck that! I was going! I'm glad I did."

"When do you find out where this is all going?"

"Mason will call me when he hears."

Later at the kitchen table during dinner with his parents, Michael's cell rang. "What's up?"

He pointed to his phone, motioning me to follow him to the stairs. "But how? All right. I'll be there tomorrow."

He hung up, baffled and anxious. "Damnit! I thought everything went so well. Mason said they're more suspicious of me now after I spoke to them. I don't get it. I have to go to his office tomorrow for strategy. I think like they're going to charge me with something. I just don't know what yet. Neither does Mason. Barb, be prepared. This is gonna hit the news."

My heart picked up pace a few beats, gut churned. I should've been much more upset, panicking, but wasn't. Cool, hardened from the past, whatever was going on had nothing to do with me. It was out of my hands. My vow still stood. "No matter any decision Michael makes, I'm gonna make damn sure I protect myself and my boys."

One day at a time.

10

The News

Friday morning, October 7, 2005, a minute after the boys left the truck for school, lowering my tween-blasting radio, I turned it back up.

"Michael Mastromarino, a former dentist residing in Fort Lee, New Jersey, is accused of stealing body parts, grave robbery, and forgery. More charges to follow. He is deemed the 'mastermind' of this operation, spanning Brooklyn, New Jersey, Philadelphia, and Rochester. More on the 'Ghoulish Body Snatcher' in later news."

My thoughts scattered all over the highway, trying not to crash. "Michael! What the hell is happening? They're saying you're the 'mastermind' of all these terrible crimes! Tell me what's going on! Is it true?"

Michael's voice was firm. "Barb, calm down. I told you it would hit the papers and I had no part of this."

"Did you know?"

"No."

"We'll talk when I get home."

Every station had its news flash. I turned it off, wanting to turn off the world.

My cell rang. "Mom, Dad, I'm okay. I'm not home yet. The boys are at school. I just heard it too. He said he didn't do it, and I couldn't imagine that he did. Tell everyone I'll call them later. Will let you know what's up when I know."

"We're here for you, baby. Anything you need."

"Thank you. Love you."

Maria. "Baby! Big happenings with your hubby! You told me to look out for something. But this? Holy shit! What I need to know is, are you okay?"

"Hey, love. A holy shit hit me, too! As okay as I can be, I just don't know what this all means yet. Call you later when I know more. Love you, girlfriend."

Rayne. "Barb! Are you okay? You know I'm here for you! Tell me what you need! I'll make some calls. Attorneys! Investigators! Anything!"

"I'm fine, beauty. Thank you! Let you know when I do."

My phone didn't stop. Call after call, keeping it brief. I stopped answering, needing to decompress. My boys, only eleven and eight. Hadn't we been through enough because of him? Rolling toward my house, a swarm of reporters, cameramen, and photographers clamored outside my front door, on the driveway, in the street. They all peered into my truck. I smiled and drove past my home as if I didn't live there. Thank God the boys were in school.

"Michael! Do you see what's outside the house? I drove right by!"

"Keep driving," he said. "Stay away for a while. Will let you know when it's clear."

They knew he was in there. Was gonna be a long wait, all hoping for their scoop. I informed the school. They knew, everyone was on guard to keep them safe. In my truck waiting to pick them up, numb. Was I paranoid, or was everyone staring, peering into my window from a distance? Not the first time brushing Michael's trouble off, this was serious news. Some who knew me approached and offered help with the children. Some waved with sympathetic smiles. Others stared, pointing, whispering. Are they fucking kidding?

My good, sweet, unknowing boys dashed to me. "Mom, can we play wall ball for a few minutes? Please?"

"Okay, but not for long. Mike, football tonight. You have to eat soon, Houston's." Fingers crossed, by that time, the coast should be clear at the house.

"Excellent! I love that place! The steak is awesome!"

"You can't eat too heavy before the game, honey."

Mike and Gerry ran off to play with their friends in my plain sight. He was not missing this game for Michael's bullshit, a starting linebacker. No hiding from this, Michael and I need to tell them together. At the restaurant, my boys enjoyed their food, excited for the game. They had not a care in the world, just being kids, adorable and funny. That would all change. The "Last Supper" of their innocence.

"I have the boys. Good to come home?"

All gone for now, I closed the garage door as I pulled in. "Boys, no playing outside the house today. I'll tell you what's up when we go inside. Let's find Dad."

They fled, running inside to seek out their dad. My babies had no idea what they were rushing to. The boys on either side of him at his desk, he knew to let me tell them.

"Boys, Daddy did business with people who did bad things breaking laws and needs to prove he did nothing wrong." I wasn't quite sure exactly what Michael was accused of. I wasn't sure I wanted to know.

"If I can't, I might have to go to jail for a while."

I shot him a look that told him to shut the fuck up. Gerry, silent, came by me and climbed on my lap, my arms around him like armor.

Mike pulled away to the far end on the couch arm, his concerns brimming. "Dad, what exactly are you accused of?"

Michael looked at me to answer.

Knowing but a glimpse, my only choice, make it bearable for my children. "Baby, it has to do with them not asking permission to do what Daddy does to help people."

"You mean cut dead people open and take their body parts to give to people who need them?" Out of the mouths of babes.

"Yes, but careful what you say! You'll scare them away!"

We laughed, inside infuriating me, my young son's knowledge of the gory depths too keen, thanks to Michael!

* * *

Michael was able to spend more time at home, which was nice for the boys. "Barb, I'm taking Mike to the track. Then, we're heading to Brooklyn to see my parents for a couple of hours. Be back later."

Gerry protested. "I wanna come!"

"Not this time, buddy. Next time, promise."

"I wanna see Grandpa!"

Thanks, Michael. Where was his Dad brain?

Diverting a very angry Gerry as they left. "Hey! How 'bout we make our own pizzas!"

Balls of dough from the pizza place, my marinara sauce, and mozzarella could always be found in our fridge. The kids loved it!

"Awesome!"

Later, Mike came in so pale, as if he had seen a ghost, his pants wet in his crotch area. I scanned him, no marks, not trusting his father who flounced into the library. What did he do? Mike buried his head in my shoulder.

I couldn't have hugged him tighter. "Baby, what happened? Talk to me."

"Dad took me to the funeral parlor and made me his assistant to cut a dead body open."

My boiling blood immediately shot to my head! "He what!"

"He talked me up that I could do it and take over his business one day. I put the gloves on, and he gave me a knife. I thought I wanted to but got scared. I couldn't do it, so, he left me outside that room alone with all the caskets until Grandpa came to get me. I heard noises. It was so dark and creepy! Mom, I was so scared, I peed my pants."

"I'm sorry, honey. It's okay. Go upstairs, shower and get changed." I gave him a squeeze and let him go.

Breaking open the library doors, my entire being was on fire! "Are you out of your fucking mind? He's eleven! I told you to never take him anywhere near that! Any of it!"

Michael chortled. "You shoulda seen how scared he was!"

Oh, how I wanted to hurt him! "And that's funny to you? You took him to cut up a dead body and left him alone in a room with caskets!"

"He's fine."

"You let him hold a knife! What if he'd cut himself? Who knows what that person had?"

"It wasn't sharp."

"Really, just shut up! Don't say another word! You sound like a negligent asshole of a father!"

"Watch how you fuckin' talk to me. I'm warning you."

"You've got to be joking! You shut your fucking mouth and listen to me! I'm warning you! You put my son in harm's way again, and you won't have the chance again! You watch how you fuckin' treat my son! He is never to go with you on a case again. Do you understand? Think!"

He shrugged it off. "It was no big deal, but okay."

* * *

Mike continued his inquisition.

"So, who didn't ask permission?"

"The funeral homes."

"Those assholes! I hate them!"

"Michael Anthony!"

"But, Dad curses. Why can't I?"

Shooting a dagger at his father, maddening how arduous Michael made it to parent, worse than a child.

"Dad is an adult and makes his own decisions. You're my child and it's unacceptable. When you're an adult, I can't help what you decide. Right now, don't or no Xbox, got it?"

Michael chimed in. "I'm sorry, pal. I won't curse anymore, promise."

He wasn't gonna break any more promises to these children if I could help it. "Daddy promises to try really hard."

"Got it, Mom. Why can't we shoot hoops outside?"

"Mike, I'm sorry, it's for your safety. I can drive you down the block to your friends' houses, but no kids are to be around the front of this house. Your friends' moms know. Between angry people that might believe the news and reporters that want to make the news, I want them nowhere near you."

Mike's eyes widened. Gerry curled into me.

"Boys, if anyone in the neighborhood or school says anything to you bad, or asks too many questions, you need to let me know. No one will get in trouble. If some friends stop talking to you or aren't as friendly anymore, it's not because of you. You have done nothing wrong. Their parents might be keeping their distance."

Mike nodded, rising, not intimidated. "Ma, don't worry. Nobody around here is gonna bother me or Gerry. They wouldn't have the nerve. And if anybody doesn't want to talk to me, that's their problem. I have my friends that love me anyway." So proud of my young man.

I also gently divulged their dad's past drug problem, ensuring they heard it from us first. Mike had a knowing look, as if all his questions finally found answers.

"Ger, honey, do you get what we're talking about?"

He retreated into his shoulders with a tilt. "Kinda."

"Are you okay, love?"

He gave one nod. Giving him a hug, I stood him up, took his hand. "C'mon, boys! Mike! You gotta get ready for your game! Let's go!"

Mike leaped onto the couch. "Yeah! We're gonna kick their—" He shifted at me. "Butts!"

Hugging him, not wanting to let go until it was all over. "Give Dad a big hug. He needs one."

Later at the game, Joanne, my trusted friend, stayed close to me. Mike and Marco were best buds in school as well as teammates. Avoiding eye contact was useless—people flocked to me, grilling me, giving condolences, offering help, even strangers. Michael was on the front page that day again. He had become a regular.

Joanne, my wing woman, helped me deflect, then pulled me aside. "Barb, plenty of these people don't really care about you. They want to become a part of your husband's celebrity through you. Be very careful. You gotta be a bitch sometimes. Cut 'em off."

"Celebrity? Shit! They can take the whole damn thing! Hell! They can take my husband!"

We laughed as we made it to the sideline to watch our boys play. There was no escaping—gossip chirped all around, inevitable. Michael and his dad stayed behind the players' bench with the coaches, one of them, Marco, Sr., Jo's husband. Gerry played with his friends close by, Jo's older daughter, Sabrina, glad to keep an eye on him. We all looked out for each other. I loved that about Fort Lee, feeling safe. My children were embraced, not shunned, for their inescapable circumstances. Even Michael had support from the dads.

Mike made a tackle with his shoulder and helmet into the receiver just yards from me. "Yes! He got him down!"

The crowd cheered! Mike was still down. The coach, trainer, Michael, and team doctor ran out to the field, just off the sideline. The crowd grew silent, all players from both teams kneeled on one knee, their helmet on their thigh. As a multi-sport mom, I knew the unspoken rule. Mothers do not run onto the field when their son is down. Fighting the urge to join my son, his pain and my fear shot through me as they checked him out. To hell with the headlines, these were the things that got to me. Just weeks ago, a boy on the senior team broke his neck during practice. Thankfully he survived but his promising football career was over. He was lucky if he walked again...let alone lived. I had cried for him, for his parents. Now, my son was lying there.

Phil, the trainer, jogged over as my whole being was clenched, still not able to breathe. "Barb, I think it's a broken collarbone."

"Does he have neck movement?"

"We told him to not move right now, but yeah."

Relief ran through me.

"The mask of the helmet must've smacked his collarbone when he nose-tackled the kid. The paramedics should be here any minute. I can't swear to it without an X-ray, but I'll be surprised if it's not broken. He's okay though. Tough kid! Hey, he went down with a good play!" He ran back over to Mike.

A broken collarbone I could live with. Sabrina brought Gerry to me, his face frozen with fear, big brown eyes wide.

"Honey, Mike is hurt, but he's okay. The ambulance is going to take him to the hospital. I'll be in there with him. You stay with Grandpa, love. he'll take you home and we'll be back home a little later."

Tears in his eyes. "Is he really okay, Mom?"

"Yes, baby, promise."

"But he's not getting up."

"He will, honey. Watch."

Gerry gaped, glued to his brother, waiting. They got him up! He was standing! I started breathing again. The crowd applauded as Mike slowly hobbled off the field toward me in a sling. The game continued.

"Hi, Mom."

"Hi, baby. I'm coming with you in the ambulance. It will be here in a few minutes."

Gerry looked at his brother teary-eyed, staring, afraid to go near him.

"It's okay, Ger bear. I'm good."

Gerry smiled through his tears. "I love you, Mike."

"I love you too, bro."

I walked him to a chair by the entrance to the fields. His pads off, shivering, his body in shock, I gently placed my soft thick sweater on his shoulders. "Better, honey?"

"Yeah, thank you. It hurts so much, Mom."

His pain was killing me. "I know, honey. I'm sorry."

Joanne whispered. "Your father-in-law has Gerry. God bless you, how the hell are you so calm? I'd be a wreck!"

With a grin. "Jo, this ain't nothin' but a collarbone. And thank you." She smiled, catching it.

The ambulance arrived and Phil talked to the paramedics. They strapped him onto the gurney, needing both paramedics back there. My heart pulled, having to ride up front. Michael followed behind in my truck. As we sped off to the hospital, all the severe current events in our life ran through my mind—the red flashing lights, loud sirens, speeding through traffic. My son injured, my husband in trouble, the allegations, the news. All so surreal.

We got Mike back home with his sling and confirmation of his broken collarbone, little they could do for it. Gerry greeted him, but couldn't hug him, so Mike gave him a soft pound with his good fist. After I helped Mike get washed up and changed, I carefully put him in bed, trying to situate him comfortably, a pillow under his arm.

"You need anything, honey?"

"Not now, thanks, Mom."

Michael peeked in. "Barb, can you come inside? I need to talk to you. You rest, pal. Mommy will be back in a few."

What now? Following him to our bathroom suite. He locked the door, peeked out of the peephole window, and ran the shower. I sat on the cold marble ledge of the jacuzzi tub. He sat across from me, inches away in the Roman chair.

His big voice was barely audible. "I think we're being bugged, be careful what you say anywhere."

"I have nothing to hide, but okay."

"Barb, do you think I should run?"

For a second, the shock hit me. But wait, it was Michael. I had almost forgotten how weak he was. "Did you do it?"

"No, but I don't know if I can get out of it. Plenty of innocent people have gone to jail. Remember *The Fugitive*, with Harrison Ford?"

Yeah, and I remember the character's wife being murdered. Secretly, after seeing that movie, the fear of attack because of my husband's business never left me.

"If you're innocent, you should stay and fight for your freedom. How could you walk away from that? Be a man and fight. Justice prevails, I truly believe that. If you run, you're admitting guilt, even if innocent."

"I could go to an island. I would never expect you to come. It's not fair to pull the children out of their lives."

"Damn right! If you go, you go alone! You might as well sign the divorce papers right now! You'll never see us again. Living under a microscope because you choose to run away, not happening! I will make sure we are cut off completely!"

"Tell me what to do! I'll listen to you!"

"I just told you. If you stay and fight, even if you lose, you'll always have your family."

His voice quivered. "You mean you won't leave me?"

Taking his hand. "I'm here for you. I love you. But you need to stay clean. You've done great for a long time now. Please don't weaken to it."

"Are you crazy? The only way I would take it is if I end up in jail, or if I have a terminal illness. Or if you went first."

I opened the door. Mike stood in his sling, distraught, frozen. Michael's face turned to rage, lurching toward him.

I held him back. "Don't you dare touch him!"

"What the fuck are you doin'! I hate when you sneak around, eavesdropping! Don't you fucking do that again! You little cocksucker!"

A barrier between them, my eyes told Mike everything was okay. "Honey, go into your room. I'll be right in to take care of you, promise." He disappeared from the doorway.

I pushed Michael down where he had been sitting with complete disgust. I hated him! In one moment he was a scared, pitiful soul. In the next, an unbearable monster! How could I have loved him enough to stay? Did I hate him for loving me so much that I did stay? Could he ever steer clear of trouble? Wasn't it enough already? Damnit! "Michael! If you ever go after him like that again, you will never see us again! And if you touch him, I will make sure you're thrown in jail! Do you understand? What the hell is wrong with you? Are you out of your mind? Do you have any idea of what a bomb we dropped on that kid? And you keep pulling me away for secret talks, leaving him in the dark? What do you expect from him? That poor child is terrified! He thinks his father is going to jail! His world is turned upside down! And now you go after him? He's got a broken bone, for Christ's sake!"

"I wasn't gonna touch him."

"You need to tell him you're sorry and reassure him you're not going to hurt him! Your temper is for shit! If we're being bugged, guess what! You're gonna have big problems with Child Protective Services, along with the Brooklyn DA!"

"I'm sorry. You're right."

"Take a step back and listen to yourself! It shouldn't take me holding you back from your innocent child and yelling in your thoughtless face for you to realize how wrong you are! You're a grown-ass man! You sound so fucking selfish! It's all about you, isn't it! What you're going through! What you need to do! How you feel! Everybody needs to be there for you! The world revolves around Michael! Once again! I'm going to my son. Don't follow me!"

Closing the door behind me, it was all still in my face. Tucking Mike back in bed, sitting next to him, caressing his head, he leaned on me. Michael knocked and walked in. I felt Mike stiffen as I comforted him.

"Mike, I'm sorry. I didn't mean to get so mad and curse at you. And I swear I was not going to hit you. I'm under a lot of pressure, pal."

Mike, scared of his father, yet brazen. "You broke your promise. You said you wouldn't curse, and you cursed at me."

"I'm sorry. I won't do it again." He caught my eyes. "I mean, I promise I'll try my hardest. I love you, pal." He reached down to kiss his head.

"Me too, dad."

Forgiveness, until the next time, right? He left the room. Relief blanketed me hearing him thump down the stairs.

"Mike, I'm going to make a pact with you. This is between you and me, okay? Just us."

Mike nodded his head, bright-eyed.

"I know you're scared of what's happening, honey. And I don't blame you. I would feel the same thing. No more sneaking around anymore when we're talking. He doesn't want you guys to know what's going on. Let's not give him a reason to get mad again." I held his hand. "I promise I will tell you everything that's happening. If I don't answer some of your questions, you need to trust me, it's not for you to know. But you will always know what's up. You must promise me, you do not mention anything I tell you to Dad or anyone, or our pact is over. Deal?" A gentle handshake with his good arm, and a soft hug.

"Deal. Thanks, Mom."

That week, Michael's parents moved in. How could I not agree? They would stay in the guest room where they usually stayed when visiting. Everyone needed to pull together during this difficult time. His parents wanted to be close to their son, as he fought for his innocence. His father was selling their house to help him take care of us and his legal defense.

He sat me and his parents down. "The DA must be using me as a fall guy to get to a bigger fish. They're not letting go, clamping down tighter."

His dad was a trooper. "Keep fightin', Mikey."

His mom was clueless.

He started to cry. "I am so sorry! What was done to those poor people and their families, at my hands!" Pledging to us and himself, it seemed. "The only thing I can do is keep doing the next right thing, and that's exactly what I'm going to do." Déjà vu. He said those exact words when he was in recovery after William Farley rehab years ago. Here we were again.

Sunday, at the kitchen table with Mike and Gerry, GM was letting his grandsons win at blackjack. They loved playing cards with him, as well as Grandpa from upstate, my dad, all the time. Suddenly, GM felt dizzy. The color flushed from his face, white as a sheet. Michael carried him to the couch as I called 911. He was having a heart attack! The kids were beside him. We gave him some water and kept him alert until the ambulance came. Thank God they arrived quickly. Mike and Gerry clung to me, scared. Michael's mom came to the banister from upstairs. She glanced down at her husband on the couch and saw them carrying him out.

"They're taking him to Hackensack Hospital. Are you going with him and Michael? Or coming with me in the truck?"

"I need to take a shower." With that, she ambled away.

"Okay. Let me know when you're ready to go."

What? Sometimes, there was no use trying to make sense of it.

Mike blinked at me, stumped. "Did Grandma just say she needed to take a shower?"

"Honey, just go with it. Grandma's way. She needs to take a shower." He nodded, knowing she was a little *pazzo*.

Joanne came right over to take the boys, who were happy to hang with Marco and Sabrina. In the meantime, Michael's brother and sister were on their way to the hospital. His mom was finally ready to leave.

On our way, Michael called. "Barb, the reporters are blocking the front entrance trying to get up to his floor. They think I had the heart attack! Go through the emergency room. Give them your name at the desk, we have a list."

"How is he?"

"They're still trying to keep him stabilized. Barb, his heart literally stopped in the ambulance, he was dead! They tried to revive him for a few minutes and brought him back!"

One week later his dad was released, thank God. In the weeks following, Michael remained the top story in the news, accused of grave stealing, forgery of family members' consents to the donation of their deceased family members' body parts for transplants and research, fraud by changing dates of birth and causes of death, and hiding illnesses such as HIV, AIDS, cancer, hepatitis, diabetes, etc. The charges seemed to grow endlessly. I avoided reading or seeing much of anything trying to keep normalcy at home, hard to ignore.

Michael continued to give us details of the DA framing him. The real culprit, a mystery to him. "Just because they're on the right side of the law, don't let them fool you! The DAs are worse than criminals! They're trying to bring me down to pin someone else, and they'll break the law to do it! Mason was a DA before he was a criminal attorney. My problem is I have nothing to tell them! It's not gonna stop them from making me the fall guy if they can't get who they want! Hell, I'm not gonna make it easy for them! Justice, my ass!"

He was cracking under pressure. His rant sent my mind reeling. Did Michael have any knowledge of what was going on despite the responsibility of the funeral home directors? Was he in on it? Or maybe he had a fleeting suspicion, but didn't question? Or did he have no clue at all? How could he *not*? He was Michael!

But this man, by the grace of God, had lifted himself up from the ashes of his addiction, his own destruction, and reinvented himself. He'd come so far, not hindered by lying because of drugs. How could I doubt him? Everyone he talked to believed him—Mason, his family, friends. He seemed so sincere. And he didn't run!

11

The Search and Seizure

"Barb, I need to warn you, they're going to search our house very soon."

"What could they possibly want from here?"

"I don't know, but I don't trust them for shit! They could confiscate anything they want. If you have anything valuable, get it out of the house."

"Would they take my important documents, like birth certificates and things like that? Do you think they would take the kids' Xbox or PS 2? They're like computers."

"Anything is possible. Just get it out."

"What if something is missing? Can I file a claim against them?"

"Are you kidding?"

Halloween Day, I packed the back of my truck with the boys' systems, my jewelry, my important personal files. What was my life being reduced to, again? Hiding my valuables for a potential search warrant in my home? Hiding my boys away in their own neighbor-hood to protect them? Gerry's school was waiting for me to help him and his classmates with their costumes for their school parade, and their lunch party afterward. I promised Gerry I would be there. As I closed the trunk, Michael threw a shopping bag in.

"What is that?"

"Just some of our personal papers."

It didn't feel right, nothing did, but I was gonna be late! As I pulled out of the driveway, two tinted sedans pulled up behind my truck and three in front of my house. My stomach jumped, remained calm in my panic. The search. I hoped they wouldn't confiscate my things! Pull-ing forward, I got out of the truck, surveying the scene of my current circumstances. Everyone looked official, some actual police officers, others had patches on their jackets. It was hard to make out who was from where. Two approached me. The others went to the front door.

"Good morning officers, I'm Barbra Mastromarino. I had put my and my children's personal things in the back of my truck. I didn't want them confiscated or disappearing. Forgive me, I've probably seen too many movies. I didn't want my children to suffer. I have my jewelry in here." I handed them my bag to check.

They smiled but remained serious, perfectly understandable, given they were there to find evidence for a case against my husband. "Ma'am, please stand with us while we check the back of your vehicle."

They checked through everything. They turned around with Michael's last-minute shopping bag in their hand. "What's this?"

That motherfucker.

I hoped they believed me. "I don't know what's inside. Michael put it back there before I closed it up and said it was personal papers. He can attest to that."

If they ask him, he better not lie! Wait, they wouldn't believe anything he said anyway. They looked through the bag like they found gold.

"Excuse me. If you don't mind me asking, is that not personal?"

"No, ma'am."

From the corner of my 20/20, it looked like bank statements as they went through it. Had to be one of his business accounts. They took the bag.

"Do you need to take family documents or the kids' game systems?"

"No, ma'am."

Relieved. "Thank you."

"Will I be able to leave after the truck search to go to my son's parade at his school?"

The female officer had a wand. "Ma'am. I'm going to have to search you. And I'm sorry, but you must remain on premises for the house search."

Damnit! If I only left ten minutes earlier! My arms out, she searched me. Clean. I was so upset I couldn't be there for my son... breaking my promise because of Michael! I wasn't the promise-breaker! He was! "May I call the school?"

"Yes, ma'am."

"Thank you." Apologizing to them that I couldn't make it but not telling them why, I sent my son hugs and kisses. Thinking of Michael and the bag, my mind reeled, then froze. Oh, no!

* * *

Michael had started his new tissue recovery business in our duplex after rehab back in 2003. He called me up to his office. I put the laundry down and brought him up coffee.

"Barb, I need you to sign some of these forms."

"What are they for?"

"They're witness forms for the donors. You know, when you hear me on the phone for the cases speaking to the funeral home directors? It's easier if you just sign it here since you heard me."

"But I'm not a part of the business. How could I sign?"

"It's absolutely fine. That doesn't matter. You're still a witness. But just sign your maiden name so it doesn't look so much like a husband-wife thing, y'know?"

Signing Barbra Reifel on the witness line seemed harmless enough. He asked me to sign on occasion, when he was on the call for a case. "Did you speak to the family yet?"

He had earned back my trust in him, something I thought was not possible.

* * *

Everything seemed so legit. He would never put me in harm's way. He couldn't have known or done this. He would never. After searching me and my truck, the officers thanked me for my cooperation and patience, and escorted me into my house, my eyes shooting daggers his way. He looked puzzled. Was he kidding? They detained Michael, me, and his dad in the hallway by the front door, while they searched and photographed the entire house, tagging and confiscating property. They allowed his mother to remain in bed, due to her hip, which was decent of them. They could've made her get up and wait on a chair in the hallway upstairs. I was a prisoner in my own house. Unbelievable. All the officers were very civil, making it as bearable as it could be. All but one.

This little fucker strutted into the house, with a snide smirk and tone that I wanted to knock off his face and out of his throat! "Yeah! Really nice digs you got here, Doc! Lotta nice things you got! Fancy!" Mocking asshole!

"Thank you, sir."

"Thank you, sir"? Michael had pushed his nauseatingly perfect manners too far. To a dick like that?

Gritting my whisper. "Overkill! You sound like you're putting on an act!"

He gave me a "WTF" look. "Quiet!"

"Go to hell."

All at once, so many emotions rushed through me, boiling below the surface—so violated, so trapped. Yet feeling cold as a stone, hardened by my state of affairs. As if my hands were tied behind my back by a fucking thief, I glared at them marching up my stairs, carrying things down my stairs and out of my house, probably never to be seen again, tearing at my insides. My laptop! My throat was on fire, wanting to speak up! It had my first drafts of my children's books to be published one day, and my child and pregnancy fitness certification information on it! By the time the officials left, I missed everything at Gerry's school, but thank God the children missed all of this.

With Michael later on the stairs, I unleashed on him. "Damn you! I could get in trouble, too, can't I! They took that bag you put in my truck and it looked like I was hiding something! What was in there? What about those forms you asked me to sign as a witness at our duplex on Warren Avenue in your office when you first started your business? Were they fraudulent, too?"

"Barb, don't worry. You're not going to get in trouble. That was so long ago, those may be clean."

"What the hell does that even mean?" Loathing him like I never had before, I shouted, "My children need their mother, you selfish shit! We shouldn't have to suffer because of your bad business decisions! Not like this!"

"Honey! Take it easy. Nothing's happened. We'll discuss it with Mason."

Nothing's happened? He just takes a shit! Everywhere, on everyone, and tells us it smells like roses! Like he really believes it! The minimizer!

It was all too much. Breathing, needing to calm myself, I told myself that I was good. I believed everything would work out the way it was supposed to, always did. Keeping the faith hadn't failed me yet. More thoughts attacked my brain. The hairs stood up on the back of my neck. Those freezers in our tandem garage, the black bags.

Michael took me in the back of the garage.

"Barb, don't let anyone back here. No one is to open these freezers. No one! This is my research material."

"Not again. Why is this all here and not at your lab? You have an entire floor."

"I don't want anything getting mixed up at the lab between the tissues. I feel better that it's kept entirely separate."

"A separate freezer in a separate room separate from our home might work. At your lab!"

"Just don't fuckin' question me! It needs to stay here right now."

"Get it out soon! Or I will!"

* * *

My fury mounted, thinking of the possibility of his alleged illegal tissue being on my premises. The only tissue at my house shoulda been for our noses and tears! Did this man have any sense of discretion at all? Getting restless, he schemed like a mad scientist trying to figure out ways to make money. He spent hours upon hours in the basement in his office, his eraser boards and flow charts on the walls. I nicknamed him "Spidey Brain." His boards made me dizzy! His ideas kept branching off and off into oblivion. His papers had this obsessive-looking scribble, words traced over a hundred times each, like a madman. Michael told me he had an opportunity to gain a profit from a real estate venture in Jersey City with this couple he met while walking Duchess one day in Overpeck Park.

"I haven't been indicted, so I can invest my money."

"Check with Mason on that one. Anyone who's seen the news in the past few months may not want to take a chance on business with an alleged world criminal. What'd ya think?"

"These people are willing. We have it structured so everybody is protected. I don't want to tell you who they are or anything about it. I don't want even a chance of you getting in trouble."

"Why would I get in trouble if this is all legal? I don't want to know, and don't ever ask me to sign anything, ever again."

"Barb, just trust me."

"Trust you? No."

The less I knew, the better in case he did something stupid again. He would own it all by himself. Self-preservation was my goal, if I could help it. He had put me in the path of enough danger.

Speaking of danger, a couple of weeks later, I was driving my boys over the George Washington Bridge Plaza on our way to KFC, Mike in the front, Gerry sleeping in the back. Suddenly behind us, lit up with what looked like a thousand flashing lights, came a thundering voice. We pulled over to get out of their way. They rode my ass. I lowered the radio volume to hear.

"Put your hands out of the window! Both of you put your hands out of the window now!"

In the mirror, a fleet of officers crouched, guns drawn! At us! The panic on my son's face tore through my insides. Gerry slept still, lying flat on the seat, seatbelt on.

"Mike! Open your window! Put your hands out!" I did the same. "Just hold them there. Everything will be okay."

What the hell was going on? I did nothing wrong. I wasn't speeding, I used my signals. Did they think I was Michael? Crouching, they approached our windows, guns pointing at my truck. Having those guns pointed at me and my child's face burned into me. Instantly, they dropped their guns down. The men at our window waved the other officers away, all retreating back to their vehicles.

"Ma'am, we are terribly sorry. Bank robbers got off at this exit with your truck's exact description. We need to carry on. Again, so sorry!"

They hustled to their vehicles and sped off to find their criminals. And so the flashing lights left us.

Stunned and grateful, Mike and I took the deepest breath of our lives. "Holy shit, Ma!"

Gerry popped up. "What?" Mike and I burst into laughter.

* * *

I knew the time would come. February 2006, Michael sat me down, alone. "A formal indictment is coming down. Mason arranged I turn myself in, so they don't come to our house to get me. He has word that bail will be one million dollars. Ten percent won't be acceptable because of the severity of my charges. We have our house, since it's in your name, and the down payment was with the disability money. Call your parents about putting their house up. I'll talk to my dad and John. That should more than cover it."

"My parents' house should be the last resort."

They didn't have the bank Michael's family had. Their house was all they had. But I asked them. For me, they said yes without question. We all put our livelihoods on the line for Michael. We believed in him. All paperwork was in order. All bonds were signed. He would take his "perp walk," enter the courthouse to be arraigned, plead not guilty, be detained, then be released on bail.

The day came. Wednesday, February 22, 2006. Michael planned to turn himself in. He met Mason at three at his law office in Staten Island, his father and brother there, his mother completely unaware and recuperating from hip surgery in the rehab center. My boys were not to know until it was time. Michael and I said our goodbyes to each other. Michael cried, couldn't stop as he drove away. I remained oddly cool. Later, in the kitchen preparing dinner, five o'clock news on my little TV by the stove, his indictment had already happened. I was clueless of the outcome. My cell on the counter next to me, I stared as if I could will it to ring. All other TVs off, both boys were distracted and fed in their rooms on their computers, playing World of Warcraft. A news segment flashed—Michael in his blue-collared shirt, glasses, handcuffed, guard on each side, perp-walking to the courthouse, the media frenzy surrounding him.

Frozen in time, I stepped out of myself, as if watching someone else's life on the screen. Sinking in hard, my mind was drowning in Michael's cesspool of trouble. Inescapable. That was my husband, an alleged notorious criminal, for the world to see. He transparently relished his newfound celebrity, his autograph in random places, pictures taken with him, handshakes from strangers, *Primetime* interview not yet aired. I had seen enough.

Look at him now. It has all come to this. I don't think he's getting out of this one so easily. Formal charges take his troubles to another level, innocent or not, media and all.

Finally, my phone rang. "Hey, Barb. It's Mason. Michael is on a bus heading to Rikers Island right now." Mason's voice was matter-of-fact.

My heart sunk into my stomach. My innocent husband is going to the worst place on Earth! "What! Why!"

"It turns out fifteen minutes before we walked into the court-house, Jason, the DA, told me they're requesting two-million-dollar bail. I didn't think the judge would agree. He brought it down to one-point-five million. Barb, you need to raise more bail as soon as possible, or he stays in. They kept everything. The bail bond outfit we're with now has some strikes against them so they need more like two-point-five million in collateral. I'm sorry. I was unaware of her record."

"I'm changing bail bondsmen."

Maria took the kids to her house to hang with her daughters, their friends, until my parents came to take them upstate. Beyond grateful for all the love and support we had, all for Michael. I hoped he felt the same gratitude. On autopilot, I was on a mission. I didn't stop, not even for sleep. Maddie and Reid told me about this solid bail bonds-man they spoke to, Tom. He had a popular HBO show called *Family Bonds*. The vibe was good with Tom instantly, feeling secure with transferring it to him, wishing this had been in my hands in the first place. Set up for Michael's new bail, we would have enough. Every-thing had to be redone, then put in front of the judge to be signed off. Mason expedited it as fast as he could. Every extra minute Michael needed to stay in that terrible place was too long.

Truck parked in the Rikers lot, bag of allowed necessities in hand, dozens of us waited for the bus to cross the bridge to the facility, in the dead of winter. Rikers is actually an island...not exactly the island Michael wanted to run off to! Frigid and windy, a half-hour later, the bus finally came, at full capacity!

"Are you kidding me?" So many thoughts ran through my head as I stood still, waiting for the next bus to hell. *What happened to my life? How did I get here? How much do I tolerate? How much!*

Finally, a couple of buses later, I squeezed into the overcrowded bus. Traveling over the bridge, the rough water below with high layers of barbed wire surrounded this captive island, my husband's current residence. Immediately off the bus, my ID needed to stay handy for the many lines awaiting. Lockers were available outside for cell phones and electronics, any liquid, gum, objects sharp or considered a weapon, and any belongings that were on the very long list of things not allowed in. Daunted, we were allowed no form of communication entering a prison with the worst criminals pooled together, only separated by guards, bars, and plexiglass. After waiting on line in the herd in the freezing cold for an hour and a half, I made it through the door. Immediately through the entrance, all coats, shoes, belts, jewelry, hair clips, and pins off, everything on the belt to be scanned.

My turn came. "Step forward. Arms to the side." Standing inside, the cylinder lit up, humming whirling around me, scanning from head to toe. Beam me up, Scotty! I passed, inching on to see them rummaging through my bag to find something they saw. Seriously? They took my mini Tweezerman! There was no getting them back, since they were considered a weapon. Gone. When we finally got inside, I went through three security checkpoints to get on the bus to his building, and another three to get to the visiting area, with the same screening all over again, drug dogs and drug tests randomly throughout. The security was extreme. They'd seen it all. It took at least half a day to get on the inside for an hour-long visit with him. What the hell was I doing there? Never in my life! Damn him! Treading with dread to his window, my gut tightened.

In his orange jumpsuit, cuffed and shackled, blocked off by plexiglass and a small round triple metal screen, visibly so broken, pathetic, he was a sorry sight. Conflicted, I could do nothing for him. Whatever he'd gotten himself into, he was not getting out of this the same man. Neither was I.

"Bail?" he asked.

"Not yet. Tomorrow. I left clothes for you."

"I'll call you later. I'm sorry. I love you." He lifted his hand to the plexiglass.

I put mine against his for a moment. "Love you." As I said the words, their meaning forever changed. Desolate pity.

Sadness came over me, his lost eyes watching me leave. The process to leave was the same in reverse, grueling and unreasonable. That night, Michael's *Primetime* segment aired. How convenient, they played his segment when he was stuck in Rikers, defenseless. Twisted, the entire segment portrayed him as completely guilty, "alleged" not used even once. They told him and Mason it would be done in all fairness. That was not fair! A fierce protector of my unprotected, the letter I sent objecting to their one-sided portrayal spouted Mason an earful when he called to ask for a copy of the segment.

In turn, he gave me an earful. "Though I appreciate you, call me before you think about 'protecting' Michael again so I don't get my ass handed to me again. Okay, Barbarella?"

"Damn. Haven't been called that since college!"

The next day, Michael's brother, John, came with me to visit Rikers. He'd visited friends in the past and was familiar with protocol, but this was his baby brother. John and I were sent to wait for Michael in the juvenile ward where they had moved him. They put us in a bullet-proof room with floor-to-ceiling windows until they brought him in. Visions of mothers, their children torn from them, only able to see them in that horrible place, broke my heart. I prayed it was my last time to ever visit that ward. Down the long hall, Michael shuffled toward us, his wrists and ankles in shackles, surrounded by correction officers, and a cameraman. His every move outside his cell needed to be documented for proof of his safety since he was not yet convicted and very high-profile, basically covering the prison's ass from a lawsuit. The guards searched him, then let him in. Michael and his brother's emotional reunion filled my eyes. Yet I felt calm, numb.

Michael hugged me. "I'm sorry. I'm so sorry."

Silent, his "I'm sorry" meant nothing anymore. After the visit, John headed home.

I stayed, my mission not complete until his release, calling collect from the payphone. "Mason, I'm here. When are we getting him out of here?"

"I'm sorry, Barbra. It's the weekend. Courts are closed. No judge wants to sign off on it. None of them want his release on their head. I have one shot with one judge. Call me later."

If I hear "I'm sorry" one more time.

"I'm not leaving here until he's released. Please make it happen."

The guards in the main area were so accommodating and protective. They all knew who I was, saying Michael was famous there, a true celebrity. Famous? Celebrity? Kinda made me ill. For the sake of my safety, I took it. At three a.m. he was finally released. I was on "empty"—there was nothing left, only pity. As we sat and waited for the bus, another inmate just released asked us for three quarters to get a drink from the machine.

"Gimme three quarters and a five," Michael instructed. Out of my bag, as I gave him four quarters and a five, he handed it to the man. That was sweet.

"Money gets you anything you want. I'm a celebrity in here. The head of the Bloods looked out for me. He said, 'Anything you need, Doc. Any trouble, you come to me.' People want to do things for me because my bail is so high. It's a sign of prestige in here. They know it means I have money."

Did he just brag about the high bail? Was he fucking kidding? Answering was not even worth the effort. I let it go.

"We really have nothing. They confiscated everything and froze the rest."

"Not yet."

The ambiguity that lay between his natural confidence and his ignorant arrogance drove me mad! Anything to survive on the inside, I supposed. A pro at twisting truths, it sounded like Michael would survive no matter what happened. He didn't run and complied with everything asked of him, as an innocent man would. But my belief and feelings for him were muddled. Again, why was I always chasing the truth when it came to Michael?

Home, the house was quiet. He showered and lay in bed as if it had been forever, yet he had insisted we sleep in the guest room. I went with it.

He clung to me so desperately it seemed, his body quivering. Tears came, sobbing, he crumbled. "I can't go back there! It's so horrible! I'll kill myself before I have to go back there!"

"Hopefully you won't. Whatever you need to face, you'll do it."

His mind snapped into reality, long-time jail looming. Or maybe it just snapped. He calmed himself and put the TV on, raising the volume, his lips to my ear. Oh, no, sex was off the table. "I spoke to Mason. I've been thinking. If Jay is not around, it would help my case. What do you think?"

Horror followed my relief. "You mean leave the country?"

He shook his head. We were from Brooklyn. We knew people. Two and two make four.

"If you're thinking what I think you are, it's not the answer! Michael, he has a wife and a child! You do say you're innocent, right? The truth will set you free."

"Mason said if Jay and I are severed, charged separately, I would be in a better position."

"Do it in court."

"The likelihood of them granting it is next to none."

"If you are serious about what you're implying, forget the law, you'll have to deal with the wrath of God. He will take care of you. Your punishment would end up fitting the crime. It usually does."

He mumbled tensely. "Of course, I'm not. My mind was just running, talking crazy. I'm not serious."

Back in my Brooklyn girl days, in my apartment before my girls and I hit the night.

My wedding day in church.

The way he used to look at me...with such love.

Michael on our honeymoon...I was so in love with that man.

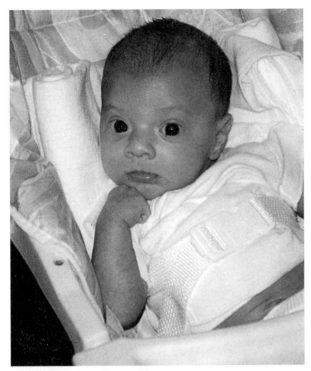

Little Mike comes home.

Before we moved, he had already started with the drugs...unbeknownst to me.

Sweet innocence.

Mike and Gerry in their superhero crater, unknowing.

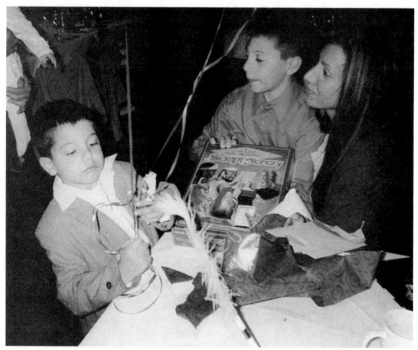

I made a conscious vow to protect myself and my children despite Michael, then and forever.

Police Surgeon's badge

Tenth chance...

Telling him how things are gonna be. Either like it. Or not—and leave.

Boys with their new cousin, Aidan.

Michael, sports dad. Gerry looks less than thrilled.

Happy again.
For a minute.

Beloved Duchess. (Passed a few years ago.)

Time together as a family. My brother Ben's Bahamas wedding.

Our last trip as a family. Disney.

Found the picture in Mike's desk drawer. I screamed in rage.

Mike's dad, moments before his heart attack.

The boys played hands with Grandpa from upstate too.

As I shaved Mom's head, thoughts of my late sister, Toni, filled mine. She was only nine when she passed...the pain.

At the worst time imaginable, my boys said I gave them the best Christmas ever...

Our visit with Michael in prison hospice proved very interesting.

Bermuda cruise...the first true vacation I was able to give my boys...a milestone.

My boys toasting to Gerry's twenty-first birthday last summer.

12

The Plea

"Why? How? Mason, I did nothing wrong! I had nothing to do with his business!" Just months after the indictment, I discovered a civil suit was filed against me through the DA for $190,000. Staggering! No criminal charges, thank God!

"You signed on Michael's annex business, Metropolitan Tissue Services. They calculated how much money ran through there."

"Son of a fucking bitch!"

* * *

Michael's business was booming. We had our life back. I had mine. He sat me down in the kitchen with some papers.

"Barb, just sign these bank papers as vice president of the bank account for the new business, Metropolitan Tissue Services, to sign for paying bills and all."

"Michael, how can I be vice president of the bank account when I'm not a part of the business? Why can't I just be an authorized signer?"

"Honey. Who would I trust everything with?"

I signed.

* * *

How did I not read them? I just signed, trusting him. Big mistake. Big! A painful, expensive, and very dangerous lesson! "I'm gonna fight that! I unknowingly signed!" I told Mason.

"I strongly suggest against it, Barbra. They have your signature on about a dozen fraudulent forms. Push and they can indict you in a second."

"But I didn't know! They know that! I've been under surveillance right along with him! What a fucking idiot I must look like! I'd like to know what they know!"

"It doesn't matter what they know. They can indict you simply for being his wife. They can indict a ham sandwich! And you are far from a fucking idiot. They know that."

"Pointless. So, basically, I'm fucked because of him, every which way."

All the air in the world couldn't help me breathe through all this. How could one person wreak so much trouble and havoc in all our lives? His father had big problems, too. The DA froze every asset and cent he had to live, and filed a civil suit against him for $250,000, almost his entire retirement, threatening to indict him for money laundering if he didn't pay. Somehow, the DA planned to wring us dry to get what they wanted from Michael. Seemed they wanted him. The less he cooperated, the more anyone close to him would suffer horribly. What did they want from him?

Oh, God, what if they use me as a pawn? Even as his wife today, divorcing him tomorrow won't do a damn thing for me. Shoulda, woulda, coulda!

The hope he might be innocent was still in us, and to hear it from him was to believe it. That summer, the DA offered him a plea of nine years.

"I can't do this to my family anymore," Michael said. "I'm going to take it. I'll be soaking our family dry if I fight."

You already did.

We sat the children down. Mike cried, Gerry stunned, as I held them. Crushed, for my boys losing their father, for my husband who would be locked away from his life, his parents and family devastated. For myself, no tears, numb, but at peace, about him and the turmoil we had been living. My children and I would be fine. Rue helped me search for rentals that would take a dog. Duchess included, or we weren't going! The cats had loving homes, ready to take them in. All the changes in our life without Michael were in motion. Michael mapped out which prison he could try to go to, learning the system like a business, as if he had a choice, livin' in his dream world. He and his dad reached out to friends on the inside and friends with people in. He still scrambled to figure out a way to make money. The stench of desperation in the air scared me.

Days after my talk with the boys, Mike woke me, shaking me. "Ma! Come quick! Gerry's choking! He can't breathe!"

Jumping up, I seized my water bottle and ran to Mike's room, frantic, shaking. Immediately sitting him up, as he grabbed at me holding his throat, I gave him a sip of water. He was able to take it. As he calmed down, another sip, he caught his breath.

"I'm okay. I don't know what happened, Mom. I just woke up and couldn't breathe!"

"You feel okay now, baby?"

"Yeah. I feel fine."

"I'm staying with you tonight. Sleep with two pillows and I have water ready. We'll get you to the doctor tomorrow. Mike, thank God you heard him and came to me right away! Thank you, honey! You saved his life! I'm so proud of you."

Comforted with me there, he slept soundly. I didn't. His diagnosis was psychosomatic stress reaction to more on top of more, and possibly a touch of hereditary asthmatic tendencies. A sleep study would help. So grateful for the sample of Advair and albuterol the doctor gave me, as both were very expensive. We had no insurance. Michael had let the payments lapse. Gerry's episodes were less frequent, nevertheless alarming. Mike and I staying with him every night helped.

At the DA's mercy, money was trickled to us to survive from GM's frozen money. Some months the DA held the payment and didn't send it, or was late, accruing insurmountable bills and late charges. Either way, I figured out how to put food on the table, cutting back wherever we could without severe penalties. Stuck in this albatross of a house, I couldn't sell if I wanted to—bound by the bail. Secretly relieved, it would remain shielded from Michael's liquidation and dissolution. In my name, thank God, security for whatever was to come. The house embodied my prison and my freedom.

As I cooked dinner, Michael floated through the kitchen to the family room and plunked on the couch, lying back. High on something but not Demerol, he was different.

Coming next to him, my voice riled, but low. "What did you take? Don't lie to me!"

He chuckled lightheartedly. So not him. A defensive Michael was usually a belligerent Michael, one of his -isms, "A good defense is a stronger offense." He picked up his bobbly head to me, his eyes slits. "What the hell are you talking about? I didn't! I had a beer to take the edge off! What do you want from me!" He let his head fall back again.

"Michael, I told you I would stand by you to fight for your innocence. If you're using, I will take the kids and leave you." I went back to my cooking.

He lifted his head, staring straight ahead. A while later, he was nowhere to be found. His mother told me he left the house earlier. Odd, I didn't hear the door chime. As I left him a calm voice message, my insides curdled with the possibilities.

An hour later, the phone rang. "Good evening, Officer Blair here, Teaneck Police. Mrs. Michael Mastromarino?"

Damnit. "This is she. How can I help you, officer?"

"We have him here on Cedar Lane. A couple of witnesses called in who saw him stumbling in the middle of the road. His truck is parked up on the curb. He's not very coherent. Do you know if he took anything or is on any medications?"

Incoherent, parked on the sidewalk, they would've arrested him. He must have flashed his police surgeon's badge again.

"Well, he is under the care of a psychiatrist. I can give you his information. I don't know what prescription he's taking. Maybe he took too much and didn't realize it?"

So glad the cop can't smell the bullshit from here.

"Ma'am, can you come down to pick him up? We can't allow him to drive. I apologize for the inconvenience."

"Thank you for being there for him. I'll be there shortly. By Astor Pharmacy, right?"

"Yes. How did you know?"

"Long story."

The flashing lights ahead too familiar, my blood didn't rise a pinch. I was so hardened. Half his truck up on the sidewalk, he'd just missed the lamp post. The officers gave me my man-child husband. My face was a stone as I drove us home.

"Barb, stop somewhere. I want a nice juicy cheeseburger with fries!"

"You're not getting a cheeseburger."

"What about the fries? Please?" Completely infantile.

"Michael, stop."

He pouted like a five-year old. "You're so mean! I'm hungry. Is there anything wrong with that?"

"I just picked you up from the police! I saved your ass from being arrested, you idiot! You drove onto the sidewalk! On drugs! You're lucky you didn't crash though a storefront window! You're not getting a goddamn cheeseburger! Now, sit there and shut up! I'm trying to concentrate on driving!"

I called his father to let them know he was okay, and we'd be home soon, then his brother and sister to tell them what had just happened.

Michael ranted. "Why did you have to call everybody? I'm so sick of it! All of it! Nothing is going right! Everybody treats me like shit! I get no respect!" He was coming down. Crazed, he tried to open the door as I was driving.

"Wait until we get to the house! You're going to kill yourself!" I was not letting him out of my sight—he was not disappearing into the night.

He took his hand off the handle as he continued rambling to himself about all his woes. As I rolled into the driveway, he opened the door and jumped out, storming away from the house. "Fuck this! Fuck everybody! I'm leavin' and never comin' back! Nobody's gonna find me! I'm outta here!"

Oh, no, he wasn't! His father was already out the front door, running after him. As he put his hand on Michael's arm, his son shoved him to the ground, raging down the block into the darkness.

His dad got up. "I'm all right!"

I ran inside! 911! He was not doing this to everyone that put all they had on the line for him! "My husband is yelling down the street. He's under the care of a psychiatrist and medication. He talked about running away and never coming back! He's out on bail! That can't happen! I need him brought back here! Please! He can't disappear!"

Suddenly, Gerry ran to me, stared in silence, and started choking!

"Oh, my God! Gerry! Breathe, baby! Hold on, please!" I dropped the phone and he started vomiting! Behind him, I supported his stomach and forehead. "It's okay, baby. Let it all out."

Sitting him on my lap with water holding him, I picked up the phone.

"Is your child okay, ma'am?"

"Yes, thank you."

"Good. I've already sent two cars. They should be there any minute."

"You're an angel! Thank you so much!"

Next call, Tom, my bondsman, who reassured me. "Ready. Say the word and I'm on it."

Minutes later, the police cars pulled up as I sat on the front stoop. Four officers started walking toward me.

A friendly face. "Nate! I'm so glad you're on this call." Been a long time. I was now under a different kind of choke hold.

He greeted me with a hug. "First of all, how are you doing? And the kids?"

"He didn't touch me, and they're okay. He shoved his father to the ground when he ranted, storming away. If you guys could just check him out, please. He's a heart patient. Mike is sleeping at his friend's house, luckily. He's seen enough."

"We got him on Briar. I talked to him. The other guys are talking to him now. He's okay. His dad is okay, over there with him. They'll bring him back in a little while. I wanted to see that you're all right."

Michael's earlier truck-on-sidewalk pharmacy incident—omitted. "I panicked. He's on some medication. He said he was running away. Our entire family would lose everything. I had to call."

"I understand. You did the right thing. Barb, please. Call if you need anything. Let me know how things are going. Tell Mike I said hello."

"I will. Nate, can't thank you enough."

Nate headed back to the next block where they were holding Michael I found Michael's extra set of car keys, scoured his car and discovered small bags of an off-white powder. A touch to my tongue didn't numb it, so it wasn't cocaine. Heroin? Crystal meth, maybe? Wasn't sure. Didn't care. It was drugs. I hid it all away, then packed our bags, ready to take my boys and I to my parents the next morning, indefinitely.

Tom comforted me, on call 24/7. "Even if we can't annul the bail in time before he runs, my boys will find him and bring him back. Trust me, there's not a fugitive they haven't brought back."

"But this is Michael we're talking about."

"This bond is in your name. I work for you, not him. You want it rescinded? Consider it done, we take him in."

"That's just too much power over his fate than I can handle. It would be so much easier to bring him in. He's one big-ass headache after another! But how would he fight for any innocence he has?"

"You are a rarity in my line of work. Anyone else woulda thrown his ass in jail already! He's lucky to have you on his side. And, yes, that's a hell of a lot of power."

"I'll use it in a heartbeat if I have to. Got my finger on your speed-dial number at all times."

The next day, no one tried to stop us. The proof was indisputable. My mother-in-law would take care of my girl, Duchess. There was no relying on Michael. At Grandma and Grandpa's upstate we'd stay, old faithful. It was summer vacation time and the boys loved it up there. My humble and sweet beginnings, I grew up in that house. It seemed my children were headed in the same direction, which was maybe a good thing. Mom's neighbors, Sal and Trina, around my age, with six kids, had that house since I was in college. A beautiful family, four of their boys were around Mike and Gerry's age, with a son and daughter just a bit older. We were all close as family. Through the boys' entire childhood, and all those times they were secured away during Michael's drug days, my savior was always visiting at Grandma and Grandpa's house.

All the kids enjoyed days spent at the pool together, trips to the beach, playing ball with Grandpa in the backyard, riding bikes and boards, video games, the normal things kids do. It was all I wanted for them. Was that too much to ask? With Michael in our lives, that became impossible. GM kept in touch with me. *Been there, done that.* They didn't blame me for leaving, always thankful I stood by him through his darkest drug time, perpetually hoping I would come back. If I left him now, they would understand. How could they not?

A few weeks passed. Gerry's choking disappeared, his trigger removed. I cleared my mind, wishing we could just stay there. His parents attested to him showing no signs of drug use. *Been there, done that, too.* Was it certain? Would it stick? He was chaos. I needed more time. Another week and he was still clean. I couldn't leave him now, so weak and alone. He was their father, still my husband, though I couldn't remember the last time it felt like a marriage.

We came home. Michael fell deeper into depression, drifting farther and farther away. I wasn't quite sure what it was. He lost his grip, grasping at schemes that never materialized—Jersey City real estate, Vegas hotel deal, metal technology, on and on. Michael returned from a meeting with Mason, doing a complete about-face from his solemn and distant despair, returning to his astronomical arrogance that I did not miss. He threw the plea off the table, determined to fight and beat this, another reason he gave us to believe in his innocence. Beating it completely? Pipe dream, honey.

A month later into fall of 2006, the DA gave me the green light to work. Would they take every cent I made? I started a new business in marketing for a radiology facility in New York City, through Danielle, one of Michael's old business contacts (one of his old affairs as well). No way in hell did I let on I knew. I played the part but I didn't trust her.

"Oh, Michael is still so handsome. I think the world of him. You're a very lucky woman." Lucky? *Wow. Take him.*

Was this bitch baiting me? I didn't bite, didn't care. On to business. Pro bono the first three months to build confidence, I swept up accounts. Danielle told me I was a natural. Michael tried browbeating me to do things his way, trying to control me. It sickened me. His obnoxious dry-erase flow chart down my throat daily was maddening.

"Barb, you need to overtake business using power, force, intimidation. That's the only way that works! Listen to me!"

"My way works just fine. The numbers don't lie."

"You listen to me!"

"No! You listen to me! This is my business! I need to take care of my family! You've done quite enough! I will do it my way! You worry about your business, and I will worry about mine!"

Once his cursing tirade started, I left the room every time. All his authoritarian attempts pushed me farther and farther away. His voice made me cringe, grating on my last nerve. Avoiding him did not stop me from being there to care for my boys. Many times, when I called for the children, Michael was out. Fighting for his innocence? I think not. Meanwhile the news was still hot, all the time, every day, every court date. Media was everywhere—in front of the courthouse, outside the courtroom, waiting for him, snapping pictures, grabbing questions. On some occasions I attended, slyly ducking out of view, evading the photographers, reporters, sketch artists inside the court-room. All of it was too much.

Whispers. "I think that's his wife. That's his wife!"

In my days marketing, at least one doctor a day would take a big dump on his professionalism and straight up make a move on me. Michael was in that club, wasn't he? I'd laugh it off as if I hadn't caught it, moving on to business. It worked every time. Some of these jokers thought they were real Casanovas, no shame in their game, giving doctors a bad rep. Many were completely respectable.

Dr. Manuel Roma, a chiropractor, was one of the good ones. Very professional, very cool, one of my big accounts. A friend set up a lunch meeting with the biggest podiatric surgeon around, a power-house, Dr. Gino Verano. "Barbra, don't be intimidated by him. I know him well, and he's a friend. He's tough, but fair."

Dr. Verano was already there. His eyes on me, figuring me out, he shook my hand. The three of us sat. He tried staring me down, tough and stone-faced, trying to rattle me. Intimidation? Not another over-inflated ego, please. How long would it take him to see past his ego? I didn't scare easy.

"So, tell me, why should I send my patients to your radiology center? My patients' care is the most important thing to me. What do you have over the others? I have one right around the corner from me. Better be a good sell."

My sell was damn good, with all special aspects we offered above the rest.

"Might not be good enough," he added, borderline taunting.

What did this guy want? Kickbacks, rather getting something back for every patient referred, and offering to do the billing on or under the table, were illegal. There was a big crackdown in the city. Trouble was not finding me, again. Not a chance.

"What is it that you're looking for? I can tell you this. I am an independent contractor, if this MRI facility can't satisfy your needs for your patients, I will find a place that will."

"I like that. You would go anywhere to find a place to meet my patient needs."

He loosened up a notch, as did the conversation. Being patient, the best strategy was to listen, picking up on some things that were important to them. By the end of the lunch his account was mine. He told me to call him Gino, but I respectfully continued to call him Dr. Verano.

My days at home, I spent quality time with my boys, making sure they were well protected, the plight and danger ever-present. Michael's combating worsened, always looking for a fight. I needed to get his damn noose off my neck! Was this the rest of my life? Not happening. Dr. Verano became the biggest account of the center, my biggest client. He wanted to discuss business over dinner. I tried for lunch. His schedule did not allow for it. Early dinner. We talked business. He told me about himself, guard down, mine up, keeping my body snatcher's wife identity secret. He let it be known he was separated and wanted to have someone intelligent and enjoyable to talk to, a friend. I tried to set him up with my friend. He wasn't interested. His eyes told me he was describing me. Respectfully, I did not "take" the hint, keeping it a business friendship.

"I insist. Call me Gino."

"I just can't. It's unprofessional, Dr. Verano."

He wrote on an imaginary pad. "Note, Barbra refuses to call me Gino. Send all patients to Omni MRI instead." His warm eyes smiled.

"Okay, Gino!"

His company was comfortable and refreshing, so respectful, and good business. He introduced me to different doctors in his area. If Dr. Verano said send all patients to my facility, they sent. It helped. After Dr. Verano and I left the last office, he confided in me about his unstable situation and his concern for his daughter. I told him who my husband was, what my life was.

He'd heard of the case, impressed. "Your husband has a brilliant mind. A great cause, just used in the wrong way."

"He causes so much trouble around him. I feel like running away with my boys, but I can't leave him like this. He's still fighting for his innocence."

"From what I've seen, it doesn't look good for him. I know judges and political heads. I'll ask them what they know."

A week later Dr. Verano got back to me, somber. "The word is he's looking at a long sentence, way more than nine years. The public wants to see him put away for a long time. I'm so sorry, Barbra."

"Michael says the DA doesn't have the proof they claim they do, that it's impossible. He insists he's not guilty with such conviction. I have to believe he must be innocent in some way."

"I understand, he's your husband. You're a noble woman."

My mind was all a rush. I'd make my way without him but stick it out the way I should. Only a support to him, he had not touched or reached out to me in at least eight months. How was that possible? Keeping my doubts at bay, this was not the time. Our only form of communication was him yelling at me, and me turning away. My business was growing, not yet seeing a cent until the three months passed. Gino agreed to a dinner meeting with the heads of the radiology center.

"I'm doing this for you, all of this. I could have sent my business anywhere. I want to help you."

Uh-oh.

"Barbra, I feel more for you than a business relationship, more than a friend."

I wished he didn't say that. "I know."

"You knew?"

"Yes, from the beginning. It was sweet, but this is business. Besides the fact that I'm a little married."

"I respect that, and you."

"I know that, too. Means a lot."

We met for the big dinner. He listened to them, at the same time texting me.

Meet me for a drink after this boring meeting.

Okay. For one drink. Go over how things went.

The Mandarin. Lobby Lounge. 35th Floor.

After the meeting, checking with my boss, all was positive. Calling Michael as I drove there, I told him it went well.

"Meeting Rayne out for a while, not sure where yet."

This was my first lie to Michael. Strategically parking out of view of the front entrance, scanning around me, I had a chill. The place was gorgeous, cool, classy, happening. Dr. Verano was sitting on a couch with a drink on the table. I joined him with a martini.

"So, what did you think? Did you all come to an agreement? I don't remember them having a meeting with any referring doctor."

"They never did business with me. You know what I thought about during the whole meeting?"

"How boring it is?"

"A kiss."

"Maybe you should try."

He did, his lips to mine, nice. Heat ran through my body. I hadn't kissed since my fling days in the city years ago. Michael never kissed me...I almost considered a kissing club! Unspoken, Gino and I both knew it would be so easy to get a room upstairs. He had too much respect for me, so did I. The kiss was enough. We needed to say good night.

As soon as I got in the truck, Michael called me. It was too coincidental, feeling as if he was following me. He kept calling, trying to keep me on the phone. Rolling to a halt at the stop sign in our neighborhood, headlights at the cross street, someone got out of the car. It was Michael. He neared my side of the truck with a creepy smile. He never smiled those days.

"What are you doing here? Were you waiting for me?"

"No, I'm just getting back from a meeting."

From my meeting? He was still grinning. Why? Like a psycho killer going in for the kill, I didn't trust it. Then again, I was flat out doing him wrong, my first time in all our years. He stroked my hair. The last time he had done that was when he high on drugs.

"How did your meeting go? Did you have a good time with Rayne? You haven't looked this happy in a long time. I'm glad." He needed to stop touching my hair, like he was going to yank it any second.

I turned my head to get the house key out of my bag and get him off me. "I have my key. Meet you home."

Two days later, at Gino's office, linking his computer system to our facility, the office staff left for the night. Trying to resist, we turned to each other and kissed, embracing, body to body, his hands roaming, wanting them all over me.

"You know you can have me," I murmured, my lips close to his ear.

"Not yet. When the time is right. I respect you too much." Respect, a refreshing change.

The doorbell rang. My heart jumped. Michael? If it was, deal with it. He saw a patient at the door on camera. Michael busting in behind the patient attacking Gino and me, flashed in my mind. Would've been a good fight, Gino a former Navy SEAL. I'd put up a good fight, as I have before. Gino tended to the patient at the front door. Locked it and returned to his office, to me. One more kiss. We agreed no more. The time would come, not now. Oh, what he could've done to me! Gino asked me for a ride to the A&P in Fort Lee to get his car at the mechanic. Uneasy, how could I say no? We didn't touch as we strolled to my truck.

"Any business arrangement with your facility is all yours, I don't need it. I want to help you, take care of you, once everything is said and done. I'll give you a salon to run. Our kids would get along. We can have a life together. You'll never have to worry about anything again."

Way too much, my mind rejected his projections. I refused to be tied down, controlled, especially owned. Dealing with Michael and his entitlement had been enough for a lifetime. Never again. But I listened, silent. As soon as we got in the car, Michael called. Coincidence?

"Where are you?"

"Is something wrong? It's only six-thirty. I'm coming back from a doctor's office. I'll be home in a while. I'm not over the bridge yet."

"Where exactly are you?"

"I'm driving out of Fort Washington. You're acting very strange. Is something wrong?"

"Do you want to meet for coffee at Starbucks?"

"If you want. I'll call you as I'm approaching. I'm gonna go. See you soon."

Driving over the bridge, in my rearview mirror, Michael's truck was wildly tailgating me! Same moment, Gino looked in the side mirror. "He's behind us."

My adrenaline kicked into overdrive. "I'll drop you off in front of A&P. I will deal with him. I don't want him to go after you."

"Not surprised. I'll be fine. Just worried about you."

Extraordinarily cool, pulling to a stop in the A&P entrance, no sign of Michael, yet. As Gino got out and headed to the entrance door, Michael pulled up and sprang out of his truck to go after him. I slammed on the gas! He jumped back in and chased after me! He caught up, sped past me in the right lane and swerved his truck in front of mine, halting me to our trucks crashing! He got out, fuming toward my driver window, my doors and windows locked!

He banged on the window with his fist! "Open the fuckin' door, you fuckin' cunt! I wanna talk to you!"

Eyeballing him, I shook my head no. Slamming in reverse, I swerved away from him around his truck and bolted down Lemoine Avenue, mindless of where I was going next. He was coming up behind me. I sped up and didn't care how fast I was going. Ducking down a side street, I turned again, and again, peering, expecting him to spring out of nowhere. I parked hidden away in the darkness, in my truck, no lights. He made me sick. I shoulda run him the fuck over! To end all this madness!

I jumped. Gino was calling, and I noticed a few missed calls. "Are you okay? Him speeding after you like that, I was worried."

"I'm okay. He crashed our trucks. I'm sitting in a dark lot, safe, catching my breath."

"I don't know about that. Do you want me to come get you? I'll take you to a safe place for a while."

I did feel safe with him. "No, I need to sit here by myself. Thank you, Gino."

Call-waiting, Michael. Ignoring, again and again.

"Please call or text me periodically to tell me you're safe. I'll be there in a minute if you need anything."

The phone rang again—home, my boys. I picked it up.

Michael's voice shook me. "Barb. I tried to call you. Who were you on the phone with? That little prick you're fucking?"

"First of all, don't go accusing when you have your head up your ass, and your dick who knows where! I never slept with him. That's your M.O.! And, yeah, it was him. He wanted to make sure I was safe. You animal!"

"That fuckin' cocksucker wants to make sure my wife is safe! I'll snap his fuckin' skinny little neck! And you didn't pick up my call! You fuckin' whore!"

Click. He called back. Ignore. A short while later, the phone rang again. Listening to the message, it was Mike.

"Hi, Mom, when are you coming home? I want you to come home now! Please! Please, call me!"

My heart tugged for my baby, then coiled. That self-seeking pig! Had he no conscience using his child? What if he threatened harm to them? No, they were safe with Grandma, especially Grandpa.

Dialing, I prayed it wouldn't be Michael. "Barb."

My voice like stone. "Give me my son. Don't say a word or I hang up."

I heard silence, then Mike's sweet concerned voice. "Mom? Where are you? Why aren't you home?"

My heart hurt so much. "Are you okay, love?"

"Yeah."

"Baby, I can't come home yet. I can't explain right now. Did Daddy tell you to call me and ask me to come home?"

"Yeah, but, when can you?"

That fucker! Disgusting!

"I'll see you later, honey. But don't worry. Mommy's safe. Go to sleep now. I love you and Gerry to infinity!"

"Love you to infinity, too, Mom."

"Barb." Click. He tried me back. Ignore.

How did I ever stay? How do I stay?

Hours passed, my adrenaline forever revved. Deep breaths worked very time. This was not my first nightmare with Michael. My eyes wanted to close. I couldn't go home. Nothing could happen to me! What would come of my children? My boys needed me with them.

The cell rang, home. "Mommy, when are you coming?"

"Honey, what are you doing up? It's so late. You should've been sleeping hours ago."

"I'm not going to sleep until you come home. Daddy's here, he wants to talk to you."

That son of a bitch!

"Barb, please come home? I'm not going to lay a hand on you. I won't hurt you, I promise. We could talk tomorrow. Just come home." His voice contrite, like a rabid wolf in sheep's clothing.

I didn't trust him, but for my boys, I headed home. The house was dark, not a sound. Passing through the kitchen, I grabbed a knife from the block, down and hidden, treading, ready, Michael's shadow on the library couch. "Barb?"

Ready for an attack, continuing past, my eyes and ears peered around and behind me. He left me alone. As I climbed the stairs, Mike's light was on. "Mom?"

"Yes, baby."

He darted out of his room to greet me with the tightest hug I've ever felt.

"No talking now, love. I'm okay, promise. Time to sleep. I'm in with you guys."

Wide awake and watching them sleep, my heart swelled, and broke, for my two angels. I hadn't told my family yet. God forbid, my friends knew what happened. This was not the life I wanted for them. Damn him!

13

The Reasons

Michael wreaked havoc, warning me he had my phone text records. A bluff—there was nothing to find. He threatened me, reminding me I owed the DA money, nobody would want to work with me. He knew info about Gino and his family, where he lived. He threatened Gino, said he'd put him out of business. He threatened Don, the director at the radiology center, if he kept me at the center, or paid me even a cent, he would tell the DA he gave Don and the company money, and they'd freeze everything! Their business would be finished! Scared, they conceded. We could've really used the money. Vile threats and all, he had the twisted nerve to plead with me to stay? All his desperate antics disgusted me. I was so ready to call Tom. Gino was not the reason, *Michael* was. Throwing him in would only fuel his destruction from the inside. Jail wouldn't stop him.

"Barbra, please. I can't lose you."

"I'm leaving."

Michael lurched into the bathroom. In front of my vanity, I stood unmoved. Behind me, towered over my shoulder, his lips to my ear, voice low and tight, pinching out the words through his clenched teeth. "From the inside, I can get to you. Trust me, I got long arms. Don't you fuckin' doubt that for a second! If I find out you end up with him when I'm away, something might just happen to one of your family members. One of them is gonna die! Understand? It could be your mother, your father, your sister, brother. Who knows?"

My eyes like ice, piercing him through the mirror, not a flinch, my voice like bullets. "You're despicable! Get the fuck away from me! Gino or not, you've killed whatever I felt for you! I'm leaving!"

It was time for Tom. Michael trudged to his vanity, leaned on the basin, his head down, defeated, sobbing. "I'm sorry. I'm sorry. You know I didn't mean that, I would never do anything to hurt your family. They're my family too! I love them!"

"Don't speak of love with me! Of the boys! Or of my family! I was right all those years ago! You have no idea what love is! You selfish bastard! You're incapable of true love!"

In disbelief. "You mean we're not going to be together? Buried together? Really?"

"It was my pity for you that kept us alive, not you! You only killed us, over and over again! I'm done! My love for you has been dying for a long time now. It's gone."

Reflecting on my words, his knees buckled, dropping to the floor. I tried shaking him, yelling, he appeared to be out cold. Was he serious? Fainting over the woman he couldn't give a shit about, abused and betrayed on so many levels?

His mother came to the door, seeing him on the floor, hysterical, crying, screaming, dropping to the floor, leaning over him as if he was dead. "My Michael! Oh, my Michael!"

As I called 911, Michael started to come around. How convenient? He probably couldn't take her shrieking anymore. His mom tried to help him off the floor. He shook her hand off. "I could do it myself!"

Nasty fuck! Even to his mother! The paramedics came.

"I don't need to be checked! All o' you! Get the fuck out of my house!" He sounded normal.

"Sir, you'd just lost consciousness. Please, let us check your vitals, and then you make your decision."

Blood pressure slightly higher than normal, all else checked out okay. Whatd'ya know?

"Sir, just for precaution, we recommend you ride with us in the ambulance to the hospital to check you more thoroughly."

"Get the fuck out!"

I escorted them out. "I am so sorry for his behavior. Thank you so much for coming."

Leaving him, would he flee? He'd lose his anchor. Panic struck. Who would watch him, make sure he stays? Revoke the bail? Would he come after me? My family? Tom didn't think he'd run, reassuring me he would catch him if he did. My call. My pity. My fear.

Bail stayed as it was, still so uncertain of his guilt or innocence, his Jekyll and Hyde actions casting doubt. Tom would be on guard for my call. His parents couldn't take the dissension between us, retreating to John and Anna's house for a while, leaving me with their psycho son.

Mike and Gerry watched a movie on the couch, staying by me at the desk. Gino called, worried for me and my children. Sorry couldn't be enough, putting him in danger. Next move, when Michael's parents returned, I would pack up and leave with the children to my parents. But before that could happen Michael busted through the French glass doors, lunging at me! He took my phone, hurling it at the wall, shattering it to pieces. The children backed away to the corner, stunned, petrified. He bellowed in my face, cursing me, lurching over me, fists clenched. Silent, sturdy, I glowered into his fiery eyes as he howled at me. He couldn't see beyond his rage, capable of anything. My boys were exposed to this horrible scene of their mother and father. Michael grabbed me around my shoulders, lifted me from the chair, and threw me to the floor against the couch! He grunted and stormed out. The front door slammed shut, shaking the house. Music to my ears...he was gone.

Showing my children that Mommy was not hurt once again, I got up, sat on the couch and slid over to them, hugging them, comforting them. "Guys, I'm sorry you had to see that. Dad was beyond wrong. He's not thinking clearly. He's lost his grip. From what he just did, I need you to use him as an example of what *not* to do."

They nodded their heads, speechless, glued to me, the fright for me in their eyes.

"We need to go to Grandma and Grandpa's now."

"Mom, can we stay? I don't want to leave. Please?"

"Why, honey? It's not safe."

"I just have this feeling, please?"

My instinct was to leave. "Only for the night."

We would leave in the morning, taking Duchess with us. I'd call his parents. The house was locked, alarm on to hear if he came in. We all stayed in Mike's room. My twelve-year-old son sat vigil in the top bunk, his hand gripped firmly on the knife tucked on the side of his mattress ready for his father, refusing to sleep, watching over me. The alarm buzzed, 4:30 a.m. Michael was home. Mike watching TV, zombie-like. He had never slept. My heart stung for my boys. We eyed each other, ready. I couldn't get us outta there soon enough. We should've left. A knock at the door, it opened.

Michael stayed at the doorway. "Can I come in?"

Neither of us spoke. He took a step in.

Mike clenched the hidden knife. "Stay right there! Tell her what you want from where you are!"

"I deserve that. You have every right to feel that way. I'm sorry, I would never hurt your mother. Barb, I'm sorry I pushed you."

"You did hurt her! You threw her!" Calling his bullying father out on his weasel words.

"Listen, I love you guys more than anything in the world. I don't want to lose you. You're everything to me. I'm sorry I lost my temper. Barb, I'm sorry for hurting you. I love you. I'll be inside. Get some sleep. Good night."

Always destroying. Always sorry. He closed the door.

"Mike, honey, you can close your eyes now."

He got up from the bed and locked his door and the door to their shared bathroom. No way in. "Now I can."

Later that morning, Michael knocked and tried the door, at least sounding calm that he couldn't enter. Mike unlocked it. Michael came in and professed his twisted love and momentary apologies again. "Mike, can you to come and talk to me in our bedroom?" Our bedroom. Repulsed me.

Mike looked at me for reassurance. I told him only if he wanted to. A short while passed before Mike came back into his room and sat next to me on the bed.

"Mom, Dad cried to me you're having an affair with a guy from work and you're leaving him for that 'piece of shit!' And breaking up our family! Is that true? He told me he cheated on you a long time ago. He's still so wrong. He asked me to try to talk you into staying."

Was Michael fucking kidding? New low! Teaching my son great life lessons from the expert of wrong! Using him again! Flaming at Michael, exploiting his son for his own benefit.

"Honey. I'm so sorry he filled your head with garbage. I have someone I do business with from work. But I did not cheat on your father with him. I'm not leaving your father for anyone but because of him and so many terrible things he's done wrong, to me, to our family."

"Like what? Tell me everything."

"The few things you've seen are enough. You don't need to know all the details. Remember our pact?"

Mike nodded. "Mom, I don't want to go upstate! I want to stay here! Please!" He took off down the stairs as if he was running away.

Instantly darting after him, I heard the garage door! And his mini-bike! Down the block both ways, Mike was gone! My heart raced faster than my truck could drive to the construction site at the end of our road where all the kids usually hung out. When I pulled up, no Mike, no bike, only the cliff. My heart lodged in my throat, approaching the edge. Nothing, thank God. Next, the beautiful open grassy landing around the corner overlooking the Hudson, spectacular panorama of the city. I took Mike there one day not long ago to talk and pacify his worries. Our pocket of sunshine in a wicked storm. My boys, my pockets of everything good every day. Approaching the dead end to the water view, in the distance there was a figure, beside what looked like a bike. Mike! He came to our spot. He wanted me to find him.

I ran up and hugged him! "Oh, my God! Baby, I can't handle you doing this! Please! You need to tell me when and where you're going. I was so worried about you!"

"I'm sorry, Mom. I just needed time. Don't worry, I wouldn't do anything to hurt myself. I need to be here for you and Ger."

I wish my love alone could wash away his worries. Why did he want to stay? His life was here, but staying over safety? Pity for his father? Did he think he could protect me from him?

Mike grabbed my arm. "I think Daddy's gone crazy. He's on something, Ma! One minute, he flips out for no reason, out of nowhere! Then, he starts crying or gets sad! And I think he's cheating on you! I'm telling you, Ma! I'm afraid he's gonna kill you!"

Every minute Michael didn't find us was a gift, and I knew we had only moments before he did.

"Mike, don't worry about me. I'm not afraid of him. I know how to handle him. You've seen too much, baby! Remember, I'm magic. But really, I have faith God and our angels are watching over me for you guys. I know they are. We should leave, honey. Why do you want to stay?"

Just then, a black truck drove up, Michael.

"Talk later, love." I hugged my pained child.

Michael got out of the truck, advancing toward Mike glued to my side, grabbed him. And hugged him. "I'm so sorry! I love you, pal."

My breath held still. Mike didn't hug him back. Michael's sorrys had become hollows of destruction. We went home, still gearing to leave. Michael's parents returned.

His father pulled me alone. "Barb! I'm tellin' ya! If you and Mikey ain't together, I'm takin' my wife and we're movin' out! And I'm takin' my checkbook wit' me! I ain't payin' for nothin'!"

My father-in-law had his fucking conditions, didn't he! For his piece of shit son! He knew how terrible Michael was to me. He knew I overstayed my own well-being. I was stuck in a very bad environment. And if I was, so were my children. Michael was a very dangerous loose cannon filled with dynamite hovering over an open flame. His capabilities were not beyond following through with any of his deranged thoughts. Top of the list was if he couldn't have me, he'd make damn sure no one would! Because of Michael our lives were going up in flames either way. My father-in-law knew I had every right to leave. For years! How could he! Resembling his son's bad behavior all too much! So much for trusting him. Only my own family, my own friends. That was it.

"You would really do that? You know the house will go into foreclosure. It will put me in deeper debt on top of what Michael did to me. I'll have less than nothing for the boys. Everything is frozen. They took everything. I'll pay you back."

"I'm sorry, Barb! You leave, we ain't stayin'!"

You know what you could do with your money!

"Your money can't make me stay."

Forging away in quiet fury, nobody was gonna buy me! I was leaving. I was at nobody's mercy for money! Money was Michael's God, not mine! Mike begged me to stay. For Mike and Gerry's sake, I agreed to not move out just yet, under the condition Michael and I would not be together. Trapped didn't begin to cover how I felt.

The following week, December 19, middle of the night, our house phone rang. Michael picked it up. I tried to make out who and what. He hung up.

"Barb. Your dad had a heart attack. They tried to revive him several times. They couldn't bring him back. I'm so sorry."

"You mean he died? My dad's gone? No! That can't be! I spoke to him yesterday! He was fine! The tests said he's fine! No! My dad can't be gone!" Tears streaming down, sobbing, I called my mom, no answer. My sister, us both weeping. "Rae? Is it true? Is he really gone?"

"Yes. They'll have him at the hospital for a while. Come now."

Michael asked if he could drive me. So out of my head, I let him. My family was there, my dad on the gurney, we all said goodbye, devastated.

Michael tried to hug me. I resisted. "He was my dad, too."

Michael's threats against my family flashed through my head. Maybe it would wake him up from his desperate, self-seeking disgusting behavior. Wishful thinking. Always wishful thinking! Saying goodbye to my dad was one of the hardest things in my life. My angel will always be with me. Michael's pleading was unrelenting. So was my no.

"You're my rock. If you leave me, they might as well put me in jail right now. I'll have no fight left in me! I will give up!"

I could arrange that. Speed dial. My position remained distant, cold, indifferent. Michael's volatile anger and violent tendencies were serious and dangerous. I had to protect myself and my kids. I needed to do what I needed to do. Michael told me he would do anything to try to make it work out between us. There was that word again, "anything." When it came to Michael, "anything" was a very scary unknown. Besides Sally, I was no actress, but I was going to put on a life-saving performance to save my family, myself, maybe the world, from him! I was stuck in this game. Countless things I could never forgive but would look past it all to get through this nightmare that was my life. Carefully placing myself as a pawn for the sake of my children and family, to give Michael a chance to free or bury himself, to keep him from running, everything stayed where it needed to be, to keep him where I needed him to be. Michael seemed to have turned over an entirely new leaf, more at ease, patient, thoughtful. It wouldn't last. Never did. How many lies to betray me? How many lies to keep me?

The new year arrived. I was hoping for a better one. For him to tell it, his deals were all coming through. Sadly, my faith in this once wildly successful world-renowned surgeon, my husband, no longer existed.

"Barb. Everything needs to be in your name."

Never!

"I can make billions! Between the oil deal and real estate deals in Fort Lee, Jersey City, and Vegas, I will be able to pay restitution off!" He was living in his own bubble of reality.

"So, you think you can buy your way out of jail? You think that's gonna fly?"

"Money can buy you anything."

And bullshit can get you anything, right?

"The Jersey City deal is close, but won't really yield much, two hundred and fifty thousand dollars."

Amazing how he threw numbers around, and we didn't have two dimes to rub together, pay a bill, or do anything, without the DA's approval.

"I ran into Jay at a diner down there. We're not supposed to talk, but we had a cup of coffee for a few minutes. He's working as a manager on a construction site down there. I'm happy for him."

"Jersey City is damn big. What a coincidence you running into him."

His deranged mind knew prison was imminent. He spent more and more time out, gone many nights. Incommunicado every time. It didn't matter. I was disconnected, though keeping my position was vital. Funny, wasn't that long ago I vied for his connection.

Months later, news hit. Jay Cello fell off a building, six stories high on a construction site in Jersey City. He was unofficially deemed a vegetable, and would need multiple surgeries.

"Michael, look at me. Did you have anything to do with Jay's accident?"

"Barb, Jay has a lot of enemies. He always got mixed up with the wrong people. Could've been any one of many. Mason said I'm off the suspect list."

"You didn't answer my question."

"No, I didn't."

If the DA didn't suspect him, I'd have to accept that. Again, uncanny. Unbelievable. When it came to Michael, the word "anything" came to mind.

May 2007. "Hi, honey, it's Mom. I went to the doctor. They took an X-ray because of my nagging cough and found a mass in my right lung. They can't say it's cancer for sure, but I need a CAT scan."

Like a ton of bricks. My troubles with Michael insignificant in a blink. Dad was only gone six months. I'd lost the best man I'd ever known. I couldn't lose her, too. I had to be strong. She had to be stronger.

Breaking inside. "Mom, you need to see an oncologist as soon as possible. I'm calling Dr. Spater to get direction, make appointments, and then I'm coming right up to see you."

On my way up, I called Raven. As soon as I heard her voice, I teared up for a moment, then gathered myself. I needed to keep it together. Mom couldn't see that. "What happened?"

"I made her go back to the doctor. She felt like she had 'a little man in her chest' for too long. Dr. Korn wasn't in. I insisted she get an X-ray. Within a half-hour the doctor called, vague as shit! She pissed me off, called it a mass but wouldn't say it was possibly cancer! Mass is a big fuckin' word!"

"Dr. Spater highly recommends Dr. Joseph Lobe, a pulmonologist. They both recommend Dr. Abraham Chanoa, an oncologist at NYU Cancer Center specializing in lung, and Dr. Spater her heart. She needs to get an MRI of her brain and scan of her abdomen. Those are the two places cancer manifests itself if it's spread."

"That's crazy! I asked friends at work, too! One of them sees Dr. Chanoa!"

Dr. Chanoa was a lively and comforting character, and brilliant! Mom, Raven, Aunt Belle, and I knew he was the one. We instantly loved and trusted him.

"Lena, you have a sizeable mass in your upper right lobe. You need surgery. Dr. Leonard Grossman specializes in lung surgery. I've known him for many years here at NYU. He's now in North Shore Hospital in Long Island. He is the man. I suggest first, a six-week course of aggressive chemotherapy pre-surgery. Research shows stats for survival are notably greater with the chemo pre-surgery."

"Dr. Chanoa, is this mass cancer? The question everyone seems to evade."

"I can tell you this. From the radiology and reports alone, I can't confirm that it is indeed cancer until Dr. Grossman goes in. But, if it looks like a duck, walks like a duck, quacks like a duck, chances are it's a duck."

"Got it."

I smelled something terrible coming from the basement, burning. Michael crouched at a table, a Bunsen burner in hand, a slew of jars and some household products spread across, one a big bottle of rubbing alcohol.

He glanced up with his lab goggles. The mad scientist! "Barb, stay right there."

"What are you doing?"

"I have something going with the Dicco Brothers. I'm making epinephrine to sell. This lab shit is a breeze! I could make a killing! Easy money!"

"You are out of your damn mind! Breeze that shit out of the house, now! Are you trying to kill us all? You're lighting up hazardous material! You're gonna blow us all the fuck up! Endanger yourself all you want, but not my children, your parents, and me! And not this house! Out!"

He turned off the burner.

"Michael, is this even legal? If it's not, are you trying to get me thrown in jail for having an illicit makeshift lab in my house?"

"Slow the fuck down! You're overreacting! I'll take it to Pete Dicco's house!"

Was that even epinephrine? There was no time for his nonsense. My energy was focused on taking care of my boys and Mom, transporting her to preoperative doctor's appointments, scheduling more scans and her mediastinoscopy, an extensive procedure to see the membrane and area between her lungs and biopsy before her surgery.

Michael still had his late nights out. Where? I did not know. I probably shouldn't know. They seemed to end at 2:00 a.m. regularly.

He explained he was doing the epinephrine lab work at Pete's house, but Pete didn't return until late.

'He can go blow up their house.'

One thirty in the morning, returning from North Shore Hospital where Mom just had the mediastinoscopy, I called Michael's cell. Voicemail. I called home. Michael wasn't home yet. I hadn't heard from him all day. I found Pete Dicco's house on Washington Avenue.

"He knew she was having the procedure today." So upset at his disregard, I couldn't imagine a good enough reason. It had been a hard day for me. Mom looked so sick. I broke down when I saw her in the recovery room. Unconscious. Swollen. Hooked up to tubes everywhere. Encased in a plastic sheath. Fighting for her life.

"Why couldn't he be there for me?"

I saw his truck parked. The house was dark. An older man answered the door in his robe. "May I help you?"

"Hi, I'm sorry to bother you so late. I'm looking for Michael Mastromarino. He's here, isn't he?"

He looked me over like a wolf waiting for dinner. "Yeah, sweetheart. Hold on." He went to a side door with stairs to a second floor, opened it and called up. "Dina! Someone's looking for Michael!"

My stomach twisted. My thoughts spiraled. He did it again! A woman with short mussed hair in rolled up sweatpants and a tank top came down, looked at me for a second as my eyes pierced her, then down and wouldn't look back up as she turned and ran back upstairs without a word. This Dina chick knew who I was.

I stayed cool. "Are they together?"

"Yeah." The man answered, as his wife appeared behind him.

I shook my head looking down, laughing in disbelief. "Oh, my God. I can't believe this."

"He's separated." The man added.

My head shot up! "No! He's not! I'm his wife!"

I imposed my way through the doorway to the stairs where he was making his way down. I looked up. His hair tussled, shirt unbuttoned over his undershirt. It looked like he just threw his clothes on! He traipses down as if I disturbed his sleep!

Something inside me fuckin' snapped and exploded! My fury drove me up the stairs! Beating on him! Slapping him! Shrieking! "I hate you! I hate you! You disgusting pig! How could you do this to me again! My mom is in the hospital and you're here? Fucking this whore?"

He grabbed my arm to push me out the front door with him. I continued my rage! I fought! Kicking him! Kneeing him! Punching him in the face! So overdue!

I screamed to them standing in the doorway as he pulled me into the street, away from the house, seeing lights go on in neighboring houses. "He's not separated! He's still very married! To me! Do you know who he is! Do you know who you're fucking? You filthy bitch! He's the body parts doctor! The body snatcher! He's a fucking criminal! But you know that already! Don't you?? Just like you knew he was married!" I never lost it like that in my life! That night was the night! I had it!

He dragged me down the block near my truck. "Barb! Shhh! Their father is so connected! If the police come, I'm dead!"

"I take you back!" I punched the side of his head and his glasses flew off his face.

In the middle of the street, he just stood still and took it, knowing he deserved it.

"I give you another chance!" Another blow. I didn't care if I broke my fucking hand!

"Over and over!" Again.

"I stand by you!" In the jaw.

"I ask my family to stand by you!" In the face.

"This is what you do to me?" In the stomach.

I wasn't done! Could never be enough! "You dirty piece of shit!" I leveraged his shoulder and kneed him in the balls. He doubled over.

I picked up his glasses. He was desperate, apologetic. "No! Not my glasses!" I twisted them like a pretzel and threw them to the ground with a fury like I've never known!

He was eerily calm. Was he on drugs too? What more? "I deserve that. But please, I need to explain. First, how's your mother?"

Still fuming. "She's okay, as if you really care! I haven't heard from you once! All day! Unreachable! I see why! Disgusting!"

His tone turned sincere and grateful. "I love your mother. I'm glad she's okay. I know this sounds crazy, but I'm glad you found me there. The truth is I was trying to make crystal meth, not epinephrine. It's in high demand and a big moneymaker. Pete returns at about two from deliveries. Pete and I needed to conjure up a reason for me to be there all hours of the night in the lab in the basement. It's his father's house who'd never allow it. A relationship with Dina was perfect."

Boy, this son of a bitch is quick on his filthy feet! The father's probably in on it! But I'm sure the wife doesn't know! She never does! Does she?

I wanted to hit him again! "Just shut your fucking mouth! Don't you dare pretend to care about my mother! Do you ever listen to yourself? What? You get off on fooling people? Even people that have tried to be there for you? You're a cruel monster! I'm so done with you! You're done!"

A car pulled into Dina's driveway. Michael pleaded. "Look at the time. It's two. I'm telling you the truth."

"Trying to hide a mountain of lies with one meaningless truth! The truth is you're married! All I've ever done is be there for you! You disgusting animal!"

"Her fourteen-year-old daughter was upstairs with us while I waited for Pete. Nothing happened! I'm glad you found me there. It was meant to be that I don't pursue that business. You're my angel. You saved me from trouble. I always told you, you make me a better person." The stench of his bullshit was so strong there was no masking it.

A master. He probably has a very different story for his bitch!

I couldn't look at him as I got in my truck. "You'll never be anything but terrible. And I don't believe you, not one word."

"Can you give me a ride home? Please? I left my keys inside. I can't go get them now. And I can't see without my glasses."

I put it in drive. "You can walk or go back in to catch some zzz's with your whore."

"Barb. Please."

Now I know how people behind the wheel run their cheating spouses over! I drove down the block.

I saw a patrol car turn onto the block in my rear-view mirror and backed up. "Get in."

The next morning he asked me to please sit and listen for just two minutes. He wanted to straighten everything out. I couldn't see it. Everything was too crooked. I wanted out. Why couldn't he make it at least just a tiny bit easy for me to stay, so he wouldn't run!

Him appeasing me was laughable. "I can ask Pete and Dina to talk to you and explain."

"I don't want to speak to your drug-dealing partner or your whore."

"But they'll tell you. You got it all wrong. I promise I will abort the lab. If you want me to abort the oil deal with Pete and his brother, I will. I want to make you feel better. I need to get my truck keys. But I should go alone. I need to apologize to them and their parents. And tell them I can't do business."

I wonder what story he's going to tell them! Probably about his crazy bitch wife! Who stalks him!

I was back there again. That familiar place, not knowing what to believe from him. Scheming liar was all I could see in him. I wanted off the Hell Ride!

Still a pawn in this, I was torn, trapped. "You don't need to abort the oil deal. I'm glad you won't be making crystal meth anymore. So, there won't be any reason to be over there all hours of the night, right? Or you have the other reason?"

His cell rang. I grabbed it and ran into the bathroom, locking the door behind me. Michael banging on the door, I answered it without a word.

"What happened?" The voice had to be her.

"You fucking bitch whore!" Click.

I came out of the bathroom. "It was her. Your bitch wanted to know what happened." I held his cell out to him, her number already etched in my brain. "Go ahead. Call her back right now. Speakerphone. Make nice. Tell her."

"Barb! Listen to me! She was concerned!"

"Concerned? You both can go fuck yourselves. Fuck each other. I don't really care. I don't want to think about this anymore. My brain hurts. Do what you need to do. I have more important things to do. They don't include you."

I was in the thick of so many bad things, all because of him. My skin was getting so tough I couldn't feel anymore. He tried to shower me with attention and affection. I tried to show him the benefit of my doubt, as a very good actress. I felt reduced, again. I let this man bring out the very worst in me, things I thought I would never think about or do in my life!

I didn't let it erode me. I was still positioned. He needed to stay put. I could make one phone call and it could be all over. But what if I put him away? And he got out? Then what? Even if I stepped out of my life and looked in from the outside, I would still be in the absolute dark not knowing where the next day would lead, not knowing truth or lie. All I did know was nothing could happen to me.

* * *

From Mom's more aggressive pre-surgery chemotherapy treatments, we managed her nausea and hair loss with medication and Sadie, her new wig. She had named it but was not yet ready to wear it.

Mike's face terrified, he asked me to come into his room, pointing to his pillow where Grandma had slept, covered with her hair. "Mom, tell me the truth. Does Grandma have cancer?"

How many pieces could my heart break into for these kids? Time for the talk. Mom and I sat with Mike and Gerry.

"From these doctor appointments, we found out Grandma has a mass in her lung. They're treating it like cancer to make sure she has the best chance after her surgery. The doctor says she will be okay, that's what he told me, promise. Right, Grandma?"

"Don't worry, boys. Grandma's going to be okay. The medicine that helps me makes my hair fall out, but doesn't hurt, and nobody can catch it, promise."

They gave her a hug so gently, as if she might break. She hugged them tighter. Our promises my boys could count on.

In the following days, as Mom's first surgery grew closer, she lost most of her hair with only a few straggling patches, holding Sadie in her lap.

"Barbra, I'm ready. Could you?"

I cradled Mom's head, feeling her vulnerability in my hand. A similar scene with Smith and Samantha on *Sex and the City* had hit my heart the thousand times I'd watched it. This? Killed me. I shaved her last strands, silently weeping. Taking a step back from my life, Michael had brought only strife for the past seven years, simply from his choices. Mom had no choice. Her husband was gone, mom gone. She had lost her daughter, my nine-year-old sister Mina, so many years ago. She had been sick. And I was sick of Michael, sucking the life out of our family and friends, feeding on their goodness just like cancer.

14

The Delusions

He worked on his deals. I didn't even know what that meant. Nothing he had done had ever panned out, one scheme after another. Nothing. All the while, he claimed to be working on the case with Mason to prove himself innocent. Since the DA had released some of his dad's money back to him, Michael used $40,000 from his dad's bank account for a wheelchair venture. Shortly after, he told us he was scammed. He didn't know if he could get it back. He couldn't. *Shocker.* Along with bail held, everyone's money was disappearing on behalf of Michael.

He summoned me to his office downstairs. At his desk, his eyes scanned his computer screen. "This online pharmacy business looks good. I know these guys from Brooklyn, global distributors." "Global" and Michael went hand in hand. "That's where I get my testosterone and growth hormone. I can't have my name on it. What do you think?"

"Didn't everybody in that business get jail time a couple of years ago? I wouldn't do it if I were you. Don't dare ask me to sign anything. I want no part of it!"

"I don't think it's lucrative enough."

"How about legal enough?"

He decided against it, strictly about the dollars. Unaffected, he always had a web of prospects going simultaneously in his spidey brain. He really was business-brilliant, unfortunately this time his unraveling spool left a growing, messy, knotted pile. Was it all a guise? He still proclaimed his innocence. The guy did have tenacity. At home, we struggled with bills, making sure we had enough for basics, food, school and sports supplies for the boys. His prospective "deals" weren't paying for that. We needed to live in today, not in promise of tomorrow, especially not Michael's false promise. Was there a Guinness Book of World Records for broken promises?

The beginning of October, he came home boasting about his big deal coming through very soon. "Be prepared for an astronomical change in our lives."

Not much shook me, but when Michael said things like that, it scared me out of my skin! My fear directly scaled to his excitement.

"Forget about millions! I'm going to make billions! Buying my way out of my charges is gonna be a cake walk! Lunch money! If you can't beat 'em, pay 'em! Money talks. If the public needs to see some time served, I'll do what I gotta do. But I'm also working on something for cancer that would give me a governor's pardon. I won't be in for long!"

What was the sense of engaging? He didn't seem high but was head trippin' to Fantasyland! Later that night, Michael didn't come home. As usual, I left a voicemail. The hours passed. Again, what was the sense? I had no trouble putting my head down to sleep where his bullshit was concerned. So I did. Five-thirty a.m. The door chimed. He was home.

"I'm sorry, I drove up and down the Palisades, then I watched the sunset at the construction site. An incredible sight."

That doesn't take all night. I'm sure he had whore company. Again, his sorry worthlessness.

"Come on, I want to show you now."

He drove me to the lot. The sun was still coming up, beautiful, bright, shimmering on the river down below, serene. Serene sounded so good.

"You see all this? There are seven lots here. Reece owns them with his cousin Lee. I already talked to him about selling them to me and building the homes for us. I want this for us. All of it! I want this to be my legacy to my family! That house to the left I could pick up for four million dollars for your mom, sister, and aunt, that house a little more to the right I want for my parents and sister, about seven million. We could have our own street here. We can name our own street!"

He was over the edge, a mirage in his head. This was never happening. With prison looming and his reputation as a depraved monster across the world, thinking he would be pardoned, thinking all this crazy shit, he didn't sound like a guilty man. Just a crazy man!

"You and the boys will need bodyguards because of the chance of kidnapping. We'll have that much money. I want everything in your name. It should be, you deserve it for putting up with me. Eric is a cop. He will retire and be your full-time bodyguard. I'm giving him that house by the entrance. That's only a couple mill."

"No, he won't! No one is telling me where I can and cannot go! I'm not living like that! Nor the boys!"

It wasn't even worth debating. Didn't matter, none of it was gonna happen, especially one bit of it in *my* name! What was he gonna do? Knock me off to get the dough?

Michael was off to his next thought as if I never spoke. "I'm going to finance the project in Fort Lee and Cliffside Park. With the Vegas deal, I definitely need a private jet."

Mama always taught me, and I tried relaying this to Michael, "Don't count it until it's in the bank, or in your hands."

Later that day, Michael wanted to take the boys to the lots. Objecting was senseless. The boys needed an ally in me, not an adversary. I went with them, waiting to undo what Michael would do. He asked them what they wanted—basketball court, indoor batting cage for Mike, full-size track for Gerry. All their hopes inflated in front of me. Michael kept puffing thin air. I wanted to stop him but it was useless. Once he was done with his mirage I would fix it. We pulled back into our driveway down the block, motioning my boys to stay as Michael got out of the car and went inside.

"Boys, all that Daddy showed you today is not going to happen. If something seems too good to be true, it is. Daddy has a lot of crazy things in his head right now. All of it is imaginary. You can dream, but you need to keep it there. I'm sorry, I wish he never showed the lot to you. Please don't count on it. No matter what happens, Mommy will make sure you guys are okay. That, you can count on!"

They nodded, deflated, reached and hugged me as if protecting me. My heart. "We know, Mom."

The next day, he took his parents and sister to the house for sale he wanted to buy for them. Amazing how Michael made people dance around in all the false hopes he filled them with! Oh, wait! I had been one of them! It was too late to change my fate. Damage was done. He was a master of illusion and delusion. Rue had arranged a private showing, since it was not yet on the market. The owners were interested because Michael said he'd pay in cash. What cash? They got a tour while his mother sat in the sprawling kitchen, her usual hangout. The house was stunning. Michael drove his mother back to our house. Lumbering away from the house with her father, Louise turned around to glance at it once more and started to cry, tears of hope, fear, sadness, for her parents and her brother.

My father-in-law took her in his arms. "Keep lookin' for an apartment, honey. Forget you saw dis. It ain't never gonna happen."

Two days later, Michael got a call from Mason. Michael was being formally indicted in Philadelphia and needed to turn himself in there. They'd give him the weekend with his family and planned to arraign him on Tuesday. Mason said they were projecting a five-million-dollar bail. Michael's big deal was the only way to get him out. It seemed he was becoming a bigger deal. Michael was so confident the deal was coming through, convinced he would only need to spend a couple of days in jail, if that. He set me up with contact phone numbers for Tanya and Marcos, his two partners in the deal, to communicate Michael's banking information for them to transfer. The deal, the deal, the deal! It all seemed unreal! We all sat for dinner together, a rarity.

"Guys, Daddy is going to court soon and may be gone for a few days. He has to work on his case with Mason."

Gerry was oblivious but Mike furtively shot me a look. My eyes told him, "Tell you the real deal later."

The last few nights before the day, Michael was absent. He should have chosen to be home with his family, since he was going to jail on Tuesday. He seemed to talk about jail as if it was an appointment, a meeting. Once it was over, he'd be back in a jiff. I kinda thought once you go in, it's a crapshoot if you get out, especially if the world and the DAs in two states see you as a gruesome mastermind criminal. I wish I knew what they knew. I wish I knew the truth, the whole truth. Michael's last night was spent elsewhere. His parents were crushed, repeatedly asking where he was. I had no answer. Hadn't he broken their hearts enough? Not sure I wanted to know where he was, I only knew where he should've been. He was a grown-ass man with choices, the wrong ones too many times to count! Finger on the button to Tom, ready to pull the trigger. God help him if he ran.

I wanted to believe he didn't create all this by choice, that he was innocent at least in some way, not all in, that he deserved my support and was just out of his head because of this. Who was I kidding? He didn't deserve my support either way!

In the middle of the night, he walked in. *Thank you, God.* The morning came. Goodbyes to his parents, his mother hugging him as if this meant forever, his father the same. Goodbye to Duchess, to the cats. He kissed the children while they slept, as did I. We left. I was steady, collected, quiet. Michael's arrogance only grew exponentially.

My pity for his warped sense of reality grew along with it. Beyond himself, he lost all sense of humility, of reality.

"Let's get this over with. It shouldn't take more than a few days. When this deal goes through, things are gonna change. I'm gonna make Mason my attorney on retainer. He won't need to work anywhere else. He'll make sure I do everything right so this never happens again."

He sickened me, as if he could buy people, put them in his back pocket. I didn't think Mason would give up everything for Michael's Monopoly money. Who could ever be sure? Some people could be bought. Me? Not a chance. Tragically, a part of me stayed for love, of what I knew in my heart it should be. At that point, leaving him would have been like telling him, "Bye-bye! Go run!" or "Bye-bye! Go kill!" He needed to face the music, to believe I would always be there. I surely didn't stay for him treating me like a fairy tale princess, and without question not for the great sex!

"You won't listen. Nobody can make you do anything, Michael. That's obvious."

"Believe me! I'll give him more money than he could ever earn on his own in his lifetime!"

After everything, he still couldn't see past the money, the power, his ego. We drove down in my truck to a rest stop along the New Jersey Turnpike to meet Mason. From there, Michael rode with him to Philadelphia to discuss the upcoming indictment. I followed. We checked in to the hotel.

Mason was kind enough to get a suite with two bedrooms and save me the expense. "Don't worry, Barb. It's comin' outta his retainer anyway!" What retainer? The fifty-inch TV he gave him?

Serious or not, he made me laugh. I needed that. The three of us got a bite to eat, Michael's "Last Supper." He was no Jesus Christ superstar. We waited in the hotel room until it was time. They threw around conversation of such monumental proportions—counts, felonies, sentencing, five-million-dollar bail, jail, prison. I didn't flinch—it was just another day in the black hole of a life as Michael's wife. How jaded I'd become. How removed from him I'd become.

It was time. Michael gave me a brisk hug and kiss goodbye, as if he was going off to work...not remotely a goodbye kiss. His ego clouded his view of what he was truly walking into today. And walking away *from*. Two hours later, Mason returned with documents without Michael. He was held for five million dollars. Mason had to go back in a few hours.

"I have copies of the indictment, if you're interested in reading it. My copy is confidential, but this one you can take a look at."

Skimming, I read that Hellina ran the operation in Rochester, referred to in the document as his girlfriend. No surprise. She was in trouble, too. After all these years, in trouble together again.

"If he's now in Philadelphia prison, do they now release the bail from Brooklyn? That would be a great relief."

"Good question, but they won't consider releasing it until everything is settled here," Mason explained. "A lot can happen." I could only hope.

Staying an extra day to visit him and see if the deal went through was a waste. Nothing happened. Something about the foreign investor's funds being frozen. It all felt fabricated, the whole deal. I assured all at home, especially my boys, that I was okay and would be home soon. I'd never let them down. Everything was gonna be all right. *Why am I here again?*

Thursday morning, the Philadelphia Correctional Facility visiting process was a snap compared to Rikers. They brought him out in shackles.

Behind the glass, shame in his eyes. "I'm so sorry. I love you. I need to change things in my life and with us." Us? Hadn't been an us since I could remember. "I can't explain now. I wrote you a letter. You should get it Monday or so." No exchanges permitted during visits. "How are my boys? And my parents?"

"Everyone's holding up."

"Your mom's surgery is next week, right? Give everyone my love. It's hard in here. They have me in 'the hole' because my case is pending. I'm in a cell as big as a small closet with a small square window for twenty-three out of twenty-four hours. Most guys, as tough as they are, break down in here. I swear, God picked me up off the floor, and told me to keep fighting! I'm okay. I'd rather be in general population, but the warden won't let me. Something happens to me, they could get sued."

Days so long ago, I was on the outside, him so distant, me wanting so badly to be back on the inside and close to him. For the longest time now, there is nowhere I'd rather be than on the outside, as far away from him as possible.

Mason told me Pennsylvania was a commonwealth state and the laws were very strict. Only Philadelphia property could be put up for bail. Ten percent was acceptable from a Philadelphia bank account only. Did I want to raise another $500,000? Not really. More havoc? Surely. Everyone was all tapped out anyway. From him. Michael let the house go into foreclosure for nonpayment, under my name. Funny, after drug issues and lawsuits, he put it in my name to protect me. I wasn't feelin' it. Creditors and collection companies chased me for outstanding bills that he ignored. He let his life insurance policy lapse for nonpayment. So now, he was not only trouble, he was worthless trouble!

What the hell had he been using the money for? His useless schemes? His whores? The lies, cheating, trouble, collateral damage… why should I even raise the money? Scouring Michael's office, finding tax records, the urge to go into his computer pulled me. The thought of invading his privacy hadn't plagued me since just after his cheating drug days, knowing his cell phone and email passwords for years from him jotting things down around where he needed the information, little notes and intel crumbled and discarded. As the designated trash collector in the house, his actual garbage pail was a flow of information as it poured out of the pail into a bag. I kept and saved it all, hoping I'd never need to use it again.

In front of his computer, I opened AOL without using the password, clicked on Mail Saved on PC. Way more than I was looking for. My heart, hardened as it was from him, took a hit. The pain, so sharp, it took my breath away. My body trembling, adrenaline on overdrive. I couldn't pull my burning eyes from the screen, completely blown away, yet not surprised at all, disgusted by how deeply pathological Michael truly was. So past done.

There were four serious romantic, sexual and long-term relationships with other women, in at least the last year. Four! Dina, in town, real estate and oil business with her brothers. Julienne, in Florida, alias Jade, Jersey City real estate. Jane, in Virginia, keeping his bone-graft patent safe. Lita, close enough, RTC inside track, cocaine connection. All simultaneously. He had a few that had fallen off. And a couple of stragglers that hung around here and there.

The draw could not have been the sex. Impossible. Granted, he was good-looking, in great shape, but had no skills, or was just too self-centered to acquire them. His allure baffled me. His juggling skills were unprecedented. And where did he find the time? Reading on, the love, sex, escapades, gifts, plans, the promise of private jets, the bubbly, the life. The duplicity. Money, power—he talked the talk. Damn, I didn't give his deceptive skills enough credit! The last year or two of his life, at the very least, was all lies, empty boasting, empty promises, revolving around his egotistical agenda.

This was not about my loss and love of my husband. That died too long ago to remember. This was about justice, retribution, dignity. Sharpened claws, I was the predator, not sleeping until my mission was complete. None of these bitches were gonna get away with it without a word or two from me! Neither was he!

A cover letter for each whore bitch:

To Michael's Pig,

Did you really think you were special?

Here is some reading material for you from your fellow pigs in his pig pen. I've had enough of yours.

You all enjoy rollin' in the dirt, with your Pig Daddy.

You're all a bunch of dirty pigs. Just like him. Now, you can all fight over the pieces of his pig pie.

And, for the record, I was the best he's ever had!

The Wife

Each whore was gonna get to read all the other bitches' emails in her own special file, personalized just for her! Sent from his email. Send. Absolutely liberating! Satisfaction with a smile. It wouldn't do a damn thing but enlighten his whores and make me feel better. Printing three copies of every page was complete, for me, my attorney, and for Pig Daddy to reread as he sat in a cell, with nothing but his hand and his inmates. The piles sat across the desk. Laughing out loud, suddenly, my tears came, my face in my hands, crying for it all, for us all. A paper ruffled. My eyes shot up. Mike stood there, paper in his hand, reading, tears. Reaching to grab it from him, he pulled away, his eyes glued. Lost in horror and confusion, he couldn't speak. He handed me the paper:

Oh, babe, thank you so much for our perfect weekend in Brigantine. Was such a beautiful sight seeing you spending time with Mia on the beach. She loves you. I love you. So happy we found each other. Looking forward to making more memories together.

Dina, his number one whore bitch. Mia, her daughter, just a year older than Mike. Brigantine, town next to Atlantic City.

"Mike, come here, baby! I'm so sorry!"

He came to my side of the desk and broke down. Taking him on my lap and in my arms, as he crumbled into sobs, I cried with him, for him.

"Honey, I don't know if daddy was planning on leaving me, but—"

"You mean us."

"He would never abandon you. You're his children."

Tears halted, his anger came. "Ma! Wake up! He already has! He's in jail! He has another family! That's why he never came to my games anymore! Or met us at the hotel. And why he was never home! Now everything makes sense!"

I couldn't let him read anything from the other piles. Then he would know she wasn't the only one!

"Baby! I need you to calm down. Just breathe, easy. We both know there's no excuse for any of it, but your father is not well. His sense of reality is all screwed up. He snapped under pressure. Please don't take it personally. He's sick, honey."

He flared. "I told you, Ma! I knew he was doing something wrong! Remember in the summer, I thought he was cheating on you when you could never reach him! And what about when I found the straw in his gum! The coke straw! He told me it must have been from a long time ago. He's so full of shit! What an asshole!"

"You're absolutely right. Just know he does love you, even if he can't the right way." I had to make him believe, he needed to feel loved, even from his unhinged father.

"I don't want to talk about it anymore, Mom. I'll be in my room."

Grabbing his hand as he got up. "Mike, please don't leave the house right now. I'm here for you and will never let anything happen to you. So is our family. I can't handle worrying about you!"

Mike wiped my tear. "Don't worry, Ma. I won't leave you, I promise. I'll be upstairs." My son's promise I believed.

My discoveries—Michael's other life, him wanting everything in my name, promises of a future to others, a few others! His words to his bitches.

Don't worry, baby. Everything's gonna happen just the way I planned. Things will be different very soon.

What did he have planned for me? A man of immediate gratification without conscience or remorse, what was my purpose in his grand plan? A means, yet an obstacle? How dispensable was I? Bump me off, take the money and run? I laughed to myself, nervously. The more all this unraveled, the more it all plays out too much like a movie. This was my life, damnit! Was he planning to have me undetectably poisoned, and the fortune in my name left to my children in trust of him? Or drug me and throw me in a psych ward? Drugs were Michael's expertise. No! He wouldn't, I'm the mother of his children! Or would he? Even questioning, I knew the answer.

The more I watched this movie called my life, the more I wanted him to stay put away, guilty or not. Michael's speech about changing at the visit was to have me believe his love and not take his imaginary fortune and leave him, to play me before anything went down. He always tried to tug at my heartstrings, only when his hands were tied behind his back. Not this time. Now it was time for me to play with his. Sorry-ass lying loser behind bars, arrogant-ass lying loser uncaged. He was cheating all that time he didn't touch me, and I was depressed while he raged over Gino. Unbelievable! The brazen nerve! All of those times he was supposedly trying to make a few bucks, he was just making time. He lied to one whore to see another, countless times. I mapped out his web of lies. Incredible!

Saturday, finally catching up with sleep after my all-nighter, his family was mortified. They wouldn't lose me or my children. It was he who had lost us. I comforted them. "We're family. None of this was anyone's choice but Michael's."

Tuesday came. Mom's surgery was a success! God is good! Raven already had the same suspicion of Michael's plans for me. Mom and Aunt Belle shouldn't know. To add salt to all my wounds, while I was at the hospital, my accountant, Dick, informed me that after an audit on Michael, the IRS stated I owed $250,000 from our personal returns which Michael finagled! Reviewing it, my signature was Michael's chicken scratch! He forged my name to all the fudged returns! This I needed to fight. Dick said he would work on it. I had no money to pay him at that time. He alluded to other forms of payment, which I was not willing to extend, and chose to overlook. "Just find me someone exactly like you."

Laughing it off, I told him I'd be on the lookout, grateful for his help, and would one day repay him. Not with my goods! Heading back to Mom's room, there was so much I couldn't share with her, but I just needed her to be okay. We all did. My boys and Aidan couldn't visit and see her like this. Hearing her voice on the phone comforted them. The daily runs home were exhausting, but my boys needed to feel me with them.

"Test me for every disease under the sun. Please." Dr. Schwabner to the rescue again. *Clean. God, I can't tell you how good you are!*

I resented Michael for all the years he took from me, for all my time he took from my children to run around for him and his messes, for all the danger he'd put me in on too many levels. I could have had a peaceful, free life, with great sex, all not with him! Never too late!

Mom offered an analogy of the situation from her hospital bed. "He's like Pig-Pen from the Peanuts gang, a mess follows him wherever he goes."

Laughter filled her hospital room. Pig-Pen. Mom didn't know about my cover letter to Michael's herd yet...that extra sense!

"It's better than crying!" Mom was right.

Michael's letter came, with a Restoration of Marriage prayer booklet. He apologized for things he didn't mention, clueless that I knew. He said he forgave me for my trespasses, too. Gino. Restoration? After his destruction? A kiss? Really? Was he for real? He wrote of us being soul mates. I wasn't so sure he had a soul! Loving me forever, being grateful for me in his life. The funny thing was I believed he meant it. Because he was trapped in a cell! His feelings were so transient, like a chameleon, to protect himself, or prey on someone. Feeling safe with him behind bars was unspoken; meanwhile, the world spoke out against him.

Play it right. He might just get out again. Anything is possible with him. Anything. Keep him where he needs to stay, guilty, or not. I need to protect.

Later that week, exiting the elevator to the prison visiting floor, I saw him at the corner window. First, I asked the guards for paper and pen and wrote a list: Dina, Jade, Jane, Lita. At his window, standing, peering at him, I slammed my list against it!

"I know everything! About the love, the sex, the trips, the gifts! I know your whole life with these dirty whores! You filthy pig hustler!"

Michael's jaw dropped open, his tongue fumbling for words. The guards gave me a hand motion to keep it down but keep goin'!

They smiled, mouthing their words. "Mmm-hm, you go girl!"

Letting me loose for a while, one came over. "Ma'am. I'm sorry. It's time to go." She winked.

Putting my face close. "Feel very lucky you're behind this glass, motherfucker!" I strided away, not looking back.

Michael received my care package: every email to reminisce on while he sat in his hole. The postage was expensive, but priceless! He'd betrayed me so deeply, so cunningly, a sick cruel game he played in his head to manipulate me to stay. With the drugs to manipulate everyone. Now, he wanted to outsmart the world? But wait, a cheater does not a criminal make. That would make almost everybody a criminal! His dirty dick aside, he did show enough signs of an innocent man to the people who knew him.

Mason called me, having just met with Michael in Philadelphia. "I cannot divulge my conversation with my client to you. Attorney-client confidentiality. Anything Michael admitted to, I can't tell you." Code for he admitted to something or some things, and I would have to ask him directly.

Michael called the house. I let him talk.

"Michael, I won't desert you." I had my reasons. Our entire lives together he knew me to be his good Barbra. I was who I was. Discovering he was not remotely the man I believed I married and loved changed everything. It changed me. I needed to remain a pawn to keep him where he needed to stay and appear devoted, though that could never be again. I needed to wait for his next move to make mine. Knowing he was capable of anything, I was ready.

He boasted to me. "Barb, you'd be so proud of me. I had an opportunity to make good money in here and I turned it down. And Lita wrote me, but I didn't write back. I swear! You can check!"

Didn't matter. Didn't care. He hinted to something about having had an idea and keeping quiet. So vague. He couldn't say anything over the phone. Helping him try to fight or sink didn't change me leaving him, a secret until time.

Amazed at how I stood by him in one capacity or another, Mason knew it wasn't because I wanted to run for president one day! He'd known me with Michael since we were dating, through everything.

"Barbra. You are most undoubtedly, positively the strongest woman I have ever met in my life! A great woman."

"Thank you, Mason. Possibly the strongest and stupidest? I think that strength sometimes works against me, like nothing can bring me down, not even the likes of my husband, and maybe I stay too long. We don't know how strong we are until we're tested. Michael has been the ultimate test for the last decade! He's worse than a defiant child!"

This time was different than any other time. No pains to put aside. There were none. This was the end of my road with him—I was done. He could never hurt me again. I did nothing wrong. He was in jail. I was not. God, how I thanked my lucky stars and angels! I didn't care if the DA took every last dime. And they did! My freedom to take care of my boys was everything.

Michael brought on two reputable attorneys to assist Mason on the Brooklyn case, Santo and Les. Knowing Santo in social circles, I was amenable to meeting at his home.

"Tell us, Barbra," Santo said. "What do you know about Michael's wrongdoings in his enterprise? Please, be candid. You can talk to us, we're on Michael's side."

"I don't know. Only what everyone else does. I'm sure Mason knows much more than I do."

Les laughed with disbelief, as if I was hiding something.

I asserted, "Just recently, Michael did hint to me in code when I spoke to him that he might have known something. Mason told me he can't divulge what he has admitted to. All very vague. The more I didn't know, the better and safer for me."

Santo shook his head. "Les, I believe she doesn't know."

He kept his attention toward Les. "Jason told me yesterday they have a slam-dunk case against Michael. Slam-dunk! He said besides all the forged signatures and info, they have evidence through DNA that Michael matched tainted tissue with good blood."

I had to interject, directing at Santo. "Wait a minute! Are you saying that Michael saved and used good blood from his good donors that were within the criteria as samples to send to the processing companies for approval for bad tissue from diseased donors?"

"Exactly. I believe we're just working on lessening the sentence here."

I became indignant. "Michael may be crazy. But he would never endanger lives! He would never do that! Maybe the DA is baiting you with speculation."

Les shot Santo a look. "She doesn't know anything."

"I'm sorry, I'm talking off the cuff. I'll be quiet now. This is Michael's fight."

Santo jumped in. "No! Barbra, please, if there is anything you feel you need to add, please do."

I couldn't trust a soul. How does the DA divulge such info, just like that, to the opposing side? Then again, I wasn't a lawyer, and didn't know how the legal system really worked. Some of it I didn't like. Who's on whose side? Who's lying? Who's telling the truth? Who's only in it for the dollar? Who's only scrapping for career advancement or recognition? Was anyone just about the damn truth besides me? My life with Michael meant the truth always eluded me. I simply wanted to believe he was the good man I remembered so long ago, a man grateful for the second chance he'd been given. I also wanted to believe he would never cheat on me again, too. Look how that turned out!

15

The Trap

December 18, 2007, Philadelphia courthouse, Michael's Philadelphia attorney, Vic Perino, got him out on ROR! Release on recognizance! How the hell did the judge agree to lift the five-million-dollar bail? Just like that? He was still out on bail in Brooklyn. He could just roam free? Didn't sound right. Something beyond this hearing was going on. My feeling was right! Michael got out! God help us. The judge pounded his gavel. Michael needed to be brought back to the prison for processing before he was released. It would take some time, maybe into the next day. After our families went home, his dad and I had a bite to eat, waiting.

"Barbra, honey. I'm sorry, I wasn't right sometimes, but dat's my son! I couldn't help it! He's an asshole, but I love da son-of-a-bitch! You're an angel. Don't you forget it! I don't know what we woulda done wit'out you. Dank you."

Michael free for even a minute? The bondsman was in the back of my brain. We hugged, then ate. Was a long day. Was gonna be a long night. GM went home to his distraught wife. Tough spot when your child is monster. I was protecting my children against so many things from their father—they had seen too much. They would make good choices, live good lives, be good people. I felt it. Still prayed. In a hotel alone near the Philadelphia prison to pick him up when released, everyone was so worried about me.

"Please, don't worry," I told my loved ones. "Hey! I'm a Brooklyn girl! I only got tougher since then!"

Prison had thugs with bars and barbed wire. Brooklyn had thugs roaming free. I had no fear then. Now? Fuhgeddaboudit! You can take the girl outta Brooklyn. But you can't never take the Brooklyn outta the girl!

* * *

My parents took me outta Brooklyn. And what did I do? Went right back down, straight outta college into my grandparents' old first-floor apartment, all to myself, in the heart of Brooklyn-Bensonhurst, my second home growing up. A shy, insecure girl, at least I thought, but damned if I didn't sleep with a knife under my mattress, ready to strike if anyone came through that window! Protected though, everyone knew me, Castellano's Pork Store, Alba bakery, Tasty Bagels, Sid the shoemaker, even Dime Savings Bank. Grandma set up a neighborhood watch before she went back to join Grandpa in San Diego at their retirement house.

A girl walking the streets alone at night in Brooklyn was like playing Russian roulette. I carried pepper spray in my hand, positioned and ready in my bag, head up, tough with confidence. Weakness was an easy target. I saw that on a TV self-defense special, supposed to deter these dopes in the street from attacking, hoping I would never have to put it to the test. In Brooklyn, it was wishful thinking.

One dark night, walking home from work right across the street from my apartment building, these two jerk-offs came on either side of me.

"Hey baby, what you got there?"

My handbag or tits? I was gonna kick ass to protect them both! It all happened so quick. One of them put his hand on my arm, I threw my arms up and got his hand off me, then undercut him in the nuts real hard! He doubled over. I looked at the other one.

"You want some?"

I slipped my hand back in my bag, pepper spray in hand, pointing my bag toward them as if a gun.

"Don't you fuckin' touch me, you little punks! Do you know who I am? You want trouble? You gonna get it! Get the fuck outta here if you know what's good for you! Now!"

They backed off quick and ran in the other direction. I walked into my apartment building nice. Pussies! Most of them were. Thing was these low hoods thought they were so tough. But they didn't know who they were dealing with. If they pushed around the wrong someone, they were gonna be found in a dumpster somewhere by daylight. It *was* Brooklyn, after all.

* * *

There was that Brooklyn in the girl! Love my Brooklyn. I saved my own life that night and didn't even know I had it in me! We usually don't until we need to.

Mason called. "Barb, the DA is ordering him to appear in Brooklyn court the next morning after his release. He agreed to that as a stipulation of his release."

"What's he gonna do? Say no?"

"Unless he wants to stay in! There's speculation all over the press, the DA suspects he will run. They probably have eyes on him everywhere."

"They'd had eyes on him, and me, since it all first hit. He's not goin' anywhere. What do you think I've been doing for the last two years?"

We had a laugh. Levity heals the soul, just like my boys—everything good and happy. I missed them. Parked by the gate in my truck, when and where the officer had told me to wait, my eyes peered everywhere. The sky was dark. In my mirror, a shadow was walking from down the road. Double-checking my doors were locked, I saw that the guy kept walking. This time, a shadow emerged from the dark driveway behind the gate. It was him. The guard let him through. He came to me. I didn't budge. He dropped his bag and put his arms around me, trembling uncontrollably, sobbing. As he collapsed, I struggled.

He couldn't cry enough tears he's caused.

"Michael. Stand up. You're pulling me down."

All I could feel was pity for the man he'd become, nothing else. The man I fell in love with so many years ago was long gone. Did he ever exist? Did I make him up in my head? Did he make him up in my head?

He crouched, peering around, murmuring. "I'm sure we're being followed."

"It would make sense." I brushed him off me.

Authorities outside, Tom or not, his Houdini capabilities never left me. It was Michael. He wanted Boston Market and pizza, then to the hotel to take a shower and rest before we drove home that night. Next, the tough part, knowing what else he'd want to do. Ready for Act I, I had to take one for the team, filled with dread.

"Hold on. Did you take an AIDS test in there?"

"A couple of months ago during intake in the prison, was negative. I was in the 'hole.'" In whose hole?

This needed to be the best performance of my lifetime. His touch, as if the first time ever touching a woman, repulsed me. Cringing inside, I crawled out of my skin, out of my body to stomach it. Blazin' Sally! No love for him, dead inside, he killed it. I wished I was alone.

"So what exactly did you do, Michael?" Once we were at the hotel, I was certain our room was bugged.

"I had a feeling there was something going on. I let it go, never questioned it. I know it was wrong to keep quiet. The money was too good."

He was lying for someone's sake, mine or the bug's. There was more to this. How much more? He was guilty.

"I have to ask. All these funeral directors, independent of each other, have taken pleas or deals, admitting guilt. They all have one thing in common. You. How could you not be in on it?"

"I didn't do all the things they say I did. They put everything they can in the indictment and see what sticks." He didn't answer the question.

Pitifully in my arms, his voice quivered. "Barb, should I run?"

I needed him to listen to me, taking everything in me to hold him, caress his head. "Honey, you can't do that, you need to be a man, face what you've done, and fight for the rest. Our family put everything they have on the line for you. You'll always have your family."

"You won't leave me?"

Daddy always taught me, never show your hand. In cards and in life. I needed to beat him at his own game. "Haven't I always been here for you?" A question with a question.

He stayed in my arms, just where I needed him to stay. Then we headed back home. I drove. When we arrived there was a happy welcome home. The boys were happy to see him, though a bit afraid to approach him. It had been almost three months, and he wasn't "away for work helping people" this time. His parents were in tears, his mom hysterical but relieved.

We had some tea together, our usual. I brought the boys mugs in their room, and joined Michael on the loveseat in our bedroom, the door closed. Loveseat. Laughable.

"How could you do that to me again? And again? And again? All at the same time? Should I go on? You cheat. You lie. You know you don't deserve me." I had every damn right but needed to back it up, unless I was trying to push him out the door to run! "Just tell me, Michael. Why?"

He answered with his routine rationalizing. "Everything I did was for business to take care of you guys. The oil deal, real estate, patent, business. It was always about business!" Futile question. Skirting answers. "Barb! I was even in a hotel room with a guy! The CEO of the water company! Do you know how that made me feel?"

"I really don't care if he bent you over and spanked you! We all have choices, Michael! For the last eight, yours have been very, very bad! Always for your own gain! You don't think I've had choices? If I made choices like yours, I coulda laid down and gotten all your attorney fees squashed! Hell! I coulda bent over and gotten you less time! But I didn't, did I? Woulda saved us a pretty penny! You're a hustler and a liar! Plain and simple!"

Oh shit! What did I do? He can't disappear! I was praying they had surveillance outside our house! Ready for Tom, if I needed him.

He gave up, knowing he deserved so much worse, and took a pillow. "I'm gonna sleep on the couch. I know you don't want me in our bed." My bed.

Silent, my eyes told him he was right. He set up on the couch in the family room, with our big, beautiful Christmas tree and fireplace. Feeling peaceful with him downstairs, peeking over the hallway balcony to make nice with him, Mike sat with his father, talking. He wouldn't run. His boys would keep him home for the night. The morning was another day of reckoning. What crap might he be filling my son's head with? Good thing Mike saw through his father's bullshit. Reassuring, but so sad.

"Goodnight, guys. Love you."

A hug and kiss to Gerry, Mike came up the stairs waving me to his room. I followed. "You okay, love?"

He nodded. "Thank you, Mom."

"For what, honey?"

"For our pact. It helped me a lot, made me feel better to know what was going on, and for always being here for us. Just for everything, Mom."

Kissing him on the head. "You know I'm magic, love. I'll always be here for you."

Mike smiled. My son had no idea how close his father came to making me disappear, too many times to count, whether his twisted rage or his warped sense of entitlement and need for immediate gratification. Every time I told my children I was magic, I prayed that it be true. I don't know how I survived it all. I feel truly blessed.

"All that matters to me in the world is that you two are good. Love you so much. Good night."

"Love you too, Mom. Night."

I glanced in the fireplace mirror. He was there, a thousand ways for him to escape into the night surely running through his mind. At my bedside, I kneeled. "Dear God, when I open my eyes tomorrow morning, please let him be on the couch. Protect me and my boys. Protect us all."

I needed to stay alert! My eyes were winning the fight to close, listening for the door. I couldn't fight fate. The alarm clock sounded. My eyes opened to the looming clouds. The sun out of sight, still there, I felt it. Quietly dashing, one eye over the balcony, on the couch were crumpled blankets. No head or arms, no outline of his body. My windpipe shut down. Wait! The blankets moved and Michael's arm came into view. Thank you, God!

"Boys, go wake Daddy. He'd love to see you." Staying power... worked so far!

Michael asked us all for forgiveness, with his regret. His parents embraced him, his mom clutching him as if he was being torn from her. I couldn't imagine. My heart clenched for my boys as Michael hugged them.

Gerry's doe eyes looked up to his father. "See you later, Dad." Michael rubbed his son's head without a word.

Mike, pensive, pulled back from Michael's arms. "Dad, are you going to be home for Christmas?"

"Yeah, pal. I'll be home for Christmas." He pulled both boys in for one last hug before we left, his expression blank. Mike's eyes were lost, searching, knowing his father was lying again. I took my boys in my arms, cradling them, helpless. There was nothing I could do to take away the plight upon their lives. Leaving my babies at that moment was like tearing my heart out of my chest and leaving it home.

As we approached the courthouse, the press circled like vultures. Sunglasses, rain or shine, I stayed feet behind him or ducked behind his big brother, John. Reaching the elevator, people peered at him and moved away.

Mason whispered. "One of the families. Some of them are at every court appearance."

Michael guilty or not, I felt for them. Anyone with a heart would have to. When the elevator arrived, Mason motioned for them to go first.

"We'll wait for the next." Who could blame 'em?

Press everywhere, Michael sat with us in the benches before he was called up. All so encompassing, the suits, officers, reporters, video cameras. The judge's bench, gavel in view, commanded respect. Above, the words so profound. "In God We Trust." To the right was a white door. My first time in court with Michael flashed in my mind. He had shuddered, pointing out the door they took him through the day he was indicted in Brooklyn, almost two years before, transported to Rikers.

"Barb, I don't think I'm getting outta here today. They wanna keep me in. I'm not comin' out. This is it."

Searching for words, none could come, putting my hand on his. Secret hope. Secret relief. My babies and I would be safe. So would the world. As pitiful as he appeared paled in comparison to how dangerous his mind was. My heart remained lodged in my throat with every moment. I lamented how he and all of this came to pass. Inescapable. Inevitable.

The proceedings began. The DA found a discrepancy with the bail papers on my house and presented it to the judge. And there it was. They found a way to revoke the bail. We'd had the bail on the house approved by the DA and the judge since day one, two years before. To me, it was a grand orchestration to keep him in, and I was grateful they found a way. The judge then gave Tom a chance to rectify the paperwork and pounded his gavel, adjourning court until later that afternoon. By law, I guess he had to. A formality before he officially denied the appeal and revoked the current bail, I could feel it. Michael was taken through that white door to be held until we scurried around to correct the papers and reconvene later in the day. All for naught, I knew. Court resumed hours later. They brought Michael back in. The discrepancy was not met properly. The judge accused Tom of possibly lying to him. Tom was on the stake, or was he in on getting Michael in? Praying Tom came out of this okay, he only tried to help me.

The judge pounded his gavel. "Let it be known the current bail is now revoked. A new bail will be set forth."

Revoked? Do we lose everything? Do we get it back?

The judge asked the DA. "Counselor, what is your recommendation for bail?"

"We strongly recommend the defendant be remanded."

"Well, that won't do." He pounded it again. "Let it be noted bail is now reset for three-point-five million dollars. And previous set bail will be rescinded to all parties immediately."

Impossible for Michael to meet. Relief! Everyone saved. Everyone safe. Release from my own private prison! They cuffed him again to take him away. He stared at me with sheer fright, powerless.

My eyes spoke to him. "My heart breaks for you."

As I approached the truck, Michael's sorry set of circumstances saddened me, despite how relieved I was. It didn't have to be this way. I opened my truck door and on the ground was a shiny penny. I picked it up, knowing. Mom and Aunt Belle always talked about "pennies from heaven," signs from past loved ones. Angels watching over.

I held the penny to my heart and looked up to the sky. "Now, I'm a believer. Daddy, I know you're with me."

It dawned on me—December 19, 2007. We lost Dad this day, one year ago. Poetic. A shiver ran through me, still hurting to my core. My mood brightened, knowing his spirit was with me always. Smiling, making my way through traffic. To home. To my boys. My mind flashed forward, like a freight train running full speed ahead, with so many paths in front of me. Which one to take? What would be my fate? I had to tell my children their father would not be coming home. Ever. Entering the house, the peace floated through me, embracing the quiet. The eye of the storm had passed.

I gathered my boys, holding their hands. "I'm so sorry, but Daddy's not coming home."

Their eyes wide. "Ever?"

"No, honey."

Mike buried his head in my shoulder and cried. Gerry stared in shock. Both in my arms, I comforted them. They lost their father, again, a bittersweet reality, safer for them, for us all, so grateful I was still there for them.

Christmas Eve was quiet—just us. Michael's family canceled the usual traditional Christmas Eve with the whole family. Killed me for my boys to be deflated, hurt most in all of this, but I understood.

I made the best of it for them. "How about you open your presents early this year!"

"Awesome!"

They needed cheer any way I could give it. Selling what little jewelry I had gave them Christmas. I planned to sell everything I could and donate the rest. They played their new Nintendo Wii and Xbox 360 all night...selling back their old systems and games had been a big help! Mom had taught me well, though I wish I could have learned better from her how to pick a good man. Ob Christmas Day, my family came early to fill the void. The boys tore open more presents with Aidan on that bright day, so grateful. After everyone had gone, my boys and I cozied on the couch in front of the glistening tree and fireplace.

"Did you guys have an okay Christmas?"

They hugged me. "This is one of the best Christmases we've ever had. We really thought it was going to be the worst. Thanks, Mom, we love you."

Hugs and love, the three of us. "You boys will always have each other. Always be there for each other."

Visiting Michael at Rikers again, I brought him the clothes his mom cleaned and items he needed.

"Oh, girlfriend! You're better than me! If I were you, I'd take a nice shit on 'em and send 'em back to him dirty!" Maria, the one with wisdom always sprouting out of her ass like rainbows, told me afterwards.

"I know, love! Call me crazy. You know me. Keep it straight, baby. I'm still divorcing his dirty ass. I just couldn't desert him completely yet."

This time he was in general population, referred to as "gen pop." He made friends, no doubt. The real Michael reared his ugly head, humility gone, giving me orders. Predictable. I refused his calls until he changed his tune. He changed enough.

"Barb. I have a couple of friends in here that are still married for fifteen or twenty years. They make it work with family weekend and week-long trailer visits. The prison promotes family for the prisoners. It keeps their demeanor steady."

My silence told him that I needed to completely sever myself from him. To avoid the media frenzy that would swoop down on me, I needed to wait a minute. Hell, I waited this long! Feeling my distance, he grew ill-tempered and nasty, his arrogance and indignance insufferable.

Mike rocked in his desk chair, calm, thoughtful. "Ma, Daddy doesn't really love us. How could he do those things and put us in this position? Why would he go on vacations with his girlfriend's kid when he has us? Why? He had a secret family."

"He just can't love you the right way. He can't help himself. He's mentally ill. He told me to tell you he's sorry. He can't cry enough tears to show you how much."

"Yeah, that's great, Ma! He does something wrong, cries about it. Does something wrong, cries about. Does something wrong! Cries about it! Yeah, okay! He's sorry!" Out of the mouths of babes.

"I'm with you, his 'sorry' means nothing. He never changed. He's proven that."

"And Ma, you must be the stupidest wife ever! You shoulda left him a long time ago!"

"Mike, you don't know what you're talking about."

"I know enough! I know the things he did to you! He has no respect for you! I don't know why you stayed!"

"No matter what, I have never and will never lose my respect for myself! I'm still here and not going anywhere! He was not in his right mind on the drugs, but he was my husband, your father. In marriage, when one falls, you hold each other up, there to lean on. The vows we took were what I lived by. Daddy tested them all."

"He treated them like a sick joke!"

"Make no mistake, honey. I won't stay married to him. Lying and cheating, hurting is his way, never to be trusted."

"If you ever go back to him, I'll never forgive you."

"Baby, just for now, things have to seem to stay just the way they are to everyone, even to Grandma and Grandpa from Brooklyn. You get me? I'm trusting you. You need to trust me."

"Tell me why and I'll trust you."

"It's very complicated. Remember I told you if you shouldn't know the details, you can't ask me twice. I'm confiding in you. He's over the edge, his sense of reality is completely warped. The time will come soon."

He didn't need to know how dangerous his father was. I needed to wait until after his plea and sentencing in court.

"Okay."

"I've had my moments, but I don't hate him, and you shouldn't either. Hate poisons you inside. I pity him. He's a tortured soul."

"Yeah, Ma! I'm sure he felt tortured when he was boning his bitches!"

"Okay, funny guy! Got your point!"

"Sorry, Ma."

"You're right. I am so unbelievably proud of you. You're gonna be all right. Everything will be, promise. I need you to think of the good things. Look on the bright side."

"Ma, the only way there's ever a bright side is when there's a really dark side."

"How'd you get so smart? But there are still so many more good things to think about than bad. Why don't you ask him yourself whatever it is you want to know? There's no reason to be afraid. He's in jail. We're safe."

Safe in more ways than he knew.

"Will you take me to see him? And stay with me the whole time? Like every minute?"

I dreaded the thought. "Of course! Are you sure you want to? I told you how it is in there. I won't lie to you, it's not nice. Give it a day or two. Think about it. If you really want to go, I'll take you. You can handle it. Grandpa will come. But not Gerry. I'm glad he doesn't want to go."

On the bus over the bridge, elbow to elbow, everything around us felt dirty. Pointing out LaGuardia Airport so close to this criminal island called Rikers, and the different objects protruding from the water in case of a prison break, he was fascinated, as if on a tour. Reaching the other side, a long wait any way around it, we entered. Taking Mike and his grandpa through this seven-point check system was not my idea of a day out with my thirteen-year-old son.

Waiting for the bus to Michael's building, an officer came with a drug dog, telling everyone to remain seated with hands on their laps, or stand with their hands in front of them. The dog sniffed by everyone once. Then again. The dog kept going back to this one lady.

Mike had to see her taken away to be strip-searched for drug posses-sion. Anyone caught would be prosecuted. People went to extreme measures to smuggle drugs into inmates. The prison had extreme measures for detection and prosecution. Continuing the tour, I explained every step of the way, answering his questions. Riding the bus through the compound, Mike pointed out the high fences with the coiled barbed wire surrounding us, penning us in. Where in my life would I ever believe I'd find myself taking my son through Rikers Island, one of the toughest prisons known, to visit his father? This was not what I had intended for my children.

We finally arrived at the building. Another officer and drug dog. We all lined up outside to be sniffed again, once, twice, clean. All the prisoners from the windows of the building in front of us were calling out to the visitors, like caged animals in a zoo, many of them waving. Mike laughed and waved back, amused. Better he found humor than paralyzing fear. We heard prisoners shouting crude comments to a woman with a hot pink jacket.

Mike shifted his eyes to us. "That's not cool."

I nodded, hiding my fury over him being exposed to it all. Inside, the line was long and slow. The holding area was crammed, the air thick. Before going on line to get in, our turn came to check his items. The list was very stringent. Mike watched in amazement. GM remained stoic. The officers looked through every page of every newspaper and magazine, for possible blades and such. They took off mailing labels, the glue and ink, and info, all dangers. Only certain colors and types of clothes were permitted for the prisoners so there was no chance of mimicking the guards' uniforms in any way, shape, or form. Only certain types of shoes—high-end sneakers were not allowed. Inmates got killed over them. No shoelaces. Choking was a hazard.

Once again taking off shoes for another airport-style protocol, we finally got in. Then one last physical search was required for each of us. We entered the last waiting area, given an invisible stamp of approval before entering. Mike gaped at the wall-sized steel sliding door, swallowing hard. We waited, watching TV. Finally called, the steel wall opened. Mike's eyes wouldn't leave me, not letting go of my hand as we entered. My heart hurt for my child. GM's eyes were sad yet strong. I could not imagine how he felt visiting his son in prison. The door slid closed behind us with a boom, as if it swallowed us up. We put our right hand under the light. The steel wall in front of us opened. The warehouse-sized room was filled with rows of small round plastic tables, and small plastic chairs set across. The officer directed us where to sit and wait. Another big steel wall door opened, orange jumpsuits scattering into the room. There he was, jumpsuit and slippers, swaggering toward us. He looked hard, worn. Michael was elated. They hugged. Prisoners were not allowed to hug visitors for more than a second, to guarantee no chance of transferring any paraphernalia, which was a relief to me. Michael saw my eyes and stayed where he was. We all sat. Mike looked at his father, afraid to speak.

Opening the floor for my son's afflictions. "Mike, you wanted to ask Dad a couple of things, didn't you?"

He shook his head.

"Mike, didn't you want to ask him about why he did some of the things he did?"

"Go ahead. Ask me, pal."

Mike let loose. "Why did do all those illegal things? Why did you cheat on Mommy? And with so many bitches! With your new family! Why did you take the drugs? Remember? That straw I found? We found stuff everywhere in the house, too!"

"I'm truly sorry for all the things I've done. I didn't do everything they're accusing me of."

He wasn't going to skirt my son! This child needed answers from the source. "Michael, he asked you why."

He shot me a look that said an unspoken, *You fucking bitch.*

I shot him a look back with an unspoken, *Go fuck yourself and man up, if only for your son!*

"I made a mistake, pal. I just made a mistake."

I was burning with rage from his dismissive response to my pained son.

"That's it? That's all you have to say? 'I made a mistake'?" Despicable.

My son has gotten exactly what he expected from his father. Disappointment. Silent, twisted, I monitored the small talk between the three of them. A buzzer sounded, not a moment too soon. Officers called the prisoners first. We had to remain seated and wait to be prompted. Making our way back through the entire system again, I couldn't get us out of there and across that bridge fast enough.

Our asses barely touched the seat of the truck before Mike grabbed the bull by the horns. "Daddy's full of shit. I bet he's guilty of everything! He's a bullshitter, and nobody's gonna change my mind!" My son had that extra sense our family carried, too young to know it, or for me to tell him.

I let him release and curse. He had just visited his father in prison. The following week, Mike wanted to see him again. Though so angry he felt bad for him. I understood his affliction, hoping he understood mine a bit better.

"Ma, Gerry definitely shouldn't visit."

"No telling your father off, deal?"

"I wouldn't do that to him. He's in prison already, what's cursing him off gonna do?" He laughed. "I did think about it, though. How do you know everything, Ma?"

"I really don't, honey." Sometimes I wish I did.

On a new adventure to Rikers, just me and Mike, this time there was a hand scanner. The officer scanned his hands, clean, relieved. They scanned my hands. I failed! Shocked, bewildered!

Mike pierced at me with suspicion. "What did you do, Ma?"

"I don't take drugs! How could I possibly have anything on my hands?"

A witty officer chimed in. "Maybe you just carry 'em."

Oooh, my razor tongue wanted to cut this fucker up! "Nice! In front of my son! I don't carry them either!" Turning from the asshole, toward the guard at the desk. "Does it tell you what kind of drug? Is it only illegal drugs?"

"Yes, ma'am, but we can't give out that information." The officer threw me a hint, sniffing. "It could be on dollar bills, the bins when you come here, or the bus handles. "Cocaine." I waited for her to confirm in some way.

The officer nodded. In the bathroom, I scrubbed my hands three times, with the special soap she gave me with the few other flunkies, holding a paper towel to touch anything as I made my way back to the desk. Failed! Baffled! Mike looked at me with disbelief. One more chance. Fail! Something was too embedded in my skin, a mystery for now. Mike calmed down. After the fails, we had a choice of having a visit behind the glass, or none. We took the visit.

"Ma, I'm sorry. I know you don't do drugs. I was afraid they were gonna take you away, like they did to that lady."

"I know, baby. I'm sorry it even happened. I need to check my truck. Your father used it a few times before he was indicted in Philadelphia. I bet I've been driving around with this stuff in my truck and on my hands all along. I need to sterilize everything. In the house, too. No one is to go in his office, got it? Don't say a word, okay?"

We visited Michael through the glass, separated. The gravity of it all hit Mike, suddenly, breathing in his whimpers, his eyes visibly wet. I cradled him close to me. My heart was splitting in two for my baby. My eyes teared, holding it in. I had to be strong for him.

What am I doing? Taking my son to see his weak, narcissistic, sociopathic, psychopathological criminal liar of a father, that still leaves a trail of shit for me to step in and clean up! How do I deny my son to see the truth? That self-serving bastard! This is not the life they should have!

Michael, weeping, had to walk away. Just added coward to his list! We left. Later at home, inspecting my truck, minute white numbing specks and granules were scattered everywhere. What did he do, sneeze into it? Trailing everywhere Michael had been, in my truck, in the house, every square inch was wiped and sterilized, twice, as if scrubbing him away. I wished it was that easy.

16

The Resolution

Suddenly, everyone wanted to come forward and tell me the truth. Friends, acquaintances, people I barely knew, even a couple of friends closest to me felt the need to share. Too little, too late. What about when it was happening? What if it happened to them? How would they all fucking like it! Michael's cruel, self-seeking escapades surfaced from the far past all the way to the present, spanning years in an alarming surge or purge of his sexual advances and affairs. My Dear John letter was spot on! At the tanning salon and gym in town hitting on women and affairs, when he was a resident and surgeon on-call screwing around, at a barbecue at our friend's house when Mike was just a baby, trying to get his old girlfriend in the bathroom. The list goes on. My husband was a fucking man-whore! The prick was now behind bars, so now it was safe to talk? And why did they tell me? Had to be for themselves! Because if it was for me, they would've told me when it was happening! All too much to comprehend. My skin thick as oak, my backbone steel, my heart diamond hard, nothing could break me.

What a cliché! Blinded by love. Thankful for people's honesty though it was way too delayed, I couldn't be more grateful that I didn't catch a damn disease! Why couldn't just one person have told me any kind of truth? Why? Wouldn't they want to know? Where was my Carly from *The Other Woman* even once?

Reid wanted to visit Michael. Maddie was not up to it. She'd never forgive him, heartbroken. Reid's reverence of him remained unwavering, and a bit unnerving, for his sake. Michael probably filled his head with apparitions of what Reid wanted to see. Over the past weeks, I had taken Eric, Louise, and Mike. This visit was different. I was different, overinformed, provocative, and so overdone. Reid sat back and watched the show.

"Your whore, Lita, called, left a few messages. As if she doesn't know you're locked up! She 'misses you so much, baby!' She 'can't wait for you to be in her arms where you belong!' Shall I go on? Obviously, she feels she has a reason to continue, though I wrote the letter and sent her your other pigs' emails. To piss me off, perhaps? Mission accomplished!"

"Why are you doing this?"

"I am flooded with new shit about your whoring all the time! You created this with your arrogant dirty dick!"

Michael's nostrils started to flare, his eyebrows raise. He snapped. "What about Gino? You fuckin' whore!" He got up.

"You don't really wanna dare compare my kiss with your dick-swingin' hustling, do you?"

He stormed away, officers receiving him. Reid gawked speechless. A show for the whole room! Michael, by the door, waiting to go through, paced furiously.

Oh, yeah! That's the Michael I know! He'll never change!

The door opened. The officers started to take the inmates through. Michael peered back.

Done with walking on broken eggshells and broken glass. My voice echoed across the entire room. "I shoulda fucked him!" The door closed.

Tensions only grew. My intolerance for his betrayals being thrown in my face from every direction became an involuntary action. Everybody that shared had no idea what they were doing to me. All too little, too late, but better late than never. Michael called later, yelling in his father's ear, cursing me. He turned to me and explained he was furious because I didn't give him one of the newspapers he wanted and gave him one he didn't want.

"Tell him to roll up all of his newspapers and shove 'em up his ass! Like the water man in the hotel room!"

His father looked at me puzzled.

"I'm not taking his calls! Who the hell does he think he is? Let him rot there alone!"

Soon nothing would make a difference. I was ridding him from my life. Michael's darkness would no longer eclipse my light.

New Year's Eve, with my children and in-laws when the ball dropped, we celebrated with kisses and hugs. I called my family, as I always did if I wasn't with them, the world a small, beautiful place. The boys fell off to sleep. Out in the city my old stomping grounds with my brother Ben, his girlfriend, Reva and their crowd, we partied all night at this hot club, Capitale. Memories came flooding back to me, there with Tiana and her crew a lifetime ago. Ti was crazy, but she had called it, Michael would pull the same shit five years later. Neither of us would imagine how outrageous, how scandalous! The club was beautiful, hot. The company couldn't have been better. Music pulsing through my body, lights flashing, dancing, talking, drinking. My escape, I released.

My New Year's resolution came over me, like the ball dropping. "I need to live, find my peace and my path, move forward, shake it all off. Tough haul. I'm game!"

First, divorce Michael. Second, separate living with his parents. Third, sell the house. From that, pay the DA. Make sure my IRS problem was squashed. And, finally, get rid of my overpriced, over-sized, overinsured Escalade ESV, LE. One step at a time, and more from there. My house needed to sell, my only security, my only way to pay the DA. Advice from Rue and everyone told me to wait, the market too soft. But if I didn't pay the $190,000 to the DA by September 30 I would be hit with a penalty of an additional $180,000! A total of $370,000 owed because of him! It burned me up that I had done nothing wrong, unknowingly signed papers my husband asked me to, thinking life was happy once again. Only debt and strife from this man, though he did give me the two best gifts of my life. My boys, hearts of a lion, needed a fighting chance in this world. He would only poison their futures for his own gain if given a chance. My curiosity got the best of me, agreeing to visit him at the Brooklyn DA's office, prior to a meeting to discuss a plea. Though he would be away for most of his life, I needed to tread carefully. With Michael, anything seemed possible.

The couple of snacks he was allowed to have went on the security belt with my bag. There I went again, thoughtful Barbra! To the man who could not have been more thoughtless and hurtful to me, not deserving of a second of my time! But I was free. Soon free from him! Humane or idiot? Maria told me I was outta my mind and shoulda injected poison in the snacks! Off the elevator, I picked up the phone on the wall. The woman on the other end directed me. Video cameras everywhere. She greeted me at the door and took me to the reception area. I sat tight. The lead DA on Michael's case, Jason, hustled in, briefcase in hand. He knew me better than I could have or wanted any idea. Michael's shit storm needed to steer clear.

Smiling as he approached me, I stood. Jason greeted me with a sympathetic smile and a handshake. "I truly apologize for what you're going through. I wish you the best, really."

Pleasantly surprised by his genuine words. "Thank you."

"They'll come to get you shortly."

How I wanted to ask him to relieve me of the judgment since I was innocent, and if I would ever get my laptop back. The detective,

Vic, escorted me to the conference room. I recognized him from our house search, the nice one. Michael felt the chill as I entered, no doubt. The room normal, door unlocked, criminal uncuffed, Vic had to be packing in three different places. He searched my bag, snacks on the table. Maria was on to something...it would've saved so many headaches!

Vic, seated at the other end of the long conference table, broke the silence. "Did you hear about the big case, the international online pharmacy fraud case that just broke? Those guys from Brooklyn are goin' down hard."

A magnet for trouble, Michael caught my expression. Sounded like the same guys he was planning to do business with. I left that unmentioned. "Really! Wow!"

I turned to Michael and began my inquisition. "How much of what they're accusing you of did you do?"

"Barb, I'm pleading guilty. I did it. They have proof of everything. They've had it all along, I can't believe it!"

When your big bad ego blinds you, you get caught.

"You can be sure that your sin will track you down." I had read that once in Numbers 32:23.

"But I didn't do all the things they're charging me with. I came clean, told them everything."

"You did it all." He was guilty, of it all. Any remnants of his handsome mask crumbled before me. Right then, a thousand miles from him. "How could you do that?"

"Greed, I'm sorry. We did so many cremations, the families wouldn't know the difference."

With regret, yet justification? He amazed me still.

"But they do now. What Santo said about you matching the good blood and bad tissue? Is it true?"

"Yes, but the processing companies' sterilization procedures wash out any possible contamination of disease or illness, so no one should get sick. It was never anything that bad, anyway, just things like hepatitis. RTC gave me the idea!"

All I heard was *yes*. Backing away from him, I couldn't be far enough away. Blame-shifting, again, this time on a grander scale than imaginable! The bags he had in our garage freezers, diseased! It all came rushing back to me. Signatures on fraudulent consent forms and a bank account linked to his illegal business as VP, makeshift lab, ruining my business, forging my names to tax returns, abusing me physically and verbally, torturing me mentally and emotionally with lies and deceit, cheating on me countless times with no protection, likely planning to kill me once his fortune in my name materialized. Endangering me was never a second thought. I was a means to his end. Double-edged. He didn't run and was behind bars now. What the hell was I doing there?

Cool, quiet, and so done. "How do you know that for sure? You played God with people's lives, Michael."

"I'm telling you, they won't get sick."

Disgusted. "So, you're caught with your pants down, as a cheater and a criminal. If you weren't found out, you would have continued growing your business, violating so many people, just as you would have still grown your network of whores, violating me, right?"

"I'm so sorry for what I've done. I'm so sorry for hurting you. I'll never have the chance to make it up to you. I'm going to lose you, I know it."

Not a word, silent admission. Michael knew. He lost me.

"When are you pleading?"

"It won't be long. The sentencing will follow on a later court date. Will you come?"

"On your plea date, I have to sign those papers of owing them that money."

"I'm trying to negotiate that. I told them you had nothing to do with anything, and you didn't know."

"You've lied to them for years. Why would they believe you now? The bottom line is you had me sign them. Regardless of your false pretenses, that's my signature, just like on those consent forms!"

"I came clean. They should believe me." In his warped bubble of his own truth that is so far from the real truth. "It was such a perfect plan, could've worked. The assistant DA asked me why. She said I could have helped so many people doing this legally and made a tremendous amount of money. I told her 'greed and money.' I told her the truth."

Mason told me that every time the DA confronted him on a charge, he lied. They must have slapped down evidence in front of him. Caught, he came clean. He lived by that old mob adage, "Deny, deny, deny 'til you die." So selectively honest to suit his needs or goals, a master of deception, desperation sharpened his skills. Not ever enough to escape without inevitable consequence. He'd never figure that out. Aunt Belle's words rang so true. "The dirt always comes out in the wash."

"Barb, I'm also researching this special radiology-based machine that has a part in detecting and curing cancer early. Eric will research on the computer whatever I ask him to, print and send me the information. I can do everything from wherever I am. This advancement in technology will help me get out early." This once brilliant man was completely in warped delusion.

"Michael, the road to hell is paved with good intentions."

"What do you mean?" Case in point. Still clueless.

"Michael, you had a groundbreaking business that could have helped the masses, and look where you are right now because of the path you took. Who's to say you won't do it again? You tend to take the dark path."

He paused. "I've learned from my mistakes. It won't happen again." He would never learn.

The DA allowed one more visit, prior to a meeting they would have with Michael. With me and both boys. Gerry could handle this.

"Ma! The security here is a breeze compared to Rikers!" Great! My son was becoming an expert on security checks at not only prison, but the Brooklyn DA's office too! We went through security only once and the guard let us up in the elevator to the same office I had met Michael before.

Mike dutifully greeted his father. Gerry let him hug him. Michael got emotional. I didn't. They said hi to Vic at the other end of the table. What did Vic think of this show he'd been watching? Episode one, Michael's wife confronts him over his wrongdoings and discovers he is 100 percent guilty of his charges and pulls away. His efforts to worm himself out of any guilt fail. Episode two, Michael tries to interact with his children, but the boys are distracted. They explore the office and play their PSPs with each other. Deck of cards, the three of them play a few hands. This scene of my family was tragic, my precious boys, their innocence pulled out from under them and I couldn't stop it. Was I doing the right thing? Should I have taken them there? Should I have taken Mike to Rikers? Was I protecting them the way I should have? I watched the visit pass, quiet with reserve and sadness.

This day, Michael would plead guilty in court. His father, John, and I sat in the benches. Surrounded by the families and their attorneys, media, sketch artists, extra security today. Reporters from major news networks were seated in front of me. Four of them turned around to give me their cards.

I took them with a smile. "Guys, you know I've stayed under the radar for the last two and a half years, right? That's not going to change now, sorry to disappoint."

Their eyes with empathy, one reporter placed her hand on mine. "Just in case you change your mind and have something you want to say."

If I didn't sign to agree to pay, my freedom was on the line. Besides the fine and penalty, I had to agree that neither I nor my boys would go into practice in the dental or medical field, or the tissue recovery or funeral business, statute of limitations set at seven years. Mason spoke with the DA team. They called me up to sign before Michael's proceedings, decent of them, really. They could have put me in the middle of his plea. I signed, accepting what was. Done and over. The money going directly to the families, and I hoped it really would. It helped me let go of being innocent and still having everything pulled out from under me and taken away.

The judge entered. "All rise." Above him, those words again: "In God We Trust."

Somehow, they brought peace to me in such a sweeping scene. The proceedings were long and detailed, as he pleaded guilty to all counts, so many of them that it seemed endless. He signed. That was it. Remanded until his sentencing, even if he had bail to post. This was the beginning of the end for Michael and for us. All at once, the satisfaction on the faces of the family members, their attorneys, DAs, the sorrowful indignity of my husband, the crushing blow to his father, the sadness and disappointment of his brother, another chapter had closed.

As they took him away, his eyes met mine. His lips said, "I love you."

My eyes told him, "I'm sorry, but it's over."

He could tell I was already disengaged. His eyes turned to panic. Amazing how tables turn in life. They took him through the white door. It was time. The next visit, I told him face to face about the divorce. I would wait to file until his story died down. He had already been ostracized as a monster. He had just lost his life, his freedom, me. I wasn't adding to the media circus against him. Devastated, he cried. I was stoic, yet sympathetic. He was broken. He needed to leave the visit. I was good with that. Some couldn't absorb my decency to him. It was who I was. I would never apologize for it, nor regret it.

Everything does happen the way it's supposed to. He was where his choices had taken him. So was I. The words of wisdom from Kevin and Keith during Michael's addiction had been, "Don't take anything personally." I got it, and I didn't, eventually. "Save yourself." I did. Would I have been as gracious if his mess put me in prison, away from my boys? Absolutely not. Only that wasn't my fate, grateful for all my blessings. Once having love, hope, and faith standing at that altar evolved to love, hope, and faith in the least painful divorce as possible!

His parents and family understood, and would always love me, as I would them. I reassured them. "Regardless of Michael, we will always be family. None of us asked for this."

His parents were grateful and also understood our lives would need to separate. His mom asked, "Should we move out right away?"

"Not tomorrow, but eventually, yes, but we'll remain close. I will be putting the house on the market by May."

I started to live, breathing in some fresh air and life. One night, resting in my bed, alone, I soaked in the quiet, the peace, pondering what fate might bring. My kids would be just fine, would grow up to be good men. For myself, a life with family and friends to fill my love, and "special" friends to fill my needs. Solitude was safe. My barrier was high and wide, guarding my heart. Searching for something my parents had was the impossible. Jane Austen had said it all: "Happiness in marriage is entirely a matter of chance."

Mom and Dad had such a once-in-a-lifetime love. When Dad passed, we were afraid Mom was not long for this world. We'd all had dreams that Dad was waiting for her, but Dad knew it was not her time yet. All of us were beyond relieved that she was healing well, getting through it with Aunt Belle by her side. I knew exactly where I got my tough-ass warrior heart from! Maybe, I'd find my once-in-a-lifetime true love, not necessarily including marriage. Never say never, though. Signing that marriage certificate did me in. No warning labels, no red flags waving! Well, except the mishap with my Unity candle not lighting in church on our wedding day! I didn't know what I was signing, on more than one occasion in trust of him. I lived and learned. And lived smarter and better. Some hard lessons. No regrets.

A few months passed with inconsequential socializing. Dom, Mike's football teammate's uncle who tried to help me with collateral for bail for Philadelphia, asked to meet for coffee. Then a drink. Funny, my first time meeting him recently, he told me he knew who I was for a long time but was respectful because I was Michael's wife. Enjoying the sporadic conversations with him, he had some head-on good advice. Sizing him up, he seemed to have a good value system and no wife or girlfriend. I agreed to dinner. We had a great time. That night, after dinner, our passion went on for hours. Despite my ever-present internal guard, I admitted to myself I was seeing him. He was very much aware of my history and my misgivings.

One night over dinner, he took my hand. "Honey, just let it go. You can't fight the heart."

"Easier said than done."

That wasn't the only wisdom he shared with me. I used to think that all that moaning and groaning, back-arching, toe-curling sex was just an act. How wrong I was! How losing control was so damn possible! He stung my brain in the best possible way! This guy was falling for me and wanted me to be his. Being owned was a problem for me. My head had no place in that. He did tug at my heart, among other things. We enjoyed each other's company. Our time together, an escape from the reality of our own lives, one not having to do with the other.

In the midst of my new relationship, I still dealt with issues concerning Michael. When the parole officer for his sentencing called me, I spoke frankly, answering all her questions. I didn't lie but didn't tell the entire story.

"He tried to be a good father and husband." A twisted stretch, by any means!

As I dated Dom, he was not a part of my mainstream life. My children and in-laws didn't know about him. Fixed in his ways, he had his own history and set of problems as well. He made me laugh, made me feel special, beautiful, comfortable, safe. One morning I didn't receive my usual call from him. I tried him, voicemail. I went about my day with the boys. Tried again, nothing, worried something happened to him. Later that night, reclined in bed watching TV, the eleven o'clock news came on. Breaking story. Biggest drug and gambling bust in New Jersey. Fifty arrests. They worked their way up the rows of arrested. Mob family ties. Dom was one of five on the top row in the gambling bust!

No wonder why he didn't call me.

I'd vowed I would never get involved with a mobster. I also said, never say never. So glad it was just gambling, not drugs. Really, Barbra?

Two weeks later, an unknown call on my cell—Dom. So good to hear his voice. "Hi, honey, I'm sorry, I just got out. They have my cells, so I didn't have your number. I had to call the Cadillac dealership to get it. I understand if you don't wanna get mixed up with me."

"You said you can't fight it, right?"

We met for lunch. He explained. He was who he was. I was who I was. We enjoyed it while it lasted. He had no kids, yet was always so thoughtful of mine. They had no idea. He insisted on food to take home for them at every dinner, Boar's Head whole sides of cold cuts, and bought me a slicer, loaves of bread every week from Piero's bakery. Every time I resisted, he said, "It's for your boys. They gotta eat, right?"

The road to my heart always led through my boys. One time, I walked into Piero's for a cake and some pastries for Easter.

When I tried to pay, Piero pushed it away. "Your money's no good here, for anything, anytime."

"Says who?"

"Dom."

Piero's was my bakery forever, our kids schoolmates.

"Piero, if you don't take my money, I'm not coming here anymore!" Would break my heart. He was the best.

"Barbra, please. Just take it. I don't want Dom to get mad at me, please."

"Okay, but this arrangement is not lasting forever. You have a business to run. Thank you!"

"No! Thank you!"

When I asked Dom, he answered with his slick smile. "I don't know what you're talkin' about."

He could have such mean eyes with people who weren't being right. They twinkled when he looked at me. We spent time together. For how long, who knew? He would have time away. What was it with me and felons?

Michael's day of sentencing arrived. Not attending, watching on TV was good enough, the news stated he made an emotionless apology to the families and was sentenced to eighteen to fifty-four years in New York and twenty-five to seventy-five years in Philadelphia. In parole terms that meant twelve years minimum in New York and an additional thirteen years in Philadelphia, knowing my conversation with the parole officer had helped him, knowing the victim families would try to keep him in, attending every parole hearing for the rest of his life. So much for severing Jay from his case to help him. Jay had gone through several surgeries to his head and brain. They still intended to make him stand trial once he was deemed able. Senseless, all of it.

As the days passed, Dom's life got more complicated, mine showed signs of clearing. "Honey, I'm a bull in a china shop. You're this sweet soft kitten."

Our time together ended. We remained friends. The few months was nice, seeming like years in a good way. We had grown close fast. If anything, my time with Dom showed me there was hope for me. My emotions could be stirred, and my brain could be shaken, both a very good thing. A divorce attorney in place, I was on my way! Liberation, I could taste it. Maria's husband, Gary, referred me to his good friend, Martin Greer, in New York City. A perfect union, Mr. Greer's first priority was protection of the children above all else. I had some work ahead of me. We hoped Michael would not contest it. That would complicate things and be more expensive. He promised his father he would give me the divorce without a problem.

Promise? Michael? I'll believe it when I see it!

My in-laws moved out, closer to Louise in the next town. Despite Rue's confidence in how I presented my homes for an easy sell, this time, no matter how I beautified my house, the ugly stigma remained. Rue and I both knew the opposing Realtors selling houses in my neighborhood were already poisoning the minds of all potential buyers, "The Body Snatcher's home." The nerve to whisper in my house! I just needed to sell the albatross off my neck. The St. Joseph statue Rue had given me was buried in my front yard for a sale on the house, my boys and I said the prayer every day. I also prayed Michael would finally sign the papers.

Mike overheard me on the phone with Mason. "He promised his father he would sign, no question! I'm not keeping the children from him! It's their choice! If they don't want to see him, that's their comfortability and his loss! He made his bed! Talk to him, Mason!"

"Ma, is Daddy giving you a hard time?" Mike asked. "It's about the divorce, isn't it? What's he doing?"

"Calm down, everything is fine. I will handle this."

"Call him right now! Gimme the phone! I'll tell him I don't want to see his sorry ass!"

"Mike, stop! I know you don't want to talk to him. If you ever want to see or speak to him, it will not be to tell him off!"

"You better warn him! If he gives you a hard time, the next time I see him will be standing over his grave!"

"Enough! The divorce will happen anyway. Don't worry. My attorney will make it happen. And you'll see how you feel in the future about seeing your father."

"'Never' looks pretty good."

"It may be never. It may not. You'll see."

Good news: We got a bite on the house, a power couple from California. The woman came to see the house and loved it. Bad news, her partner flew out to see it too, loved it, but was confrontational on every point. Very bad news! The inspector found a small crack going up the back of my house from the patio! They backed out of the deal. The worst news! Michael wouldn't sign the divorce papers. Trapped once again, October 1, 2008, came. No sale yet and I would be owing the DA $370,000. My old high school friend of over twenty years, later turned boyfriend, Nolan, fixed the crack in the brick, and Rue helped me with other repairs. A few buyers showed interest, but none stepped forward.

"I can't thank you all enough!"

To repay Nolan, all I could do was surprise him with one of the seventy-two-inch TVs he fell in love with from my house. He was ecstatic. And a lifesaver! I was relieved on both counts. After a conversation with Aunt Raven, Mike prompted me to move us to Grandma's as soon as possible before Christmas to give me a chance to get on my feet. He had no idea what that would take. His father had buried me in debt. So proud of Mike, offering the smart and right thing. Gerry was a bit reluctant knew it was right, too. It was time.

17

The Return

My house became a hollow shell, embodying all that was lost, all that was saved. The St. Joseph prayer every day was not working, six months later! Frustrated and troubled, I stopped and dug it up, put it back in the box. I was on my way to losing the house, my only security to hopefully pay off the serious debt from my "Michael" troubles. We had moved to Mom's before the holidays. The boys settled into their new schools, adjusting better than anticipated. Thank God for Sal and Trina and their kids next door.

The Escalade Michael insisted I get was one of the nooses he put around my neck. After conversations with GMAC, I had to voluntarily repo my Escalade at the dealer in Rockland. They assured and reassured me I was clear and wouldn't have any responsibilities, besides my credit suffering from it. Months later, I was notified I owed the balance of the lease!

Mom bought a used SUV for me to get everybody around. I brought it to the service department behind the showroom. I ran into Enzo, who worked in service at our Cadillac dealership in Englewood Cliffs. I hadn't seen him in a few years.

He shook his head. "Doc was crazy! A total coke head, right? He was always coked up when I saw him. I'll never forget. One day, this jerkoff comes hot-wheelin' into the parking lot on a Harley with a chrome helmet on, like, who the hell is this guy? Could you believe? A chrome helmet! When he took his helmet off, it was Doc!"

Enzo rapidly clapped, mimicking him. "He goes like this and says, 'I gotta get something outta my car! Now!' He got the keys, went into the car, gave me back the keys and took off. Pop wheelin' and speedin' out. I don't know if it was his bike or not, though. I never saw it before."

I tried to stay calm, pressure rising. "He kept a car on the lot?"

"Yeah, his black CTS. The FBI came and confiscated it. Was a big scene. You didn't know about it?"

"No. When was this?"

"In the last couple of years. He was already in trouble."

He followed me with that car. I remember. Probably did all his dirty work with it. "Despicable motherfucker! Michael let his eighty-year-old father drive around with two bald tires on his twelve-year-old Lincoln, while he pissed his father's money away on a secret car, and possibly a bike! He knew he was guilty and undoubtedly, inevitably, going to jail! Wheelchair business, my ass! How does someone do these things to the people that love and try to help him?"

Enzo shook his head. "I'm sorry, Barbra."

"I don't know why I ask myself these questions. He's a narcissistic master sociopath."

"What do you mean?"

"He preyed on people to get what he wanted. Sociopaths mirror to you what you want to see, but only what they want you to see, selective truths to hide their scheming lies. He would confide in or trust the victim of the moment with something openly important to them, and deceive them from an entirely different angle, devastating them, without a blink of an eye, moving on to the next." Enzo waited for more. "He created a matrix of lies. He wanted to outsmart the world, living his life as if nothing was beyond him, like he was above everything—even the law. Now, everything in his life is beyond him, on the other side of the prison wall. He just can't get out of his own way." I let out a big sigh. "Okay, that's all I got."

"Wow!" We laughed.

"Tell me about it! Thank you. You helped me put more pieces to Michael's diabolical puzzle together."

Later John told me he wasn't surprised. "On my dad's account, what Michael did was unbelievable! Besides the jewelry, gifts, trips, clothes, and bills, he bought one of his girlfriends a house! He spent all my dad's money!"

"That was Julienne, alias Jade, his Jersey City real estate whore. Confiscated. I found some things he forged your dad's name to, I wouldn't doubt if that's how he bought the house, and it had to do with them threatening to indict him with money laundering, demanding money. Who knows!"

Afraid to get a job until I was divorced, Mason told me I may have implications with every lawsuit against Michael because that lowdown lifesucker actually had me sign as vice president of Metropolitan Tissue Services! The company! Not the bank account! Mason dropped that bomb on me in Chicago, an hour before I was being picked up and brought to Oprah's studio to be a guest on her show, about being married to Michael! Livid! I sat next to her on the set before the show started.

Oprah so gracious, awe-inspiring, she beat me to it as I worked up the nerve to thank her. "Barbra, I want to thank you for being here today to share your story with us."

Awestruck by this woman. "I'm honored to be here. Thank you so much for having me."

"Barbra, hold on." She put two fingers on my knee, grounding me, calming me, as she directed about nine cameramen and producers circling around us with her other hand! Incredible.

One thing Oprah said during my interview struck me and I'm sure the whole world. "My good friend, Dale, always says, 'Heed things that make you go, hmmm.'" Life-altering.

Michael's power trip refusing to sign the papers was not gonna stop me! I would sue him for the divorce. My expenses and debt increased. All uncertainties but I kept the faith. I had already sold much of what I could to give my kids the necessities. The boys understood things were tough, but we had a lotta love and support. Shuttling essentials from my house to Mom's.

Mike came in from training with Sal and the boys for the upcoming baseball season. "Hi. Mom."

"Hey, honey. How was the practice? You know I have the blue net in the garage you used at our house."

Mike's tone exceptionally irritable and angry. "They don't need it, Ma! Uncle Sal has the batting machine!"

"Watch your tone! I was just asking if—"

"Ma! Please don't talk to me right now! I'm not in a good mood. I need to get in the shower."

"Easy! Just know I'm here to talk to, love."

"Okay, Ma!" He stormed off to the shower.

In the living room, staring blankly at the TV, ruminating about Mike being next door, practicing with someone else's dad, because he didn't have his. My ears perked, hearing a faint cry. I tiptoed to the bathroom door, shower running, my heart stung with his every weeping word.

He wailed openly as if shut off from the world. "Oh, God! Why did my dad do all those terrible things? Why? Why? The world thinks he's a monster! The whole world hates him! My dad!" I let him release. "Please, God! Please! Make him a better person! Please! I can't take this! It hurts so much! Why did he do this?"

I was behind that same door at fourteen, Mike's age, sobbing, asking God why He had to take Mina, my nine-year-old sister. It should've been me instead. Mina died of an acute liver disease within a month and half of getting sick and being diagnosed, devastating our family. Mina was such a burst of life, just what I called Mike.

His sobs were so severe, I finally knocked as if I didn't hear a thing. "Mike?"

His voice straightened up instantly. "Yeah, Ma."

"When you come out, I just want to talk to you for a minute, okay?"

His tone tight, not angry. "I'll be out in a couple."

"Take your time, honey." I waited on the couch.

His head down, face sullen, he sat close to me, his head on my shoulder. "I'm sorry, Mom."

"It's okay, baby."

In my arms, he wept, completely releasing. "I'm so scared. How are you going to be able to take care of us? The whole world hates Daddy! I have no dad!"

I held his head against me. "I am going to make damn sure we will be okay. You and your brother will have a bright future. Trust me, love. Never lose the faith. My biggest job is to make sure you guys grow up to be happy, good people. You'll figure out what you want in life. Unfortunately, you've learned the hard way what not to do to go after it. Love and life before money, babe. We are so lucky to have so much love around us."

Mike lifted his head and looked at me in panic. "Ma. I don't wanna become like him! I'm scared. I can't become like him!"

"Baby. You afraid of becoming anything like him is enough. You have nothing to worry about."

"Yeah, you're right. Thank you, Mom."

Gerry walked in, looking at us, puzzled.

"Come sit." My arms around both. "Mike, you are not him. I need you to just be a kid, cooperate, give Ger a hug once in a while instead of your usual 'love' for him. Through everything, we have each other. I know it's hard for you to be around your friends with their dads sometimes, practicing next door with the boys and Mister B."

He put his head into me again with tears.

"Baby, just know I understand, but, you'll be okay. You're already so much stronger from all the things you've gone through."

He stopped crying and lifted his head high, as if just remembering how strong he was. "I love you, Mom. I love you, Ger."

"I love you both so, so much."

"Me, too."

They gave me a hug sandwich, though we couldn't call it that anymore. At eleven and fourteen, I'd get, "Not cool, Ma."

Gerry hadn't had a choking fit since Michael was put in prison. Dr. Shea, an ENT doctor in Rockland, retested him. "Gerry doesn't have asthma. Toss the Advair. He should not be taking it."

At my albatross of a house to bring more basics upstate, in Mike's desk drawer, an old picture jumped out at me. Michael on our couch in our Manhattan apartment lifetimes ago. My infant son, Mike, on his little belly, propped up on his daddy's chest. That beautiful innocent baby's eyes looking up at his father. Trusting him to love him, to be there for him, to take care of him. Alone in my fury, I screamed until no more sound could come! At that very moment, I hated Michael. For his love of his ego, above all else, forsaking his children. My children would be better without him, safer without him.

In my closet, something shiny caught the corner of my eye. A penny on the barren rug. I picked it up. "I know you weren't here before. I was just in here. Nothing in my pockets. My bag is on the bed inside. No one else is in the house with me. No one's been in the house but me in the last month." Kissing the penny, placing it on the island in my closet. "Daddy, I'm going to leave this penny here. Please, help me sell my house, okay? I need you, please, Daddy. I love you!"

Two days later Rue called me, shocked and ecstatic.

"Barb, you're not going to believe this! The couple that had seen the house a couple of months ago are seriously interested! I was sure it was a dead end! They want to show the house to their parents this week and measure it. They also requested a copy of the floor plan. These are very good signs!"

"Very good signs!" Closing my eyes. *Thank you, Daddy.*

Two days after the showing, Rue received an offer, lower than I needed, but I'd do what I had to do. Too many houses in my neighborhood were for sale, and the market was too scary to let this buyer go. Within a week, my real estate attorney, Sam Silver, ironed out the agreement.

One glitch, a big one. I knew damn well if Michael wouldn't sign the divorce papers, he was surely not going to sign the waiver of consent for the closing of the house. Though the house was solely in my name, he was my husband and resided in that home with me, so to complete the closing I needed his signature to waive his rights. An absolutely terrible law! I had to plan a masterful strategic divorce by default, even just one day before the closing, coordinated with precision. There wasn't much time!

My mandatory class for divorcing parents showed me the way: "All divorcing plaintiffs must make sure they schedule the court date as close to the thirtieth day mark from when the defendant was served as possible. If the opposing spouse does not include the fee with the dispute within that time, the delay in contesting the divorce buys the plaintiff time to divorce without opposition. Most defendants don't know about the fee, allowing you to beat them to the punch."

I counted on him not including the fee. Or not opposing at all. We planned court for Tuesday, March 3, 2009, the closing for that Friday, March 6. Nothing with Michael came easy. I would be in deficit of over $125,000 following the closing, after DA, bank, mortgage costs, arrears of unpaid mortgage, taxes, and penalties. Mason referred me to Stan Taft, a very well-reputed defense attorney in Brooklyn, to communicate with the DA on my behalf. The mortgage bank and DA were at a standoff. Neither budged. The deficit remained. Sam worked diligently to sway the bank. No go. Stan reasoned with the DA. Nothing. I wrote a hardship letter to both. As the big week approached, I was ready to threaten backing out of everything and let the house fall to complete foreclosure. In that case, all would lose—the bank, the DA, and of course, me.

You can't squeeze blood from a stone.

I would lose either way. I lost already. If they could come to an agreement, I would come away with nothing, but would have paid my debt to the DA, sold my house, and been able to move on. A wash. It took a week to move everything out of my house. On the last day, Mike, Gerry, and I drove away. Nothing left behind but bad juju. The big day had arrived. My very own court date. I would be free from him, at last! With my New Jersey liaison attorney, Scott Rayner, at the Bergen County courthouse, the room was small, full house, easy to pin the opposing parties in the room in a second, the peering, pointing, comments shooting across the room, a war zone. No one there to oppose me, laughing, I would trade my shadow of troubles in a second. He opposed me enough from prison! Scott had paperwork trouble three times with my documents. He scrambled to get all the kinks out before our turn.

He reassured me. "They should let everything go through."

"'Should' is not good enough, it has to!"

The judge entered. "All rise."

Though I was so damn sick of courtrooms, this was the best day in court I ever did have! He gave his verdict, case after case, holding my breath, waiting for my turn to come. Meant to be last...my time had come.

My right hand on the Bible, left hand on my heart, the judge asked, "Do you swear to tell the whole truth and nothing but the truth, so help you, God?" Did Michael's hand burn when he put his hand on the Bible and told only lies and nothing but lies?

"I do." Atonement. Those two words were ironic to me.

The judge asked me to confirm my husband was incarcerated and would remain so for a total of twenty-five to seventy-five years. He granted me my request for full custody and proclaimed Michael would be ordered to pay me sixty-eight dollars per week for child support from prison. "Ma'am, do you want to him to pay you through the court or personally?"

"What is the difference between the two, your honor?"

"If it went through the court and he doesn't have a job in prison and couldn't pay you, he would be in arrears. If the arrears reached a certain level of nonpayment, in simple terms, he would be placed in a prison within the prison with many restrictions. If you do it personally and he can't pay, nothing happens, but you don't receive your child support."

I know I'll never see a dime from him. If the prison is smart, they won't give him a job. He'll corrupt something or break out!

"Your honor, I'm just grateful to have my life and my freedom from him. I don't need his money. He's got enough problems."

The judge chuckled. "Are you sure, ma'am?"

"Yes, your honor."

"Then so be it."

The judge's last question was the toughest, but nothing was stopping me! "Would you agree to be divorced for irreconcilable differences?"

Originally it had been on grounds of infidelity, but I didn't care, I needed this to be final. "Yes. I agree, Your Honor."

The judge asked me to confirm my request for my name change to my maiden name, as stated in the documents. I did. A woman at the Rockland Department of Motor Vehicles had advised me to ensure my request for the name change in my divorce decree. Whether I decided to do it or not, it allowed me that right, and less expensive down the line. What a nugget of wisdom from a passing angel that was!

The judge asked me to stand, running through a couple of statements with me. As he lifted the gavel and started to speak, I tried so hard to quietly suppress my sobs, my eyes overflowed. I couldn't hold it in. It was finally happening!

"I now declare the marriage of Michael Mastromarino and Barbra Reifel-Mastromarino, by law, null and void."

He pounded his gavel. The floodgates opened, my sobs let loose, all eyes on me brimmed with compassion.

The judge concerned. "Are you all right? Would you like some water? Bailiff, please give her this." He handed him his tissue box.

"Thank you." Taking some tissues, smiling, this time, good tears. "No, thank you, Your Honor. I'm better than I've ever been. You've granted me my freedom. All I needed. Great day! Thank you so much!"

The judge was ready to jump over and give me a hug if he could. "Good luck to you. I wish you well, Miss Reifel."

"That name sounds so good! Thank you, Your Honor."

Following Scott to the office across the hall. The woman behind the desk handed me two pieces of paper, my official divorce decree and name change order in my possession. Raised seals and all!

"Wait! The decree wasn't signed by the judge yet!"

The woman grabbed back the paper and ran across the hall! Somebody up there was bein' funny! Dad! He was a funny guy. She came back and handed me the signed papers. I hugged her, hugged Scott, wanting to hug everyone! So thankful, bursting with elation, I floated down the hall, out of the building and to my truck. Sitting alone and recapping, more tears of joy, of freedom, of peace, once and for all! Okay, one hurdle down! Next—the house-closing dilemma, before Friday.

My real estate attorney was getting nowhere. "Barbra, I've left several messages at the bank, with no calls returned."

"I need to talk to them myself. Sam, please give me the contacts and numbers. They need to hear my plight from me, hopefully breeding more compassion for the true severity of my circumstances." This was my last shot.

Calling, I pleaded to three different departments with the story of my hardship. "I may be forced to walk away. I don't want to do that to you or to myself."

They were understanding and sympathetic to me but gave no promises. No final decisions were made yet. "No" was still a possibility. The day of my closing there was no call, and I woefully resigned myself to the fact that I would still owe the DA at least $125,000 after my closing. I didn't know how I'd pay it, but hopefully they'd accept what little I could give over time, without throwing me in jail for non-payment. So unfair. Sometimes, life wasn't.

On my way to pick up Mike from school, just two hours before my closing, Sam called. "I just got a call from the bank. Whatever you said to them worked! They accepted the short sale!"

"You mean the bank will accept whatever is left after the DA takes their three hundred and seventy thousand dollars and all fees are paid?"

"Yes!"

My voice trembled as I expressed my gratitude. My eyes were wet and red. "We did it! We did it! Sam! Thank you so much! Oh, my God! I need to call the bank and thank them! You have been so diligent and patient with all of this. I can't thank you enough!"

Get it together. He can't see you like this.

Pulling up to the school, Mike got in the car. He saw right through me, alarmed. "Ma, are you okay? What's wrong! Why were you crying? What happened?"

"It's a good cry, honey."

I told him. He hugged me, sharing in my relief. At my closing, after signing the papers, I came away without a cent, feeling blessed. It could have been $125,000 worse! What a week! Brushing those dark shadows off. A new beginning with better times to come!

18

The Call

The years passed and to comfort my babies, this became my mantra: "Boys, if you ever want write your father, I'll help you send it. If you ever want to visit him, Uncle Ben will take you in to see him. I'll wait at the hotel for you. If you don't want to, you don't have to, ever. Do not feel guilty. You guys have been through enough. Your comfort is what's important. If anybody tries to push you into it, you tell me! And I will take care of it!"

Nobody was gonna coerce my kids to do something they don't want to do! Nobody! And my boys never wanted to. So, they never did. Michael wrote them twice a year, knowing not to expect a response. Each had their reasons. Until they were eighteen, I screened every correspondence for their own safety. He squeezed in love references about their mom, as if nothing had ever happened. Another one of his tactics. Behind bars for the rest of his life, he had nothing to lose. He would never see me again. He had no right.

Five years had passed since Michael was put away, just before Christmas. Still close with his family, we planned our continued Christmas Eve tradition at his brother, John's house, just about every year since I dated Michael.

John called. The last time I got this feeling, a few years before when he had called me, his dad had a heart attack and didn't make it, on Michael's birthday, no less. My boys had been devastated. He was greatly missed.

"Barbra, Michael has cancer. The doctors say he has three months to live. Training for a triathlon in the prison, he had bad hip pain. They took X-rays and found a tumor. It spread rapidly to his lung and brain, throughout his entire body. He's in the hospice ward within the prison. They transport him to the hospital for whatever he needs. It all happened so suddenly."

"Oh, my God, John. I'm so sorry." Tears for a minute, then relief. Then, the unthinkable. "Mike was planning to go up with a friend. But, in light of this, I think the boys and I should go up together and visit as a family, forgive, make peace, say goodbye. I will break it to them and talk to them about it."

Two summers ago, Mike had told me, "Ma. When I turn eighteen, I'm gonna go visit my dad. I mean, *my father*, alone."

The boys knew when we talked about their father to please never call him "Dad" in front of me. Big difference between a father and a dad. In my eyes, he was no dad to my children. They understood and respected my word.

"Ma, when I see him, I'm gonna look at him, man to man! Eye to eye!" Mike, seventeen, grown so far to 6-feet-1, broad, sizeable, he thought of himself as a contender to settle a score, not so much Michael's son. Scared no more. "I have a few things to tell him and I have some questions for him!"

"Honey. I hope you're not expecting the truth."

"Absolutely not! He's a fuckin' liar! When I see him, I'm gonna wanna punch him right in the face!"

"If that's how you feel, maybe you should wait to visit him until you get a hold of that. I don't need you thrown in there, too, for assault! Please, honey!"

* * *

Turned out he did wait. Meanwhile, Michael accused me of keeping his boys from him. Imagine that!

"Oh, Barbra. That would be wonderful." John was elated to hear I would plan a family visit given the news of Michael's cancer. "Thank you so much. You have every right to keep your back turned on him. You're an incredible person."

"It's just the human thing to do." It was also the human thing to feel relieved. My children and I would be safe as soon as he was gone.

Mike, eighteen, was in his first year of college at SUNY Rockland and worked at the Rockland Bakery deli. Gerry, fifteen, was a sophomore in Clarkstown High School North, active in wrestling. Later that day, after school and Mike's work, I told the boys that we should visit together as a family, try to forgive him for ourselves, make peace within our hearts, and say goodbye. Gerry was wide-eyed, but okay. Mike teared up for a minute.

"Layla and Gemma will be up that weekend. So, we can visit together and hang with them."

The big draw was their cousins would be there. Layla, Louise's daughter, a magazine editor, lived in Boston. And Gemma, John's daughter, a chef at the Hilton, lived in Albany. I loved them—they were great kids. Though they were young women, they would always be kids to me. I came into their lives when they were five.

"They're really gonna be there?"

"Yep. Reach out to them. Or we'll see them Christmas Eve. You can talk about it more, then!"

"Yeah, I'll go."

"Ma, I'm glad we're going together. Are you okay going?"

"Absolutely, honey. Was my first thought." Not exactly, but one of them.

Gemma saved me with her rates for the hotel in Buffalo by the prison. My hands were still tied financially because of Michael, between jobs because I was still working on getting out of my $250,000 tax problem with the IRS from him forging my signature on fudged returns. His dark shadows still followed me.

Christmas Eve came. John and Anna always gave the best holiday of the year, since my nieces were the little ones. Then they grew up, and my kids came along and became the little ones. Michael's mom was still a bit nutty. Isn't every old-world, Italian mother? She stayed nice and comfortable in her own little bubble of her own reality, a little extra, a little trouble, in the family at times over the decades. But all in all, harmless. Michael's bubble had been a whole different stratosphere of dangerous, globally! The night was filled with a lotta love and laughs. It was our time to catch up and bond. We visited with John and Anna's girls, Gianna and Gemma, and Louise and Ted's girls, Kate and Layla. Despite all that happened, I would always be their Aunt Barbra. Beyond everyone's bright mood, the truth was it was bittersweet.

Christmas morning was spent with my family in Rockland, and we saw Max, his life partner, Vita, and his boys for lunch in the city. Max talked to me about Michael. He still hadn't talked to him in years, since he unearthed Michael's betrayals against him once he was put away.

"The boys and I are going to visit him in a couple of weeks, but there's a lot of red tape to schedule. I know how you feel, but if there is anything inside you want to settle—make peace, tell him, ask, forgive—think about going. He doesn't have much time."

"I don't know, Barb. He really cut me deep."

"Oh, he cut a lotta people deep! Alive or dead! Across the world! It's a wonder I still have blood in my veins!"

We laughed. "How about you let me know how it goes for you and I see?"

"Deal, I will keep in touch while we're up there. In the meantime, just give it some thought."

Over these years Michael was away, I was Max's go-to about Michael. He had so many unanswered questions racking his brain. They were best friends since Max was eight and Michael was six. I fell in love with Michael when I was twenty-three. That was a lot to choke on. Were there signs? Did we miss something? Was he always that way? Or did he become that way? Was it the drugs? Or did the drugs uncover? Did we ever really know him? We would just hash and come to the same conclusion every time. There was no clear answer, no explaining it, and we were not crazy, nor terrible judges of character. The small obscure signs, who would even notice when we were young? But through life he honed his slippery skills, becoming a master of deception. It all just evolved a certain way, to fool us all, which was hard to swallow. We remembered Michael in happier times, but accepted what was, and what he had become. Michael was a case study for the books! And for anyone that was close to him in his life.

Mom, Aunt Belle, Raven, and Ben always made sure Mike, Gerry, and Aidan had a warm, loving Happy Hanukkah and Merry Christmas. We celebrated all in our family, so grateful for them, for their love and support. Mike needed more support because he had seen more, dealt with more, had more issues and more anger. He had a kindred bond with Aunt Belle, because she understood all too well. Most paled in comparison to Michael's level of bad, but her father was bad too. She was also the oldest and her mom died when she was just twenty-two. Aunt Belle was Mike's go-to, a godsend.

19

The Visit

Destination: Wende Correctional Facility in Buffalo, N.Y. We drove up eight hours in a snowstorm. Anything to do with Michael was still a damn struggle, even on his deathbed! We arrived at the hotel, snow stopped, our visit set for tomorrow. The girls met us and we headed to the Anchor Bar, the original Buffalo wing place in the country! The kids loved it! They needed every good memory they could get. After the visit tomorrow, we planned to see Niagara Falls on the border between the U.S. and Canada, so beautiful at night, like aurora borealis through water. Too bad it was the dead of winter. We all said goodnight and went to our rooms. The boys just chilled watching TV, perfect time to prepare them.

"Guys, your father is in the hospital building of the prison, on the hospice floor. He's not going to look like the man you remember. He lost a lot of weight. He's very sick, bedridden, nothing that any of us can catch. We all have everything to be angry about, but let's put it all aside, and get through this together."

Mike rested his head on my shoulder. "Ma, I don't know how I'm gonna feel when I see him."

I kissed his head. "I know you'll be strong, probably have a tear, but you're gonna be okay, honey." This was a big deal.

And this damn man made me go back on my word. *He was to never see my face again, but I am willingly visiting him. I was to never shed a tear over him again. Now, he has to go and die.* Go figure. Life was filled with more twists and turns than I knew how to keep up with. So many ironies I could've never imagined. It all started with him. My noble knight in shining armor turned to a weak, cheating, drug addict criminal. My white picket fence turned into prison bars!

The girls had visited him a couple of times before, so they showed us the routine there. Mike and I knew the drill, too, from Rikers, the hardest of the hard. All electronics, money, jewelry, hair clips or bands, belts, just everything, to be left in the car. No underwire bra, nothing metal. If Gerry had braces, what would happen? Would he not be allowed to visit? We waited in the little house outside the prison walls and barbed wire, a long wait as expected. They called us. A bus took us to the main building where we waited in front of the ten-foot iron gate. We were buzzed in and escorted by correction officers through two more locked doors into the main holding area. Yes, that was what it was. It certainly was no visiting area.

"Boys, don't feel insulted in any way. Bottom line is we are here to visit a criminal, and they have to treat us as criminals until we prove ourselves not to be."

Shoes off, jackets, everything on the belt, empty pockets inside out. We put our head down and shook our hair out, body scans, hand stamps, checked, rechecked. Only three at a time and the girls let us go first. We knew it would be an all-day ordeal. Rikers still had the edge on the worst. Our bus finally came and we were taken to the hospital building. Sick or not, the security was fierce. At times, we had to stream by cuffed or shackled prisoners with guards, a breath away, too close, so unnerving, rubbing shoulders with them. Who knew their stories, but they were there for a reason. Wende Correctional Facility was a long-sentence prison.

We got to his floor, led to an office to wait, feeling the sickness and darkness in the air. Across the hallway, the visiting room had men in wheelchairs, attached to oxygen tanks. Michael was so sick that we had to visit him in his room. His counselor, Randall Pearce, came in to greet us, unspoken, nothing would be discussed in front of the children. I appreciated that. Giving me his direct extension, he surely would be hearing from me. A guard came and directed us to follow him, my boys close to me. At his door, told to wait, I caught a glimpse of Michael through the window, speechless. Mike walked in first, always protecting his brother and Mom. Sitting up in bed, oxygen in his nose, so frail, bones and skin, Michael was literally half the man he was. Aged thirty years in only five. Sadness and pity filled me.

Michael's face filled with joy and sorrow all at once, he started wailing. "Oh! My boys! My boys! My wife!"

My wife? Now wasn't the time. In his hysterics, he waved his hand for the boys to come to him. Both looking to me for reassurance, I nodded. "If you're comfortable."

Leaning in on either side of him, Michael grabbed them in for a hug. Mike started to cry, Gerry somber. I fought it.

Damnit! He has no right to see me cry over him again!

The boys' heads buried in their father's sunken chest, and Michael, nothing but a skeleton of a man, was one of the saddest sights imaginable. The human relationship can lift one up, bringing joy, happiness. Or it can tear one down, destroy one's life and heart. Michael and I were polar opposites. They calmed down. Mike asked to have a few minutes to talk to his father. A guard waited with us outside his room.

Gerry sat by me as I stood, keeping my clear shot through the window, listening. "Why, Dad? Why?"

"Mike, I did this all for you boys and your mom. I only wanted to give you everything!"

"What about your other family?"

"I had no other family! You're my family!"

Mike would see through his father's horseshit. Gerry and I walked back into the room. "You okay, babe?"

"All good, Ma." He winked.

My son winked at me! He had his father's "number." I situated in the corner, the farthest point from Michael, Gerry closer to me, Mike between me and his father.

"I'm sorry, pal. I really wanted to get you your first car when you got your license."

His first thought, a material piece of metal for his son? His priorities were still upside down, reaching. Has he truly realized the magnitude of what he'd done? To his children? To me? To everyone?

Mike handled him, already knowing his father had a warped sense of priorities. "I have a car to drive. I'm good."

"I'm sorry for everything, guys."

Their eyes shifted to me, speechless. His sorry null and void. "What's done is done," I said. What more could I offer?

"Y'know, the priest purged me! I'm washed of my sins."

Really? Just like that? It must've taken a good month! Couldn't have been a one-shot deal.

"Good for you. It didn't purge my two-hundred-and-fifty-thousand-dollar problem with the IRS from you fudging personal returns, forging my name."

"I'm sorry, Barb. Is Dick helping you? I can call him!"

"So he says. But nothing so far. No, you've done enough, thank you. I'll deal with it. The boys are doing well in sports and school."

"Gerry, you still running in track?"

"Nah, wrestling."

Michael gleamed at Mike and chuckled. "Mike, how are you around the track, bud? Still slow as shit?"

"Michael! Cut it! Now! Or we leave," I snapped. Michael always bragged about how fast he was in college football, second fastest in the league, riding Mike for not being a speed demon like himself. Not slow, his forte a strong power player over speed, football and baseball. Michael never let it rest. "I see you're still an asshole," Mike noted. "Nothing's changed."

What was Michael gonna do? Jump out of bed and beat on him again? Mike was right. Sick, eaten away, dying, he was still an asshole. "Mike, please, honey."

My dad used to talk up Mike to tease Michael. "All right, big shot. I bet you, your son beats you in a sixty-yard-dash when he's fourteen. You'll be an old man!"

"Never happen," Michael had responded curtly.

Mike was only ten at the time, unaware of the bet. Never to happen, Michael was in prison a year when Mike turned fourteen. Mike was eighteen now, faster, stronger, but not into sports the way his dad was. He attended college and worked. Life took a different road of priorities than Michael, all around, thank God. This visit was a tug of war of emotions, as predicted.

"Guys, I'm telling you. I really shouldn't be here! The solution I made preserved the integrity of tissue like magic, like nothing else on this Earth! It didn't matter if the donors were sick. My solution and the processing company's sterile technique eradicated that."

Is this sick son of a bitch trying to tell my kids he did nothing wrong? That he doesn't deserve to be in prison? What a fucking role model!

I needed to interject. "But you're here for reasons. You did things wrong and against the law. That's why you're here."

Gerry shot me daggers. Sparring against his sympathy for him was gonna be tough. This deranged man was damn sure not going to poison these boys' minds! I would battle until his last breath!

The fucker threw a line, they bit. Gerry had the scientific engineering brain. "So, what's this magic solution?"

Michael tapped his temple with his wiry finger, a villainous smile on the skull that was his face. "It's all up here."

"Can you write the formula down?"

"I can't write. I'm too weak." That was true.

"Tell me, I'll write it down."

"I can't think right now. My head gets jumbled."

That could have been true, too. He did have tumors in his brain, hip, lungs. The tumor in his neck cracked one of his vertebrae, and the ones on his arms and shoulders were so pronounced through his thin skin—they were wrenching to see. Michael snowing my children to look like a genius hero, working them, playing on their sympathy, on their curious, fresh minds, was not gonna fly! Deprogramming would commence back at the hotel! He showed them how brilliantly he rigged his warming pot to boil water, which was *not* allowed, since it could be used as a weapon to burn someone's eyes or face.

"They never let me work in the library or with any equipment or machines, because of the computers and all. With my brain, they know what I'm capable of."

Something to brag about. A big dangerous liability.

The subject needed to be changed. "John told me that you're best friends with Richard Chandler."

Makes sense they'd be drawn to each other. So much alike, it was scary. Tall, dark, handsome, charming masks. Narcissistic, dangerous sociopaths beneath. Chandler was the Preppy Killer, who choked his girlfriend to death in Central Park, decades ago. So young, he was nineteen! Tragically she had only been eighteen. The vision of them joking about Michael choking me made me think, I musta been flirting with death since I met him. Amazing what one moment of one wrong choice could do. God help my boys to always make good choices.

"Yeah, good man. I haven't seen him since I've been in here. They won't let him visit me. He helped me get through it in here. Y'know, I was working with the authorities. Did Mason tell you? I was possibly going to get out in two years. Did you know that?"

"Mason had said something about five years, but it was a real longshot, at best."

"Oh, no, it was happening, but doesn't matter now."

Just like the seven-lot legacy and becoming a billionaire from zero with one deal.

"And you know the first thing I was gonna do?"

The boys in unison. "What?"

He turned his head to me, with his sinister sunken eyes, and a devil's smile. Purged, my ass!

"I was going to find you, my pretty."

Shivers ran up my spine, laughing through my words. "Oh, no, you wouldn't! And, by the way, when you speak of home, my home is not your home. Maybe your sister's or brother's. You and I are not family anymore."

The boys laughed hard.

Michael still grinned like a psycho amusing himself. "Why? I thought we had a good marriage."

Mike and I busted out laughing harder! "Now, that's funny, Dad! You *so* did not! It was terrible! You were terrible!"

"I was? Oh, all right." He sounded like his mother!

That whole scene strangely felt like a family moment, warped, so far from reality, but he was a dying man. Grateful, I let it be for the time.

"If it took me dying to see my family again, so be it."

How sad, and ironic, that Mike helped his father sit up, rubbing his back and shoulders for him gently. With any pressure, Mike could have literally snapped his bones with no effort, something Michael had threatened to do to both of us. The human relationship was damn puzzling, from beginning to end. We switched with the girls and Gerry stayed with them for the rest of the visit. Waiting in the car, Mike started sobbing. My baby, there was no stopping him, only comforting him. On my cell, I called Max. Crazy timing. He could hear Mike crying.

My voice trembled. "We just got out. Max, I'm glad we came. It was the right thing to do. If you really want to make peace, come see him, even just once."

"I will."

We all got back to the hotel, grateful to the girls. I just held my boys, like the hug sandwich they used to give me when they were little.

"Boys, please don't believe your father's words. He did so many things so wrong to go to jail. Everything he did was illegal, and hurt people, putting people's lives in danger. Do not let him convince you he's not guilty. Don't lose sight of the truth, please."

"Ma, trust me, I know," Mike said. "He was still full of shit!"

Gerry shot me that look again. "Mom! The guy is dying! Cut him a break!"

I had no choice. "Dying or not, he lied to your faces! I won't allow him to manipulate you! I have protected you your whole lives, I'm not gonna stop now!"

"But he made that solution."

"Gerry, honey, this is what I mean. His solution was not magic. Anyone could have easily taken it to a lab to have it analyzed to break it down. You're a tech kid. You know that's possible. Any way you cut it, he still broke multiple laws violating people's rights and endangering people's lives."

A knock at the door was perfect timing. At the restaurant, the girls enlightened us. "Uncle Michael wanted us to start a fund for the inmate families through the state. The money would funnel through our company and we would take a fee."

"That doesn't sound kosher. Tell me you didn't do it!"

"We researched, and it was not legal!"

We all cracked up. "Were you surprised? I cannot believe he tried to use you two as a front for his shady business! Thank God you two are smart girls! He knew. He makes things sound so legit and appealing, right? Master con man."

My boys were riveted at the revelation. They heard it from their cousins and received validation. Watching the four cousins together, smiling, laughing. After everything, a bright refreshing scene.

"Yeah, I know! We told him what we found out. My dad told him no more bright ideas!"

The next day, Niagara Falls was breathtaking. The lights glowed off the Falls in the darkness of night, the hum of the rushing water, good for the soul, healing. The next day, I declined Mike's offer to help drive home. Therapy. Warfare aside, the vision of Michael, of how he dwindled away to nothing, in pain, dying, the tragedy of our lives from beginning to this end, still saddened me. When the boys fell asleep, I wept.

Mike had woken. "Mom, please, don't be sad."

"But it is sad, honey. Not because I love him, but loved him for a good part of my life, though he fooled me our entire time together, I had a life with him, children with him. To look at him now, it's hard to see."

"Ma, I think my father ruined you for all other men."

"Baby, I'm just smarter. My heart still works just fine. Look! Tears for the most terrible man I could have ever chosen! Though it brought me you two, his family, and dear friends. I have no regrets."

Max called me after his visit. "I confronted Michael about the things he did to me he had no idea I knew. I told him, 'This is your chance to come clean.' Barb, he looked at me from his deathbed, and fuckin' flat out lied to my face!"

"Max, did you expect anything different? He's been in his own bubble of truth since I can remember, like he really believes his lies. Are you glad you went?"

"Yeah, without a doubt, for my own peace and confirmation. He is and will always be out of his mind. But I loved the guy!"

"Me, too."

John called. Michael stopped chemo. The Priest read him his last rites. They gave him forty-eight hours. We visited one last time, emergently. Forty-eight hours later, he was still kickin'! John had to get back. I stayed. Really? Visiting again? Was I out of my damn mind? My process, I supposed. And truth be told, I needed to see him actually pass. No tricks. No witness protection program. Nothing could be put past Michael. Randall, his counselor, didn't think it was healthy to visit too many days for my own sake. Apparently, it was a shock that I visited him in the first place—to Randall, the guards, his family, some family, and friends. My immediate family had no doubt.

"Barb, can I hold your hand for a few minutes? Please?" I let him.

"You know, you're the love of my life. I will love you forever."

"I love you, too, Michael." I lied to him, giving him the semblance of a family. Being decent for my boys, his family, even in some way, for him. When he fell asleep, I took my hand back.

He woke and dropped a bomb. "They're trying to get me this experimental miracle pill like chemo, y'know."

My nerves were knotting as the words spilled from his mouth. Miracle? My miracle was a little different. "You mean they're testing it on you?"

"It's really hard to get. Been a while. It's not likely. My case would be documented. I feel tired, like I just want to go, but I would want you to be here if I did. Could you?"

"Don't be afraid. If you feel like it's time, let go."

Now would be okay.

"I've tried! I even asked them on the sly to give me a slew of my pain meds, so I could just do it. They won't."

John, too, wished God would take him to spare his little brother from that pain to live like that, to spare us all.

"Maybe I can talk to Randall. Be right back."

I left his room to Randall's office down the hall, so glad he was there. "Michael is holding on by his last breaths. Is there any way to make it ethical to 'help' him? Extra doses or IV of his pain meds, maybe? Michael wants this."

"I'm sorry, Barbra. There is no way. The prison would be liable."

"What if the aide gives it to me and I give it to him?"

He smiled a no.

"Hey, I had to ask."

Michael was sleeping. I sat back in my chair, much closer to his bed than my first visit. *How did I get here?*

I just stared, tired, perplexed, conflicted. Why not help an ex out? As he slept, I walked over to his bedside, my back to the hallway window, no intentions of exposing myself to him. He didn't move. I wrapped his pillow around his face, held it there. He struggled for what seemed like seconds. It was over.

My eyes opened with a jolt. I was still in the chair! He still lay there, sleeping in bed! What a dream! It would've been so easy, but I could never. He was at God's mercy, not mine. If I hadn't killed him already, it wasn't happening!

A couple of days later, he was still holding on. This was the last time, doing what I could. Again, no regrets. And no pillows! I drove home. The final chapter to this saga was closing, bringing me relief with not an ounce of regret. I had evolved into a very different woman, more wisdom than I thought I could handle at times. My fairy tale morphed as life happened. Turned out I was my own hero. My two princes were my light, angels close and all around. Michael, in disguise for too long, was my antagonist, my darkness.

After all the visits, it felt so good to be home. Michael may have led a path of destruction through my life. But he was never gonna take my womanhood. Beyond grateful I had no disease after years of his free, uncovered, dick-swingin' ways, everything else was gravy. In no rush to link lives with a man again, I had too much to settle, too much to accomplish. And honestly there was no man that measured up—not his dick, his character! The man for me needed to rival my backbone, preferably outrival. Not sure that was possible. Michael still hung on, calling the boys once a week, if he had the strength. Someone had to hold the phone to his ear.

Mike came to me. "Ma, my father told me I shouldn't go to Panama and stay a couple of weeks to see if I want to live with Uncle Max to help manage his restaurant in Panama City. He said I need to stay here to take care of you and Gerry."

Furious with this presumptuous man! Even on his deathbed! Trying to insinuate himself into my boys' lives, telling Mike what to do? The sage himself? Where the hell was he for them when he was home? My blood was boiling!

"Honey, you listen to your mother! You take whatever opportunity you want, and you go! Do not listen to your father. Look where his decisions have led him."

His best decision was giving me two beautiful boys. No regrets, simply for the sake of them.

"Mike, I want you to fly and thrive! If it's Panama where life takes you, go! Give it a try. You always have home to come back to. You'd be living with Uncle Max. He'd take you under his wing. He trusts you, and you trust him."

Mike's eyes had doubt. "But Mom, do you think Uncle Max sees my father when he looks at me?"

"Honey, I'm sure there are parts of you that bring back fond memories for him. They grew up together. He loved him. He knows your character is everything your father's is not. Your godfather sees the exceptional young man you've become. And you'll listen to him. He and Vita invited me to dinner one night, asking if I was good with it. That means a lot to me. Certain things can show so much about someone's character, their integrity. With my blessing, I told him how grateful I was. I'd rather you boys be given opportunity over a dollar any day! He's a great family friend, and uncle!" Mike hugged me. "Again, I repeat. Forget what your father told you. Put it out of your mind! I'll miss you, but we'll be fine, just a plane ride away. The world will just become a smaller place. You go live your life! I will always be here for you, love."

With Mom at Aunt Belle's post-knee surgery rehab, my cell rang. Michael. The boys didn't pick up, so I did.

"Barb! You wouldn't believe! They started giving me that experimental cancer pill a couple of weeks ago. And my tumors are starting to shrink! It's a miracle!"

Oh, shit. Stricken with fear, my head wanted to explode.

Mom and Aunt Belle were puzzled, concerned at the terror on my face.

"Really? Wow! But your cancer is so advanced. It's still throughout your body, right?"

"Yeah, but if it keeps up, I'll be outta here in no time!"

He'd better be bluffing, or completely out of his mind!

"And tell Max I wanna talk to him about Mike!"

"I'll tell him." Max had a one-visit limit, face-to-face or phone.

All my gestures were for a dying man! He would have never ever seen me otherwise!

After I hung up, I told Mom and Aunt Belle the news, not holding back. "Oh, no. He's got to go! I never wished him harm or death. But, damnit! He was dying by God's will. What the hell happened? I need to speak to his counselor."

My wisdom-wielding ladies had no words, scared as I was.

To Randall, masking my fear didn't work. "He said 'full recovery,' and 'getting out in no time.' What are the most extreme possible effects of this pill? Sounds too unbelievable."

"Don't worry, Barbra. This pill may extend his life a few months at best." He saw right though me.

"By rights, he should've been gone already. Your family visits may have given him a boost, but he's too far gone. Between your visits and the pill, he only bought a little time."

"So, Michael is delusional? Or just trying to scare me?"

Randall chuckled. "Wherever this pill takes his mind helps him cope. Hope is never a bad thing. I commend you for all that you've done for him, considering your position. And I also understand your position in light of his news."

"I truly appreciate that. I'm a good person. Sometimes, the thoughts I have about Michael are not in my character. In my life, opposing him, he brought out a side of me that I should never see in my life again, the thoughts I had, the things I did to combat him. They were surreal and out-of-body. Life with him was a horror. Right now, I'm not having pure, godly thoughts about him."

"Barbra, I have been doing this for a very long time. I truly understand. You are above and beyond a good person. Don't beat yourself up about any of it. Please call me with any concerns as you go."

Mom and Aunt Belle knew. Clasping my hands together, eyes closed, I prayed in silence. When Michael started telling Mike what he should and shouldn't do, he had already started that fucking pill, no doubt. Scary Michael was making a comeback. It was only the beginning, but not too far from the end, I hoped. A week later Michael called. Again, the boys weren't answering. I picked up reluctantly, a bad feeling about this one.

Michael emitted a surge of power. Scary, authoritative power. "My tumors are still shrinking! Listen, get a pen and paper. Take this number down and get in touch with this attorney. Reach out to Mario after your conversation. I need to talk to Max. I need to go over something with him about Mike. He needs to listen to me. Make sure he calls me. I need you to send me some magazines and newspapers."

And with this bellowing voice, reminiscent of his lambs to slaughter dream. "Things are gonna change!"

Oh, this fucker is in full bloom! He better wither soon, before I have him knocked off myself!

"You just hold the fuck on! I don't know who the hell you think you are! Or who you think you're talkin' to! But I'm not your lawyer! Your secretary! And I am certainly not your wife! You call your attorney to take care of this shit for you!"

Silence.

"And you back off those boys! You let them live their life! You just love and enjoy the moments you have left on this Earth with them in yours! I'm warning you! You will never hear from any of us again! I mean it! Leave them alone!"

Click. He didn't try to call back. Good decision.

"Randall, he has become scary Michael again! His behavior has become unbearable. He may be out of his mind, but that doesn't mean I have to put up with it. I don't ever want to speak to him again. I don't know what to do. He's dying. I'm sure the kids will still speak to him. But I can't go back there."

"The COs and aides have complained about his growing overbearing and abusive behavior. You're not alone. It is your decision if you choose to or not. You make the boundary."

"You just brought me back to Al-Anon. *Boundaries.* Wow. I'm back there again, whether I want or not." For Al-Anon, I was eternally grateful. "And no miracle recoveries, right?"

"Boundaries are important. And no."

How did this sliver of life of a man have so much tyranny busting out of him? The boys needed to know about their father's behavior and not hand me the phone if he called. They understood. This was all so hard for me. Granted, the world probably wished I let him die years before on my loveseat, a simple drug addict overdosing, woulda saved everyone a whole lotta trouble, including myself. But he was a life, my children's father. Who could have ever guessed? The strangest thing to know someone's M.O., to even predict it, but be completely perplexed by it. To anyone who knew him, Michael was an enigma. To the world, a flat-out dangerous monster. To me, both.

20

The Light

"Ma, I spoke to him. He said they're moving him to a prison closer to his family, Fishkill. How far is that from us?"

How the hell did this man manipulate his way to a prison to suit him? How does this happen?

"Seriously? Your father never ceases to amaze me. About twenty minutes. It's a good thing for Grandma, Uncle John, Aunt Louise, and your cousins to see him."

"We don't have to visit him all the time now, do we? Ma, I really don't wanna."

"Mike, you and your brother have done more than you ever had to, more than your father deserves. You've given him a relationship he killed a long time ago. You did a good thing, baby. If you never go again, you're good. Even if he was five minutes away, dying or not, I told you, your and Gerry's comfort is the only thing that matters."

Relief came over my son's entire being. This poor child, constantly needing to be reminded that he can't live his life through the guilt he can't shake inside him, conjured from his father, the one who deserved to drown in his own guilt! Gerry was different—younger, less impacted, easier to protect. He had his mom and his brother. He was good.

Though I wouldn't allow him in any interview at only fifteen, a producer once asked Gerry if he was angry. "I'm not angry about my father. What's the sense of being angry now? It's in the past. We're okay." His logic always astounded me, since he was little.

How I wished Mike could find his own peace. That couldn't happen until his father was gone from his life, from existence, though the scars would always remain. Since the news hit of Michael dying of cancer, the media swooped and scooped, unkind. Karma was the word. I preferred, "you reap what you sow." Newspapers wanted statements from me, producers from shows contacted me, so adamant.

My response the same. "At this difficult time, to respect his family's privacy, I must decline."

Maybe this is all a ploy, his death staged, bringing him to almost death, and then bring him back, to bring down the big billion-dollar companies. Again, to fool the world! And then hide away in witness protection. His tumors are shrinking, right?

Had I seen too many movies? Or had I lived too much life with Michael? Was this all really possible?

Mike called me into his room, holding out the phone. "Mom, he wants to talk to you."

Putting my hand up, shaking my head no.

"Please, Mom? For me?"

Taking the phone took everything out of me.

Scary Michael in sheep's clothing sounded meek. "Hi, I'm sorry. How are you?"

"I'm fine."

Back in my Al-Anon days, FINE stood for Fucked up-Insecure-Neurotic-Emotional. Now, it was more like Free-Invincible-Namaste-Empowered. "I'm at Fishkill now, y'know." "I know."

Offering up a visit wasn't on the table.

"Can I call you to wish you a happy Mother's Day?"

"Sure."

Phone back to Mike. I had reached beyond making amends with him yet keeping my boundary. My amazing grace was at it again, though he didn't deserve a moment of my time. I knew the clearing of the dark clouds was not far off.

July 7, 2013, thirteen years to the day since Michael's arrest, my confirmation of Michael's drug addiction and affair, the day before Mike's birthday, it was John who told me the news.

"Barbra, he passed this morning." Uncanny timing.

"I'm sorry, John." That was his baby brother, after all.

"You have been an angel. I gotta tell you, I don't know how you did it. Could never thank you enough, for everything, all those years."

"You know me, I just did what I needed to do when I needed to do it. What happens now?"

"Everything is set. One thing, it's not pleasant, but there's a solution. The first of kin needs to accept his remains and the last of his belongings. That's Mike."

"That can't happen."

"If you notarize a letter relinquishing all rights to Louise, problem solved."

"Consider it done."

A sunny scorching summer day, quiet, our immediate family and family friends gathered at the gravesite. My family there, a testament to them. He would be buried next to his father. We all waited. And waited. And waited. The elders were escorted to wait in the air-conditioned cars. The rest of us sweltered, trying to find patches of shade. He was late. Another cruel joke, compliments of Michael, even from beyond the grave probably laughing at all us fools.

John made an announcement. "We have a problem. The funeral home doesn't have all the proper paperwork to release Michael. They're working on it. It should take within the hour. It's only ten minutes from here."

So close, yet so far.

Light chatter echoed in earshot. "This is just like Michael!" "Causing trouble from his grave already?"

Every time a hearse drove close, we hoped. Nope, it kept going, and the next, and the next. An hour later, his hearse drove up to the site.

"Hallelujah!"

Time to put him and all his mess to rest. They carried the casket out. The end was near. A close call too many times, the fear never left me, from the news of his illness, the miracle pill, the news of his death, to the casket in front of me. Was Michael part of a higher conspiracy?

In a low whisper, I needed to know. "John, please, forgive me for this, but did you see him?"

"Yes, he's gone, Barbra. I understand."

He hugged me. Closure. All I could do was believe. I prayed for his tragic soul, for our peace!

The service was solemn. Tears were shed. My heart felt for his mother, his family, for my boys, bittersweet. We paid our respects to my father-in-law. Both boys cried for their father, for their Grandpa. All the relatives said goodbye to Michael. His mother lingered, broken. My heart felt for her. We walked away, leaving it all behind us.

"Ma, let me drive home." Mike was the man of the family and had been for a while.

But right then, he was my wounded child, needing to heal. "You look so tired, honey. You have work early tomorrow. Why don't you let me drive and you take a nap, please?"

"Okay, Mom. Thank you. I love you."

My hug couldn't take away their pain. I drove home, forward, taking us to a better place. In the rearview mirror, Gerry asleep. Beside me, Mike reclined, turned away, rustling to get comfortable. It would take a while.

He turned to me. "Ma, so, this is it? No more?"

"Yes, love. No more. Peace from this day forward! You can close your eyes now."

He smiled, turned over, and slept like a baby.

May Michael rest in peace. May we live in peace.

The light was so bright. It felt warm, happy, safe.

We made it.